Adaptation to the United States Academic Culture for International Students

First Edition

MEI ZHONG

San Diego State University

Bassim Hamadeh, CEO and Publisher
Seidy Cruz, Specialist Acquisitions Editor
Gem Rabanera, Project Editor
Christian Berk, Production Editor
Jackie Bignotti, Production Artist
Trey Soto, Licensing Coordinator
Natalie Piccotti, Director of Marketing
Kassie Graves, Vice President of Editorial
Jamie Giganti, Director of Academic Publishing

Copyright © 2020 by Cognella, Inc. All rights reserved. No part of this publication may be reprinted, reproduced, transmitted, or utilized in any form or by any electronic, mechanical, or other means, now known or hereafter invented, including photocopying, microfilming, and recording, or in any information retrieval system without the written permission of Cognella, Inc. For inquiries regarding permissions, translations, foreign rights, audio rights, and any other forms of reproduction, please contact the Cognella Licensing Department at rights@cognella.com.

Trademark Notice: Product or corporate names may be trademarks or registered trademarks, and are used only for identification and explanation without intent to infringe.

Cover image copyright © 2013 Depositphotos/Belchonock.

Printed in the United States of America.

ISBN: 978-1-5165-3623-8 (pbk) / 978-1-5165-3624-5 (br)

Adaptation to the United States Academic Culture for International Students

CONTENTS

INTRODUCTION	**VI**
PART I INTRODUCTION	**1**
CHAPTER 1 INTRODUCTION TO CULTURE AND COMMUNICATION	2
1.1 WHAT IS CULTURE? HOW DOES CULTURE AFFECT COMMUNICATION?	3
BY ALEXIS TAN	
CHAPTER 2 INTRODUCTION TO COMMUNICATION	8
2.1 WHAT IS COMMUNICATION? INTERCULTURAL COMMUNICATION?	9
BY ALEXIS TAN	
CHAPTER 3 UNDERSTANDING CULTURAL DIFFERENCES IN COMMUNICATION	28
3.1 WHAT IS CULTURE? HOW DOES CULTURE AFFECT COMMUNICATION?	29
BY ALEXIS TAN	
PART II ADAPTING TO THE U.S. ACADEMIC CULTURE	**45**
CHAPTER 4 CROSS-CULTURAL ADAPTATION TO THE UNITED STATES	46
4.1 THEORIES OF INTERCULTURAL COMMUNICATION	47
BY ALEXIS TAN	

CHAPTER 5 HOW TO INTERACT WITH AMERICAN PROFESSORS   78

    5.1 INTERACTING WITH PROFESSORS   79
        BY ANDREW ROBERTS

CHAPTER 6 HOW AMERICAN STUDENTS PREPARE FOR COLLEGE   93

    6.1 BE AN ADULT   94
        BY SAN BOLKAN

CHAPTER 7 EFFECTIVE STUDY STRATEGIES AND ACADEMIC HONESTY   124

    7.1 CONCENTRATION AND STUDY ENVIRONMENT   125
        BY ROBIN ROACH GILLEY

    7.2 LISTENING IN CLASS   134
        BY SAN BOLKAN

    7.3 NOTE-TAKING GUIDELINES AND FORMATS   144
        BY ROBIN ROACH GILLEY

CHAPTER 8 ACADEMIC HONESTY AND PLAGIARISM   153

    8.1 PREVENTING PLAGIARISM   154
        BY KATE L. TURABIAN, GREGORY G. COLOMB, AND JOSEPH M. WILLIAMS

PART III UNDERSTANDING CROSS-CULTURAL INTERACTIONS   161

CHAPTER 9 LANGUAGE AND CULTURE   162

    9.1 LANGUAGE AND COMMUNICATION   163
        BY PAYAL MEHRA

CHAPTER 10 NONVERBAL CODES AND CULTURE   180

    10.1 NONVERBAL MESSAGES   181
        BY PAYAL MEHRA

INTRODUCTION

Adaptation to the US Academic Culture is a course offered at some large American state universities, such as San Diego State University, and some small colleges, such as Snow College in Utah.[1] Like other colleges that rank high in the number of students who study abroad, we at San Diego State University, also welcome many international students who come to the US from all over the world. These incoming international students visit us via a variety of programs, such as semester abroad programs, year abroad programs, or as degree-seeking students.

Southern California offers many attractions to visiting international students, and although they see American students around campus daily and take classes with them, many visitors feel it is difficult to actually "meet" American students or form meaningful friendships with them. Most international students come to the US expecting they will become immersed in American culture and make American friends; however, upon arrival, they often find their life in the US is separate from that of their local peers. Indeed, research[2] "has revealed that international students encounter challenges in their academic adaptation process while studying in a foreign country," (Park, 2016, p. 888) and programs designed to address these adaptation challenges can be valuable in enhancing the international academic study abroad experience (Poyrazli & Grahame, 2007).

Two key concepts of academic cultural adaptation have been defined by previous researchers. Academic acculturation is "the dynamic adaptation processes of linguistically and culturally diverse students engaging with the academic study" (Cheng & Fox, 2008, p. 309). "Academic adaptation is a process of appreciation and acquisition of the target culture in an academic situation" (Park, 2016, p. 889).

---

[1] See https://www.snow.edu/academics/humanities/esl/syllabus.html?subj_code=ESL&crse_numb=1000.
[2] See Cheng & Fox, 2008 and Spack, 1997.

When international students arrive in the US, they need to put in great effort to adapt to the broader American culture—and specifically, the American academic culture. Everything seems different: from food to music to transportation to entertainment to how people greet each other and resolve conflicts. Moreover, they are here to attend an American college, which is part of a very different system of higher education than the system they experienced in their home countries. They quickly realize that just about everything is different here, including how to register for college classes, how to navigate around campus, how to communicate with American classmates and professors, how exams are conducted, how papers are assigned and graded, and much more.

As an illustration, one major difference faced by international college students when studying in the US is that many American college professors are focused on active, rather than passive, learning, and they aim to develop the student into an independent, rather than a teacher-dependent, learner (Zhang, 2013). Instead of the instructor "professing," lecturing, or providing a knowledgeable monologue, American professors engage in a dialogue with students, asking them questions and expecting to be asked questions by students.

As a visiting Chinese student, "Lin" told Zhang:

> "I did not experience dialog in a classroom before. I was familiar with a one-way communication style in class and did not know how to involve myself in a class discussion. I was puzzled when trying to figure out when it would be appropriate for me to speak, and how to express myself better. I realized that there is a difference in the classroom. I observed and imitated what my American classmates did." (2013, pp. 117)

This more equitable classroom structure where both teachers and students are engaged in a collaborative teaching and learning experience can be quite intimidating to the international student who is used to attending class, paying total attention to the professor, taking extensive notes, and regurgitating the knowledge gained in exams.

The dialogical classroom experience is part of a pedagogical strategy designed to create college students into independent thinkers. Again, Chinese student, "Lin" told Zhang:

> In the United States, the teacher acts more like a facilitator, and they give students lots of autonomy. Students are required to be familiar with the course content and raise questions for debates and discussions in classes. Students are likely to learn from the self-directed

> study rather than from the authorized teachers. Therefore, independent learning is a significant feature of an American learning style. American teachers believe that the responsibility for learning lies with the students. (2013, p. 96)

However, this set of apparently more democratic educational power relations has also been claimed to mask a more insidious US global dominance, since these power relations "based on knowledge and language operate in a global education environment to shape cultural attitudes as well as daily interactions and ... [they operate] as the daily embodiment of the global hegemony enjoyed by American universities" (Kim, 2012, p. 455).

Research (Lustig & Koester, 2013) has documented that effective adaptation to a different culture is dependent on one's ability to communicate with indigenous members of that culture. Therefore, understanding verbal and nonverbal communication codes and their appropriate use in various contexts can contribute to better communication competence.

Courses like the one offered at San Diego State University and websites such as the ones offered by Suffolk University and the University of the Pacific are designed to facilitate the adaptation process of international college students who are studying at a US higher education college or university.[3] The main purpose of these courses is to help visiting students learn and understand cultural differences between their home culture and that of the US, particularly as this relates to the system of higher education.

Existing research has summarized certain key challenges facing the international student in American colleges and universities and identifies tips to help overcome them. First, it takes time to adjust to the US academic culture, and doing so, as we saw in the example from "Lin," requires observation, insight, and reflection. Indeed, adaptation is the end stage of a process that begins with the initial honeymoon period of awe and amazement. This is followed by a fall into shock, sometimes depression, and a missing home stage which precedes adaptation.

Second, the dialogical approach to teaching and learning requires active participation by the student; it is not constructed for students to maintain a passive role because doing so misses much of what it means to have an American higher education. Active participation is not facilitated by large formal lectures with rows of seats facing a lectern or podium from which the professor "professes." Rather, to engage in dialogue, a smaller seminar-style, face-to-face learning environment is required. This is to facilitate conversation using both verbal and non-verbal communication,

---

[3] See http://www.suffolk.edu/academics/25623.php and http://www.uopinternational.org/7-tips-adjust-us-academic-culture/

which is necessarily more informal than formal. "Students might dress informally or eat in class. Professors might sit on their desks while talking or ask students to call them by their first name. This doesn't mean students don't respect professors, or that professors aren't professional and smart" (Fechtelkotter, 2017). Students are also encouraged to participate in group projects or discussion groups, and students, like the teacher, are expected to make presentations to the other students, typically using a PowerPoint presentation.

Third, as previously mentioned, the aim of American higher education is for you to become an independent and, preferably, an innovative and creative thinker. This means challenging and questioning knowledge, even from professors. This needs to be done with civility, but American college professors generally prefer students who want evidence and a basis for the knowledge they share with you. Accepting everything they say at face value because they say it may lose your professor's respect for you. A good American student is one who asks for more information, asks lots of questions, and respectfully challenges professors to show how and why they think what they do. To do this effectively, an American student must take control of the knowledge production process. He or she will need to read in advance of classes, be familiar with the topic, know the key researchers or authorities on it, become aware of the different lenses with which researchers view a topic, and know where they agree and disagree. Reproducing what the instructor tells you without having a critical take on it will get you no more than an average grade (a C or C+). Disrespecting the academic learning environment means not behaving respectfully and civilly to the instructor or other students, not being open to suggestion or others' ideas (being closed minded), or being distracted by cell phones, being on social media, or listening to music while in class!

Fourth, the grading system uses different standards in the US than in other academic cultures. Letter grades, including pluses and minuses, are used; grades tend to be higher with sometimes more than 50% of students getting A grades (perhaps a result of "grade inflation"); students typically take four to five classes a semester; classes only typically last one semester (which is 16 weeks). Some colleges still use a quarter system which is like the typical term system used in Europe or elsewhere. Finally, overall grades from classes (the term for a course) are composited into a grade point average (GPA), which is a running index on a 4.00 scale of how a student is doing overall. Straight B students have a 3.00 GPA, straight A students have a 4.00 GPA, and average students range between a 2.5–2.7 GPA. Most American colleges and universities place a student "on probation" and develop an individualized remediation program to bring up a student's GPA when it falls below a 2.00—if that fails, the student has to leave the university.

HOW TO USE THIS READER

In this reader, I hope to achieve three goals: 1) introduce students to a way of analyzing and discussing cultures and cultural differences, so they have the tools to express themselves in terms of what they see and feel as culturally different; 2) cover some information and techniques that will help students survive and succeed in the US college system, including how to interact with American students, how to relate to American professors, how to attend classes, and how to study for exams, etc.; and 3) help build cross-cultural communication skills and, ultimately, help students achieve better cross-cultural competencies. Accordingly, the structure of this textbook covers these three areas.

Part I discusses basic information and definitions of culture, communication, and cultural differences. Tan's chapters cover these three areas clearly and concisely. Chapter 1 is a good introduction of cultural concepts. Chapter 2 provides a set of terms and concepts regarding human communication. Chapter 3 gives a general survey of the main cultural differences an international student will find when enrolled in an American university.

Building on these foundational concepts, Part II of the text examines cross-cultural adaptation. It begins in Chapter 4 with Tan's research findings and theories regarding cultural adaptation. Then, the focus turns to introducing specific topics of surviving in the US academic culture. These include Chapter 5 by Roberts which discusses interacting with American professors and Chapter 6 where Bolkan focuses on how to be a college student in the US by acting like an adult and managing one's time while in college. Chapter 7 combines two articles, an article by Bolkan and an article by Gilley, to cover topics on how to attend college classes and study effectively in the US, as well as how to concentrate while studying. Chapter 8 by Gurabian, Golomb, and Williams introduces to international students the idea of "academic integrity" and how it is highly emphasized in the US compared to some other cultures, which, according to American standards, may allow a degree of plagiarism.

Part III returns to cultural differences, especially regarding communication characteristics. Chapter 9 features Payal's publication on the relationship between language and culture, while Chapter 10, also by Payal, focuses on nonverbal communication codes and culture. These two chapters give students a good understanding of how people interact with each other differently in the US compared to an international student's home culture. The hope is that students will reflect on their communication behaviors towards the end of the semester and be able to understand and even analyze how they interact with American students and how American students act and react with them.

This anthology text is designed to accompany courses offered to facilitate international students' adaptation process while studying in the US. Studying abroad is considered one of the highest impact activities during a student's college career. The experience and knowledge gained in this process is long-lasting and often life-changing. It is hoped that this text and course can help enhance the international student's life-long learning experience while living in the US and after he or she returns to his or her home country. This text will provide students not only with a structure containing an organized set of concepts, but, along with the course, it will also provide a series of applied activities through which visiting international students will engage while studying at their host college or university. Students, then, will be able to reflect on these concepts and apply them to their experiences even after they return to their home culture.

I am grateful to Dr. Stuart Henry for his generous guidance and encouragement throughout the process of developing our International Studies minor at San Diego State University as well as this text. I would also like to thank the College of Professional Studies and Fine Arts at SDSU for the support in offering this important course that contributes to more effective study abroad experiences for student visitors to American colleges.

REFERENCES

Cheng, L., & Fox, J. (2008). Towards a better understanding of academic acculturation: Second language students in Canadian Universities. *Canadian Modern Language Review*, 65(2), 307–333.

Fechtelkotter, K. (2017). 7 Tips to adjust to U.S. academic culture. *University of the Pacific*. Retrieved from http://www.uopinternational.org/7-tips-adjust-us-academic-culture/

Kim, J. (2012). The birth of academic subalterns: How do foreign students embody the global hegemony of American universities? *Journal of Studies in International Education*, 16(5), 455–476.

Lustig, M. W., & Koester, J. (2013). *Intercultural competence* (7th ed.). New York, NY: Pearson.

Park, E. (2016). Issues of international students' academic adaptation in the ESL writing class: A mixed-methods study. *Journal of International Students*, 6(4), 887–904.

Poyrazli, S., & Grahame, K. M. (2007). Barriers to adjustment: Needs of international students within a semi-urban campus community. *Journal of Instructional Psychology*, 34(1), 28–45.

Spack, R. (1997). The acquisition of academic literacy in a second language: A longitudinal case study. *Written Communication*, 14(1), 3–62.

Zhang, H. (2013). *Academic adaptation and cross-cultural learning experiences of Chinese students at American universities: A narrative inquiry* (Doctoral dissertation). Retrieved from (3595874, Northeastern University). ProQuest Dissertations and Theses, 190. Retrieved from https://search-proquest-com.libproxy.sdsu.edu/docview/1446718357/fulltextPDF/DBF5D8EFB0664A48PQ/1?accountid=13758

INTRODUCTION

PART 1

# CHAPTER 1
INTRODUCTION TO CULTURE AND COMMUNICATION

WHAT IS CULTURE? HOW DOES CULTURE AFFECT COMMUNICATION?

BY ALEXIS TAN

[...] intercultural communication is communication in general, with one important distinction: the participants bring with them differing worldviews, values, behavioral norms, and communication styles to the interaction. Let's take a look at culture in more detail and see how culture can affect communication.

In doing the research for this chapter, I came across two quotes originally cited in the book *Management Across Cultures* by Steers, Nardon, and Sanchez-Runde (2013) that tell us something about culture:

"We do not see things as they are; we see things as we are."
—Talmud Bavli, Ancient Book of Wisdom, Babylonia

"Water is the last thing a fish notices."
—Lao Tzu

What do these quotes tell us about culture? To me, Bavli says that how we see the world (our realities) is influenced by our cultures; Lao Tzu reminds us that we may not be aware of this influence at all.

DEFINING CULTURE

If culture is such a powerful force on how we see and make sense of our environment and other people, then how can we not be aware of its

Alexis Tan, Selection from "What is Culture? How Does Culture Affect Communication?" *The Intercultural Communication Guidebook: Research-based Strategies for Successful Interactions*, pp. 29-33, 47-48. Copyright © 2016 by Cognella, Inc. Reprinted with permission.

influence? Before we can answer this question, let's define what we mean by culture. This won't be an easy task, considering that there are at least 150 definitions, by one estimate (Kroeber & Kluckhohn, 1952), in anthropology, sociology, social psychology, and communication. Here are some examples:

> Culture … is that complex whole which includes knowledge, belief, art, law, morals, custom, and any other capabilities and habits acquired by man as a member of society. (Taylor, 1871, p. 1)

> Culture may be defined as the totality of the mental and physical reactions and activities that characterize the behavior of individuals composing a social group collectively and individually in relations to their natural environment, to other groups, to members of the group itself and of each individual to himself. It also includes the products of these activities and their role in the life of the groups. The mere enumerations of these various aspects of life, however, does not constitute culture. It is more, for its elements are not independent, they have a structure. (Boas, 1911, p. 149)

> Culture means the whole complex of traditional behavior which has been developed by the human race and is successively learned by each generation. A culture is less precise. It can mean the forms of traditional behavior which are characteristics of a given society, or of a group of societies, or of a certain race, or of a certain area, or of a certain period of time. (Mead, 1937, p. 17)

> Culture has been distinguished from the other elements of action by the fact that it is intrinsically transmissible from one action system to another by learning and diffusion. (Parsons & Shills, 1976, p. 172)

> Man is a biological being as well as a social individual. Among the responses which he gives to external stimuli, some of the full product of his nature, and others to his condition (culture). (Levi-Strauss, 1949, p. 4)

> Culture … is ways of thinking, the ways of acting, and the material objects that together shape a people's way of life. Culture can be nonmaterial or material. (Macionnis & Gerber (2011, p. 11)

> The term culture refers to what is learned ... the things one needs to know in order to meet the standards of others. (Goodenough, 1971, p. 19)
>
> The culture concept denotes an historically transmitted pattern of meanings embodied in symbols, a system of inherited conceptions expressed in symbolic forms by means of which men communicate, perpetuate, and develop their knowledge about and toward life ... (Geertz, 1966, p. 89)
>
> The collective programming of the mind that distinguishes the members of one human group from another. (Hofstede, Hofstede, & Minkov, 2010, p. 3)
>
> An integrated system of learned behavior patterns which are characteristic of the members of a society and which are not the result of biological inheritance. (Hoebel, 1976, p. 2)
>
> The collection of beliefs, values, behaviors, customs, and attitudes that distinguish the people of one society from another. (Kluckhohn, 1949, p. 1)

As you can see, there is no lack of definitions for culture. From these definitions, let's identify the characteristics that stand out and about which there is agreement.

1. Culture is a characteristic of people who identify with a group. This identification may be based on shared geographical boundaries (such as a country); a shared demographic category, such as race or ethnicity, religion, or socioeconomic level; or simply shared interests and goals, such as a corporation or student club (organizational culture).

2. Since culture is dependent on group membership and identification, the individual must be aware of the group's existence and acknowledge his or her membership in the group.

3. Culture includes agreement within the group about how to make sense of or assign meanings to its environment, which behaviors in response to the environment are acceptable, what is important in life, and how to feel about other people and objects in the environment. These components are the *dimensions* of culture: beliefs and worldviews (to make sense), action norms (acceptable behaviors), values (what is important in life), and attitudes (how

to feel). Culture is manifested in these nonmaterial human tendencies, but also represented in material artifacts such as art, language, architecture, laws, rituals, literature, and so on. Our concern in this book is nonmaterial culture.

4. Culture therefore guides an individual's response to and interpretation of the environment. Its influence is distinct from our natural human tendencies, which are hardwired into our genes, such as, according to some scholars, the tendency to be prejudiced or to favor in-groups over out-groups.

5. Culture is a pattern of shared dimensions, each related to and reinforcing the other. For example, beliefs are related to attitudes, attitudes to behavior.

6. Culture is shared by group members using signals, verbal and nonverbal.

7. Culture is transmitted over time from one generation to the next through a process of socialization (discussed later in this chapter).

8. Culture can change, as a response to changes in the environment, such as economic growth (Inglehart, 1997), encroachment by other cultures (Inglehart, 1997), proliferation of foreign media (Tunstall, 1977; Scotton & Hatchten, 2008), and migration (Inglehart, 1997).

Incorporating these commonalities, here is my simplified definition that applies to intercultural communication:

> Culture is a pattern of shared beliefs, values, attitudes, behavioral norms, and worldviews shared by members of a group and transmitted over time from one generation to the next. Although generally resistant to change, culture is malleable, as a response to environmental changes. The major form of transmission is communication.

My definition of culture, as well as the other definitions I cited, share a common problem: How do we know that a worldview is shared? One hundred percent agreement? (highly unlikely). By a majority? What about those who don't agree, the outliers?

Scholars have taken different approaches to solving the problem. Some, like Hofstede (1984) and Hofstede et. al. (2010) use statistics (i.e., means, standard deviations, factor analysis, and correlations, which I discuss later in this chapter) to analyze results of surveys, looking for commonalities within a group, in his case, countries, and then comparing groups. Kluckhohn (1951) also used statistics to compare indigenous groups in the United States on several dimensions of culture. Others have used critical analysis of the artifacts of culture to identify themes representing cultural dimensions, such as in law, literature, the mass media, and observations of everyday behaviors and activities. Still others (Wood & Smith, 2004; Schwartz et al., 2001) have analyzed culture both at the individual and group levels, looking for individual differences in how cultural dimensions are internalized and demonstrated. In this latter approach, outliers, members of a group who deviate from cultural norms, are given special attention by analyzing possible reasons for their deviations. In intercultural communications and other interactions, there is a risk in automatically ascribing to a person a group culture simply because of membership, which is a form of stereotyping. (Perhaps we are interacting with an outlier.) While these generalizations are a useful guide, and in fact they are often accurate in describing a majority, the prudent approach is to use culture as a guide while being cognizant of possible individual differences or deviations. [. . .]

REFERENCES

Boas, F. (1911). *The mind of primitive man.* New York, NY: Macmillan Publishing.
Geertz, C. (1966). Religion as a cultural system. In M. Banton (Ed.), *Anthropological approaches to the study of religion.* New York, NY: Routledge.
Goodenough, W. (1971). *Culture, language, and society.* Reading, MA: Addison-Wesley.
Hoebel, E. A. (1976). *Cultural and social anthropology.* New York, NY: McGraw-Hill.
Inglehart, R. (1997). *Modernization and postmodernization: Cultural, economic, and political change in 43 societies.* Princeton, NJ: Princeton University Press.
Hofstede, G. (1984). *Culture's consequences: International differences in work-related values.* Beverly Hills, CA: Sage.
Hofstede, G., Hofstede, G. J., & Minkov, M. (2010). *Cultures and organizations: Software of the mind.* New York, NY: McGraw-Hill.
Kluckhohn, C. K. (1949). *Mirror for man: The relation of anthropology to modern life.* Berkeley, CA: Whittlesey House.
Kluckhohn, C. K. (1951). Values and value orientations in the theory of action. In T. Parsons and E. A. Shils (Eds.), *Toward a general theory of action.* Cambridge, MA: Harvard University Press.
Kroeber, A. L., & Kluckhohn, C. K. (1952). *Culture: A critical review of concepts and definitions.* Cambridge, MA: Peabody Museum.
Levi-Strauss, C. (1949). *Myth and meaning.* New York, NY: Schocken Books.
Macionis, J., & Gerber, L. (2011) *Sociology.* New York, NY: Pearson Education.
Mead, M. (1937). *Cooperation and competition among primitive peoples.* New York, NY: McGraw-Hill.
Parsons, T., & Shils, A. (Eds.). (1976). *Toward a general theory of action.* Cambridge, MA: Harvard University Press.
Schwartz, S., Melech, G., Lehmann, A., Burgess, S., Harris, M., & Owens, V. (2001). Extending the cross-validity of the theory of basic human values with a different method of measurement. *Journal of Cross-Cultural Psychology, 32*(5), 519–542.
Scotton, J., & Hachten, W. (2008). *New media for a new China.* New York, NY: Wiley.
Steers, R., Nardon, L., & Sanchez-Runde, C. (2013). *Management across cultures: Developing global competencies.* Cambridge: Cambridge University Press.
Taylor, E. (1871). *Primitive culture.* London: John Murray.
Tunstall, J. (1977). *The media are American.* New York, NY: Columbia University Press.
Wood, A., & Smith, M. (2004). *Technology, identity, & culture.* New York, NY: Psychology Press.

CHAPTER 2
INTRODUCTION TO COMMUNICATION

WHAT IS COMMUNICATION? INTERCULTURAL COMMUNICATION?

BY ALEXIS TAN

To understand intercultural communication, we must first understand the general communication process. Let's start with a model developed by two electrical engineers, Claude Shannon and Warren Weaver, who published *The Mathematical Theory of Communication* in 1949. Although this model—commonly referred to as the *mathematical model of communication*—was developed over 65 years ago, it still has considerable influence on communication researchers today because it provides for a precise and quantified measure of information sent and received. This enables the researcher to measure the accuracy of transmission of information from sender to receiver and to identify the conditions that could increase, or decrease, accuracy in communication.

A MATHEMATICAL MODE OF COMMUNICATION

Shannon and Weaver (1949) were primarily interested in technical problems in electronic communication, such as the relation between the speed of transmission of a message and the fidelity of its transmission and improving the quality of transmission of the human voice over the telephone

Alexis Tan, "What is Communication? Intercultural Communication?" *The Intercultural Communication Guidebook: Research-based Strategies for Successful Interactions*, pp. 11-28. Copyright © 2016 by Cognella, Inc. Reprinted with permission.

(issues that still exist today). The model they formulated can be applied to most forms of human communication today, including intercultural communication. This model is shown in Figure 2.1.

Figure 2.1 A Mathematical Model of Communication

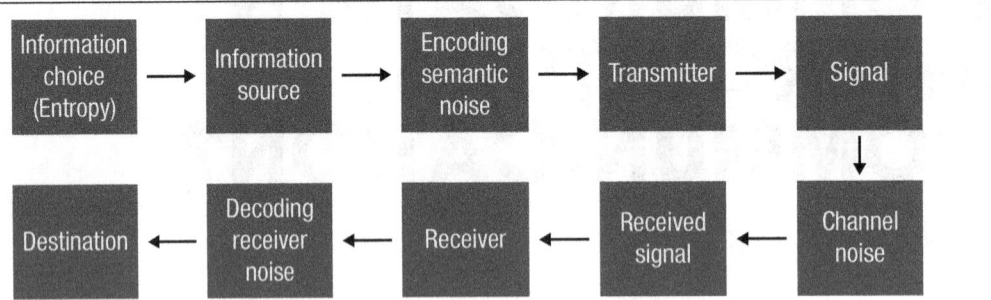

Source: Adapted from: Claude Shannon and Warren Weaver, "A Mathematical Model of Communication," The Mathematical Theory of Communication. Copyright © 1949 by University of Illinois Press.

In Shannon and Weaver's model, an information source selects a message from a set of available messages. This message is changed by the transmitter into a signal, which is then sent over the channel to the receiver, which changes the transmitted signal back into the message and then sends it on to the destination. When I talk to you in the classroom, for example, my brain is the information source, my vocal system is the transmitter, varying sound pressure is the signal, the air is the channel, your ear nerve is the receiver, and your brain is the destination. In the process of transmission the message may be unintentionally distorted or changed. These distortions are called *noise*. Distortions often occur in the channel, such as static in a radio, a fuzzy picture on your television or tablet, or a garbled voice over your cell phone. Noise could also occur as the information source encodes the message for transmission. This is called *semantic noise*. Examples are distortions of meaning unintentionally produced by the source, such as misleading or confusing use of language and other symbols. A third source of noise is in the receiver. *Receiver noise* is message distortion arising from decoding of the message. Subjective—that is, in the interest of the receiver—language or symbol interpretations are a major cause of receiver noise.

The Shannon and Weaver model measures the accuracy of message transmission in a defined communication system; that is, a system in which the source, transmitter, and receiver are clearly identified. To do this, they introduced the concept of entropy, which is a quantitative measure of information sent and received.

Information, according to this model, is the amount of choice or freedom that the source has in constructing a message. Sources can transmit more information in a message if they have many instead of only a few messages to choose from, or if there is greater "randomness of choice." Shannon and Weaver refer to the degree of randomness as *entropy*. When there is high entropy, the receiver will find it difficult to guess correctly what the message of the source will be because many messages will be sent. Thus, high entropy leads to greater uncertainty in the receiver. This uncertainty can be reduced by a message—a singular one chosen for the moment—from the source. The amount of information in a message is the amount of uncertainty it reduces. The greater the uncertainty, or entropy, reduced, the more information transmitted by a message. Let me illustrate with an example:

If all I could say was yes or no to answer your question, and if each word were equally probable to be used in my message, then you would already have a 50% chance of guessing what my message will be. In such a situation, there is not a great deal of uncertainty or randomness in what I could communicate to you since my choices are limited to two words with equal probability. Entropy is low, and any message I send to you would be low in information content (you would be able to guess the correct message 5 times out of 10). Suppose, however, that instead of only 2 words, I could say 10 words, such as "Yes," "Maybe," "Conditionally," "No," "What?" and so on. If my message consisted of only one word at a time, and if all the words were equally likely to be used in my message, then your chance of selecting the correct word (message) would only be one-tenth, or 1 in 10 times. There is greater randomness of choice in my choice of a message. Any message I send to you will contain more information because more uncertainty is reduced.

Shannon and Weaver use this notion of uncertainty or entropy to measure information in probabilistic terms. In the simplest communication situation, where all the messages are in code and consist only of combinations of two signals (e.g., "1" or "0" or the "dit" and "dah" in the Morse code), then for a message n signals long the total number of distinct signals that can be sent is 2^n. For example, if we wanted a message of only two signals, and each message would be a combination of two signals ("1" or "0"), then the total number of distinct messages would be 2^2, or 4. These messages would be 10, 01, 11, and 00. If we knew that there were 2^n different messages possible, and if they were all equally likely to be sent, our chance of correctly guessing the contents of any one message would be one in 2^n. We could take the number 2^n as a measure of the amount of uncertainty, entropy, or information. However, to facilitate comparisons between different messages, Shannon and Weaver suggested that instead of taking 2^n, in our example, we use the logarithm of that number. Using this procedure, it becomes possible to compute the amount of information for each signal or message from any source in which the occurrence of one signal does not influence the occurrence of another. This allows us to calculate source, channel, and receiver information capacities and to determine the accuracy of information transmission from source to destination. Perfect communication, according to this model, is when the amount of information transmitted by the source is equal to the amount of information received at the destination. When these amounts are not equal, the channel may not be capable of transmitting the information, or there may be sources of noise leading to message distortion.

As we have seen, Shannon and Weaver's mathematical model provides us with a system that measures communication effectiveness in purely objective terms; that is, as the amount of information that is sent and received. It also introduces us to the concept of noise, which is anything in the system that reduces the amount of information received. Although the model defines noise as resulting from technical problems in the system (Shannon and Weaver were, after all, engineers), more recent communication models have used this concept to refer to human interference, of which culture is a major factor. So, this seminal model has contributed to our current definitions of communication. However, we should not forget that it deals only with the technological aspects of communication and with the amount, not the content or substance, of information. Meanings of messages are not considered. So it is possible to have "perfect" communication, as defined by the model, if the amount of information sent equals the amount of information received, even if the meanings sent by the source do not correspond at all with the meanings received by the source. Clearly, a symmetry of meanings is important in intercultural communication. When two entities (such as individuals) from different cultures interact, meanings assigned to a message are affected by their values, beliefs, worldviews, and notions of what is acceptable behavior. Another limitation of the Shannon and Weaver model is the presumed linearity of the communication process—it has a starting point (the source) and an end (the receiver). As we shall see in the following sections, most models used today in the communications field, including intercultural communication, define communication as an interactive, transactional process.

AN INTERACTIVE MODEL OF COMMUNICATION

Let's now take a look at an interactive model, shown in Figure 2.2, that was developed by Horace Newcomb, a social psychologist. In this model, which is often referred to as the *ABX model*, communication is an interaction between two people or groups of people about an object or topic of communication. The model considers how interpersonal relationships such as liking or disliking between the two participants, and their evaluation of the object or topic, such as approval or disapproval, liking or disliking, affect how much communication occurs and what the result will be. As shown in Figure 2.2, two persons or groups (A and B) exchange messages about an object that is the topic of communication (X). A and B are both communicators because each can send a message to the other, making the process interactive and two-way, as indicated by the bidirectional arrows. For communication to occur, A and B will need to be aware of or recognize X as the topic of communication. Communication cannot happen if A and B don't have this common recognition, such as when they might be talking about "different things." A and B will have initial or pre-communication feelings about X, such as like or dislike or agree or disagree, or, they may not have any feelings at all about X. These orientations or feelings toward each other may be liking or disliking, or simply ones of neutrality or indifference. The interactive model explains and predicts how pre-communication orientations toward X (AX and BX) and pre-communication orientations between A and B (AB and BA) influence whether A and B will engage in communication and the frequency and intensity of communication, intensity being indicated by the effort put into the interaction by the participants. Also, the model explains how these pre-communication orientations might result in changes in orientations of A and B toward X and toward each other. Thus, Newcomb is not so much concerned with how much information is transmitted (as in the Shannon and Weaver model) as he is with whether the two participants will engage in communication; the duration, frequency and intensity of engagement; and the effects of communication on participant orientations toward the topic or object, and toward each other.

Figure 2.2 An Interactive Model of Communication

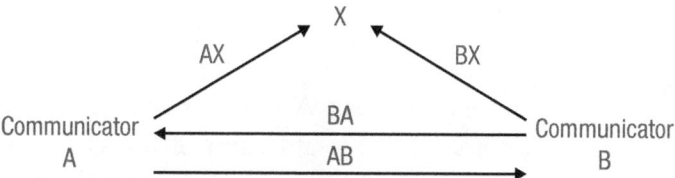

Source: Adapted from: Theordore Newcomb, "An Interactive Model of Communication," "An Approach to the Study of Communicative Acts", Psychological Review, vol 60. Copyright © 1953 by American Psychological Association.

According to the interactive model, the objectives of communication are to define, clarify, establish, and maintain a clear orientation toward one another and toward the object or topic of communication. Orientation is first, cognitive awareness, and second, affect. *Cognitive awareness* refers to knowledge of the object (or topic) and the other person. *Affect* is how the participants feel about each other (liking, disliking, or indifference), and how they feel about the object or topic of communication (liking, disliking, indifference, agreement, disagreement). Communication allows the participants to know what these orientations are.

The first objective of communication, according to the interactive model, is to establish a common cognitive orientation, a common awareness of the topic of communication. We ask, are we talking about the same thing? Do we have a common understanding of what it is that we are talking about? Once this common cognitive orientation has been established through communication, the participants can move on to the second objective, which is to achieve symmetry.

Symmetry is agreement on our (assume you are A and I am B in the model) affective orientations toward X; that is, how we feel about X. Once we have established that we are communicating about the same thing (X), we ask, do we know how each of us feels about X? Do we agree on X—for example, do we both like X, or do we both dislike X? Symmetry can be illustrated in Figure 2.2 when the valences (signs, + or −) are equivalent or the same for AX and BX. If both signs are positive, A and B like or agree with X; if the signs are negative, A and B dislike or disagree with X. Symmetry is present in both these cases.

Asymmetry, the opposite of symmetry, is when you (A) and I (B) do not have a common understanding of X; that is, when we are talking about different things or when our definitions of X are not the same. Even if we had a common understanding, asymmetry also exists when our orientations toward X differ, such as when we disagree on our evaluations of X (you agree and I disagree; you like X and I don't like X).

To illustrate, let's say that X is the United Nations (UN). You and I are about to engage in a conversation about the UN after a talk by a former ambassador to Afghanistan on the role of the UN in promoting international peace. We were in the audience, sitting next to each other. After the talk, you take me aside and ask, "What do you think?" For symmetry to occur, we must first establish that we are talking about the UN, and not about any other international alliance of countries, such as NATO or the Arab League. Second, we must establish that we have a common understanding of the UN; that is, that it is an international organization open to most all nations, with headquarters in New York, but it is not an American organization. Once we have established this common cognitive orientation, you and I, according to the ABX model, will assess how each of us feels about the UN; this is affective orientation. Symmetry is present when we have a similar affective orientation toward the UN. For example, we both agree that the UN is doing the best it can in promoting world peace, and that it deserves the monetary support of the United States. Or, we could agree that the UN is a waste of resources and that the United States should not support it.

In our communication interaction about the UN, you and I will also be assessing how we feel about each other. Do I like you and do you like me? Is there mutual dislike? Are we indifferent toward each other (no strong feelings)?

According to the ABX model, cognitive and affective orientations toward X, and participant affective orientations toward each other, are established by communication. By establishing these orientations, we are setting the stage for future effective communication.

The ABX model predicts that in a communication interaction there is a "persistent strain" toward symmetry, which means that A and B are motivated to arrive at similar evaluations and understanding of X. There are several reasons for this desire to achieve symmetry. First, symmetry allows each person to calculate readily the other's behavior; that is, interaction between A and B will be more predictable and will require less effort. It is easier to interact with another person when there is agreement than when there is disagreement. Second, symmetry reinforces A and B orientations toward X. A can convince himself that he is "correct" about X because B agrees. Thus, agreement or symmetry is reassuring and comfortable.

The strength of the strain toward symmetry according to the ABX model varies with attraction or liking between A and B, and with how important X is to A and B. The more A and B like each other and the more important X is to A and B, the more A and B will be motivated to continue communicating with each other until symmetry is achieved. In contrast, if A and B don't like each other, and if X is not important to them, there will be little motivation for communication. Increased communication to achieve symmetry when there is disagreement can result in one of the following outcomes (assume that you are A):

1. Arrive at an agreement with B regarding X (to achieve symmetry).
   a. By changing B's orientation to agree with yours through persuasion;
   b. By changing your orientation to agree with B's (you are persuaded by B);
   c. By convincing yourself that B really agrees with you on X (often referred to as *cognitive distortion*).
2. Changing your orientation toward B.
   a. Decrease your attraction or liking for B ("I really don't like B that much") so that disagreement is more easily tolerated.

Newcomb's ABX model is useful because it tells us when communication is likely to take place and the possible effects of communication. A weakness is that it does not explain how communication works. To be competent in intercultural communication, we should, as the model suggests, make sure that we, the participants, are talking about the same thing and assigning equivalent meanings. It is also important to assess our orientations toward each other and the object of communication so we can adjust or manage our interaction accordingly. For example, if I sense that you disliked me because of pre-communication stereotypes, and if it's important to me to persuade you to agree with me on the topic of communication, what can I do to change your opinion or stereotype of me?

The model is particularly applicable to intercultural communication. When two people (A and B) from different cultures communicate, they often do not have a common understanding of X because their understanding of X depends on language, values, and worldviews [. . .]. Also, A and B will have strong orientations toward each other (stronger than when A and B are from the same culture) because of implicit biases, stereotyping, and prejudice, and simply because A and B more likely will perceive each to be "different" from the other. These are sources of noise, barriers to effective communication [. . .]. Therefore, effective intercultural communication is more of a challenge than intracultural (within the same culture) communication because the ABX orientations are more likely to be asymmetrical than symmetrical.

A TRANSACTIONAL MODEL

The transactional model includes the concepts of entropy and noise from Shannon and Weaver's mathematical model, the ABX orientations from Newcomb's model, and adds an analysis of how messages are sent and received in the context of a transaction between source and receiver. The model (from Tan, 2015) is shown in Figure 2.3.

Figure 2.3 A Transactional Model of Communication

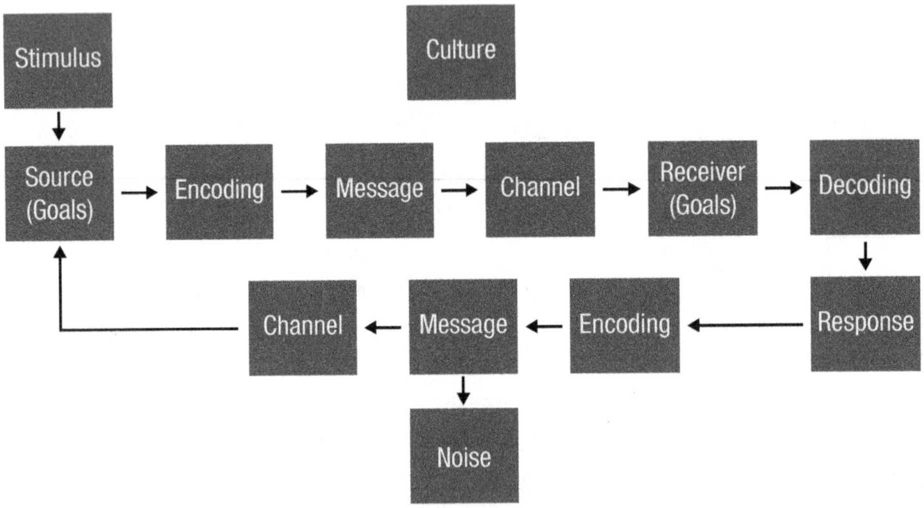

Source: Adapted from: Alexis Tan, "A Transactional Model of Communication," *Mass Communication Theories and Research.* Copyright © 1985 by Macmillan Publishing Company.

To understand this transactional model, let's define its components, as shown in Figure 2.3.

1. The *stimulus* is the topic of communication. It can be anything in the natural environment (anything that can be sensed; that is, seen, heard, or felt) or in stored memory of the source. Examples are another person or group (such as Muslims, the UN); a political or social issue (such as immigration policy, gun control, foreign aid, climate change); or just about anything that the source is motivated to send a message about to a receiver. One motivation is to reduce entropy, which is uncertainty about the stimulus.

2. The *source* is a person, group, or organization that sends a message to a receiver about the stimulus. Besides reducing entropy or uncertainty about the stimulus, the source will have other motivations, or *goals*, to send a message. These goals, shown in Figure 2.4, are to inform, to teach, to persuade, to please, or to satisfy receiver needs.

3. *Encoding* is the process by which the source transforms his or her response to the stimulus, a response that originates as a thought or mental representation of the stimulus, into signs that can be transmitted to the receiver. Signs can be verbal, using words and phrases, as in languages; visual, using pictures and moving images, such as in film; or nonverbal, such as gestures and facial expressions. I talk about signs in more detail later in this chapter.

4. A *message* consists of signs that represent the source's response to the stimulus. These signs are in a form, such as language, a photo, or a smile, that can be sent on to the receiver. A message transmits both information (quantity of information in Shannon and Weaver's mathematical model) and meaning (orientations in Newcomb's interactive model).

5. The *channel* is the medium that the source uses to send the message to the receiver. The medium could be the Internet (to send a text message); television, newspapers, radio, or film (to reach large audiences by means of a mass medium); or air, such as in face-to-face conversations (to talk to another person or persons who occupy the same space as the source).

6. The *receiver* is another person, group, or organization to whom the source sends the message. The receiver has a choice: to pay attention to and accept the message ("Yes, let's talk") or to ignore it ("I don't want to talk"). This decision will be based on whether a receiver goal can be met by attending to the message. As shown in Figure 2.4, receiver goals are to learn of threats and opportunities in the environment; to understand the environment; to acquire

skills and knowledge; to learn community values, behaviors, and rules; to reach decisions; to make choices; to enjoy, relax, or be entertained; to be distracted from problems; or to establish a positive relationship with the source. A receiver will accept the message when he or she expects that the message will facilitate the attainment of a goal or multiple goals.

7   *Decoding* is the process by which the receiver makes sense of the message, asking, "What is this message about?" "What is its meaning?"

8   A *response* is the receiver's evaluation of the message. Does it make sense? Do I agree? Disagree? The receiver can choose to send a response back to the original source, thereby continuing the interaction. The process starts all over again and continues until one or the other participant decides to no longer participate.

9   *Culture* is the accumulated worldviews, values, accepted patterns of behavior, and beliefs of the source and receiver based on membership in a group. [...]

10 *Noise* is anything in the model that interferes with the transmission of the message, thereby reducing the amount of information sent and its meaning. Culture is a source of noise when source and receiver do not share a culture, and when they do not understand each other's culture. [...]

Communication, according to this transactional model, is the process indicated by the arrows in Figure 2.3. A source responds to a stimulus, encodes this response, and then sends the encoded response in a message through a channel to the receiver. The receiver decodes the message and then sends a response back to the source. In the transactional model, source and receiver are motivated to participate in the interaction by the goals they expect to attain. Therefore, communication is goal directed and transactional. Both the source and receiver gain (attainment of a goal) from participation in the communication.

COMMUNICATION GOALS

In the transactional model, both the source and receiver are directed by the communication goals or purposes shown in Figure 2.4. The source may wish to inform the receiver of threats and opportunities in the environment or to simply provide knowledge that will help the receiver adapt to the environment. An example is a news report of home burglaries in the community. This information warns residents of a threat so they can lock their doors. A second source goal is to teach the receiver how to apply knowledge. Teaching goes beyond imparting information; it requires the application of knowledge, as when the source uses information about the appropriate behaviors in a culture to interact effectively in that culture. Another example is my attempt to teach you how to apply theories about noise reduction to intercultural communication. Yet another example is parents teaching their children the values of multiculturalism and how to interact with people from other cultures. A third goal of communication is to persuade; that is, to change attitudes, beliefs, and behaviors of the receiver in a direction determined by the source and usually for the source's benefit. Examples are product and political advertisements and a flyer for or against gun control. A fourth goal is to please and to gain acceptance or liking from the receiver. An example is entertainment programming in television. Its goal is to elicit positive emotions from the audience. Of course, the bottom-line goal is to convince us to continue paying attention to the programs so that the producers and media providers will make money from the program sponsors, the advertisers.

Because communication is transactional, receivers will have corresponding goals, shown in Figure 2.4, for participating. The list is not exhaustive. Neither are the discrete purposes mutually exclusive; in reality, they often overlap. However, Figure 2.4 gives you an idea about the major purposes or goals of communication in a transactional model.

Figure 2.4 Goals of Communication

COMMUNICATOR'S GOALS	RECEIVER'S GOALS
1 To inform	1 To learn of threats and opportunities; to understand the environment
2 To teach	2 To acquire skills and knowledge
3 To persuade	3 To reach decisions; to make choices
4 To please, to satisfy receiver needs	4 To enjoy, relax, be entertained

Sources: Adapted from: Alexis Tan, "Goals of Communication," *Mass Communication Theories and Research*. Copyright © 1985 by Macmillan Publishing Company.

SIGNS

A *sign* is a physical representation of a source's response to a stimuli, with the response being the beginning of the communication process. A sign or combination of signs convey meaning and information to the receiver and is sent as a message.

A sign is an object existing in the real world, meaning that both source and receiver can see, touch, hear, or otherwise consciously know that it exists (Short, 2007). Therefore, a sign can be just about anything in the environment. We shall limit our discussion of signs to verbal, nonverbal, and visual representations of the object or topic of communication.

VERBAL SIGNS AND LANGUAGE

Language is a formal system of signs and rules that people use to designate, represent, and assign meanings to objects (Thibaut, 1996). Language can be verbal or nonverbal (as in sign language and Braille). Verbal language uses words, phrases, and sentences to convey meanings (Evans & Levinson, 2009), and can be transmitted orally using voice ("speech") or in written form.

A useful tool for understanding how verbal language conveys different meanings depending on a communication source's orientation (such as liking or disliking) toward the object of communication is the linguistic category model (LCM) (Maas, 1999; Ruscher, 2001). The LCM says that a source, in constructing a message such as describing an observed event, has a choice of several linguistic categories with different levels of abstraction. Each linguistic category transmits a very different meaning than any of the other categories do. These categories, from the most concrete (i.e., description of the observed event without interpretation and closest to "reality") to the most abstract, are listed, defined, and illustrated below:

- *Descriptive action verb*: Refers to specific behavior without interpretation. For example, John shoves Bill; Susan touches Jim's arm.
- *Interpretative action verb*: Refers to a specific behavior with interpretation. For example, John hits Bill; Susan caresses Jim.
- *State verb*: Infers an actor's cognitive or emotional state in describing motivation for a specific behavior. For example, John despises Bill; Susan loves Jim.
- *Adjective*: Refers to an actor's character trait or internal disposition without referring to the specific behavior. For example, John is aggressive; Susan is affectionate.

As can be seen from this list of linguistic categories at the disposal of the source, very different meanings can be transmitted to the receiver depending on which category is used. A source's use of linguistic categories is influenced by his or her perception or orientation toward the object or person that is the topic of communication (the stimuli eliciting a response). The more strongly the stimulus is perceived negatively or positively, the more likely the source will use a higher level of abstraction to describe it. Thus, language is a powerful tool to convey meanings that go beyond describing people, events, objects, and behaviors.

NONVERBAL SIGNS

Meanings are conveyed not only by words but also by physical or nonverbal signs. It has been estimated that about two-thirds of human communication is nonverbal, including visual signs (Hogan & Stubbs, 2003). Here are some examples of nonverbal signs, excluding visual communication, that I discuss in the next section:

- *Facial expressions* refer to voluntary (conscious) or involuntary (unconscious, not controlled by the source) movement of the mouth, lips, eyes, nose, forehead, and jaw. The human face is estimated to be capable of more than 10,000 different expressions (Ekman, 2004). The expression of most emotions through facial movements varies across cultures, but facial expressions for happiness, sadness, anger, fear, surprise, disgust, shame, and interest are similar throughout the world (Ekman, 2004). Facial expressions can express negative or positive emotions. Negative emotions are generally expressed by a tightening of the jaw, furrowing of the forehead, squinting of the eyes, or "lip occlusion" (lips seemingly disappearing or appearing smaller). Positive emotions are generally expressed by loosening of the furrowed lines on the forehead, relaxation of the muscles around the mouth, and widening of the eyes (Navarro, 2008). Some cultures are more expressive than others, and some people can manipulate their facial expressions to convey emotions they don't feel (such as a leader wanting to appear calm before his or her followers). Therefore, the interpretation of facial expressions is not an exact science and should not be over-interpreted. However, it is useful to know that in some contexts, such as intercultural communication, facial expressions can and do transmit meanings not carried by verbal messages.
- *Paralinguistics* refers to variances in vocal delivery that are separate from the verbal message. Examples are tone of voice, loudness, inflection, and pitch, which can influence how words are interpreted by the receiver. The meanings assigned to paralinguistics are influenced by culture. Speaking in a loud voice may be seen as projecting authority and confidence in one culture but as impolite and disrespectful in another.
- *Gestures* refer to conscious (deliberate) or unconscious movements of the hands, arms, body, head, face, and eyes. Gestures may be used to convey messages and meanings independently of words. They may also be used by the source to add

meaning to verbal messages. As with other forms of nonverbal communication, the use and meanings of gestures are culture specific. Gestures that convey positive emotions in one culture may be improper and offensive in another (Pease & Pease, 2004). For example, in many Western cultures, gesturing with the hand is an acceptable sign to "come here please." The same gesture is offensive in many Asian countries because it is commonly used to call dogs. In the modern era of global communications facilitated by the Internet and accessible travel, the cultural specificity of meanings of some gestures may be moving toward universal understanding and acceptance, especially for young people. The point is, these gestures convey meanings, intended or unintended, and should be deciphered within the context of culture.

- *Body language and posture* complement gestures and convey additional meanings to words. Examples are slouching, towering, thrusting the jaw, putting shoulders forward, arm crossing, and leg crossing. Postures, whether conscious or unconscious, can signify emotions (liking or disliking), differences in status, and attention level or interest (Bull, 1987). An open body stance, such as a forward lean, expresses liking and interest, whereas a defensive body stance, such as leaning backwards, expresses dislike. Again, these interpretations are culturally based and influenced for the most part by studies in Western societies. Whether there is a universal system of body language and posture is debatable. We should therefore exercise caution in generalizing these interpretations across cultures. Nevertheless, we should pay attention to additional meanings that body language and posture express, but always place it in the context of cultures of the source and receiver.

- *Proxemics* refers to how people use and perceive the physical space around them (Hargie & Dickson, 2004). In general, the less space between the source and receiver, the more intimate the interaction is, and this is indicative of interest and liking. However, the interpretation of space is influenced by culture. What is appropriate space—and the intimacy interpretation of less space—in one culture may not be true in another. Although generalizations to entire cultures are often hazardous and inaccurate, research in intercultural communication has suggested some differences in how different cultures regard space. Some studies indicate that preferred distance between people engaged in person-to-person communication is much closer for Latin Americans, the French, Italians, and Arabs compared to White Americans. The principle suggested by these studies is that within parameters commonly accepted in the cultures of source and receiver, shorter distance expresses liking and interest.

- *Eye contact or gazing* is looking at the other person while talking and listening. In Western cultures, liking and attentiveness are expressed by the duration of mutual gazing: the longer the gaze, the more liking and intimacy between the communication participants (Hogan & Stubbs, 2003). However, in many cultures, such as Hispanic, Asian, Middle Eastern, and Native American, eye contact is generally considered to be a sign of disrespect or rudeness, and a lack of eye contact does not necessarily mean a lack of interest (Kirch, 1979). Also, studies of gender differences in Western societies indicate that heterosexual women may avoid contact with men because eye contact can be misinterpreted as a sign of sexual attraction (Kirch, 1979).

- *Haptics* is the study of how touching in communication adds meaning to words. Common touching in Western societies includes handshakes, holding hands, kissing (cheek, lips, hand), back slapping, high fives, a pat on the shoulder, and brushing an arm (Knapp, Hall, & Horgan, 2014). The interpretation of the meanings of touch depends on the context of interaction, the relationship between source and receiver, what touch is used, and culture. Touching that is appropriate in one culture may be disrespectful in another. For example, in the West, a handshake says "Thank you," "It's a deal," or "Glad to meet you." While the handshake is becoming universally accepted to convey these meanings, a bow of the head may be more appropriate in Japan; a slight kiss on the cheek between men may be more appropriate in the Middle East. And, in Islamic countries, any form of touching, including a handshake, between men and women in a business or social context is generally inappropriate or even forbidden.

VISUAL COMMUNICATION

Is a picture really worth a thousand words? Most communication relies heavily on visuals to make a point or simply to express feelings. To understand the encoding process fully, we must consider how meaning is transmitted by visual signs.

Visual communication is the transmittal of meanings by using still and moving images received by the eye. By one estimate, Americans are exposed to about 5,000 visual images a day (Lester, 2006). These images include pictures in magazines, newspapers, books, posters, and billboards; moving images in television shows and movies; and the images we receive on the Internet. With digital technologies, just about anyone with a digital phone and camera can send and receive images across geographical and time boundaries.

Considering the ubiquity of visual images, some scholars suggest that a worldwide visual culture, particularly among young people, has emerged. In a visual culture, people use images more than words to communicate, and they are more responsive to visual images than to written text (for example, Lester, 2006).

The proposition that visual signs are a more powerful tool for communication than language is supported by studies showing that "pictures have a direct route to long-term memory, each message storing its own information as a coherent chunk or concept" (Medina, 2008, p. 2), implying that pictures are better remembered than words. Also, some researchers suggest that humans are hardwired to respond to visual stimuli, considering that, historically, humans relied on vision to survive and adapt to the environment, for example, such as when choosing a mate or identifying predators and food sources (Medina, 2008). As a result, vision is our most dominant sense, and we absorb information much more successfully when visual signals are used, particularly when combined with words. To illustrate, one study found that 3 days after receiving a message, research participants remembered 10% of what they had heard (orally only), 20% of what they had read, and 65% of a message consisting of oral and visual signs (Lester, 2006). Besides improving retention significantly, visual signs have other characteristics that potentially can make a message more effective by improving attention and retention:

- A large number of images can be transmitted in a short time (Lester, 2006). Consider how much information can be transmitted in a 20-second television commercial.
- Visual images, compared to words, project greater realism, force, and immediacy. Studies show, for example, that emotions are more readily aroused by photos and moving images than by words (Smith, 2005).
- Visual images are capable of evoking involuntary (uncontrolled, unconscious) responses in receivers (Blair, Judd, & Chapleau, 2004). Consider, for example, the warm, pleasant feelings evoked by pictures of puppies and children.

In summary, visual images are a powerful tool for encoding messages, and should be included in the analysis of communication, particularly in the study of intercultural communication.

WHAT IS INTERCULTURAL COMMUNICATION?

We can use the mathematical, interaction, and transactional models to describe intercultural communication with one important distinction: the source and receiver are from different cultures. Here is our definition:

Intercultural communication is the exchange of information between at least two participants from different cultures to attain goals in a mutually satisfying relationship.

The potential for noise—differences in how the topic or object is understood, in the use of signals to encode the message, and in how signals are interpreted in decoding the message—is greater in intercultural communication than in intracultural communication, in which the participants come from the same culture. Therefore, effective intercultural communication requires greater attention to culture as a source of noise.

WHAT IS EFFECTIVE COMMUNICATION?

Before we can begin to talk about strategies for effective communication—intercultural communication, in particular—we must first define effective communication. This definition will depend on which model of communication we are considering.

- According to Shannon and Weaver's mathematical model, effective communication is measured by the amount of information sent and received. Perfect communication is when the amount received equals the amount sent in the system (Figure 2.1). Effective communication is facilitated by reducing the amount of noise in the source, channel, and receiver.
- Newcomb's interactive model defines effective communication as symmetry; that is, when the participants (A and B) come to an agreement about how they feel about the object or topic of communication (Figure 2.2). To arrive at symmetry, A and B should first have a common understanding of the topic of communication, and then have a sense of how they feel about each other.
- In the transactional model, effective communication is achieved when the source and receiver both have gained from the interaction (Figure 2.3). Mutual gain is measured by satisfaction of each party and by an assessment of whether goals have been met (Figure 2.4). Effective communication is facilitated by the reduction of noise, by mutual understanding of goals, and by willingness to compromise in the pursuit of goals.

Using the criteria from the different communication models, I define effective communication as:

- The transmittal of information so that the participants have a common awareness of the topic of communication (i.e., that they are talking about the same thing). The amount of information required will vary according to the situation, such as differences in the importance of context to the participants.
- Similar evaluations of the object or topic of communication, expressed as liking or disliking, or agreement or disagreement, by the participants.
- Shared positive evaluations by the participants; that is, they both like each other. The degree of liking will vary according to the situation. Participants starting out with severe dislike of each other, such is as in negotiations between wartime enemies, will not end up liking each other from the communication interaction. A minimum criterion is that after the interaction the participants will have reduced their dislike of each other or will have increased their liking of each other.
- Mutual attainment of goals, which may require compromise when original goals are not all met in the interaction.
- Mutual satisfaction from the interaction indicated by a shared evaluation that the interaction was a positive experience.

WHAT IS EFFECTIVE INTERCULTURAL COMMUNICATION?

Effective intercultural communication is attained when the criteria for effective general communication, as identified above, are met. In addition, mutual understanding of the cultures of the participants is a criterion for success. We now turn our attention to a discussion of culture and how culture affects communication.

REFERENCES

Blair, I., Judd, L., & Chapleau, K. (2004). The influence of Afrocentric facial features in criminal sentencing. *Psychological Science, 15*(10), 674–679.
Bull, P. E. (1987). *Posture and gesture.* Oxford: Pergamon Press.
Ekman, P. (2004). *Emotions revealed.* New York, NY: Henry Holt & Co.
Evans, N., & Levinson, S. (2009). The myth of language universals. Language diversity and its importance for cognitive sciences. *Behavioral and Brain Sciences, 32*(5), 429–492.
Hargie, O., & Dickson, D. (2004). *Skilled interpersonal communication: Research, theory and practice.* Hove: Routledge.

Hogan, K., & Stubbs, R. (2003). *Can't get through: Eight barriers to communication*. Grenta, LA: Pelican Publishing.

Kirch, M. S. (1979). Non-verbal communication across cultures. *Modern Language Journal, 63*(8), 417–422.

Knapp, M., Hall, J., & Horgan, T. (2014). *Non-verbal communication in human interaction*. (8th ed.). Belmont, CA: Wadsworth.

Lester, P. (2006). *Visual communication: Images with messages*. Belmont, CA: Wadsworth.

Maas, A. (1999). Linguistic intergroup bias: Stereotype perpetuation through language. In M. P. Zanna (Ed.), *Advances in experimental social psychology* (Vol. 31, pp. 79–121). San Diego, CA: Academic Press.

Medina, J. (2008). *Brain rules: 12 principles for surviving and thriving at work, home, and school*. Seattle, WA: Pear Press.

Navarro, J. (2008). *What everybody is saying*. New York, NY: Harper Collins.

Newcomb, T. (1953). An approach to the study of communicative acts. *Psychological Review, 60*, 193–404.

Pease, B., & Pease, A. (2004). *The definitive book of body language*. New York, NY: Bantam Books.

Ruscher, J. (2001). *Prejudiced communication: A social psychological perspective*. New York: The Guilford Press.

Shannon, C., & W. Weaver (1949). *The mathematical theory of communication*. Urbana, IL: University of Illinois Press.

Short, T.L. (2007). *Peirce's theory of signs*. Cambridge: Cambridge University Press.

Smith, K. L. (2005). *Handbook of visual communication: Theory, methods, and media*. Mahwah, NJ: Lawrence Erlbaum.

Tan, A. (1986). *Mass communication theories and research*. (2nd ed.). New York, NY: Macmillan.

Tan, A. (2015). *Communication and prejudice: Theories, effects, and interventions*. San Diego, CA: Cognella Academic Publishing.

CHAPTER 3
UNDERSTANDING CULTURAL DIFFERENCES IN COMMUNICATION

WHAT IS CULTURE? HOW DOES CULTURE AFFECT COMMUNICATION?

BY ALEXIS TAN

DIMENSIONS OF CULTURE

Culture is defined by its dimensions—worldviews, beliefs, values, attitudes, and behavioral norms. In this section, I discuss those dimensions that have the most impact on intercultural communication.

HOFSTEDE'S NATIONAL CULTURAL DIMENSIONS

According to Hofstede (1984) and Hofstede et al. (2010), culture has six dimensions that can differentiate between countries. Here are three of them:

- *Power distance* is the "extent to which the less powerful person accepts inequality in power and considers it as normal" (Hofstede, 2001, p. 139). In a high power distance culture, society is highly stratified into institutionalized hierarchies based on wealth and political authority. People with high power consider people with low power to be different from them; they consider the unequal distribution of power and authority to be "a fact of life," and believe that everybody has a rightful place in society determined by how much power he or she

has. In high power distance societies, there is greater centralization of political power, less participation by people with low power, positions of authority are held by people with power, and more importance is placed on status and rank.
- In low power distance cultures, people believe that inequality is undesirable and should be minimized, all people should have access to power, and people in power should be held accountable to the publics they serve. In low power distance cultures, laws, norms, and everyday behaviors minimize power distance.
- According to Hofstede (2001), Malaysia, Guatemala, Panama, and the Philippines are high power distance cultures, whereas Austria, Israel, Denmark, and New Zealand are low power distance cultures. The United States ranks 38 out of 53 countries (53 being the country with the lowest power distance). These rankings were based on a survey of IBM employees in over 50 countries in the late 1960s and early 1970s by Hofstede and his colleagues (Hofstede, 2001).
- *Individualism/collectivism* is a cultural dimension that measures the degree to which members of a culture use the group or the individual as a basis for personal identities (Schwartz, 1994). In collectivist cultures, the group is the most important identity source, meaning that people's identities are anchored on group memberships. Therefore, there is greater emphasis on needs and goals of the in-group; on collaboration, shared interests, and harmony; and on preserving the "face," or positive image, of the group. In contrast, in individualist cultures, personal goals take precedence over group goals, independence of the individual rather than reliance on the group is stressed, and an individual's personal identity and self-image are more important than group identity in guiding behaviors and interpersonal relations. Hofstede et al. (2010) identified the United States as the most individualist culture among more than 50 countries in the IBM surveys, followed by Australia, Great Britain, Canada, the Netherlands, and New Zealand. The most collectivist cultures were Guatemala, Ecuador, Panama, and Venezuela.
- *Uncertainty avoidance* refers to the degree that people in a culture are uncomfortable (or comfortable) with situations that are unstructured, unpredictable, unknown, unfamiliar, or unclear, and the extent to which they are willing to cope with and tolerate these situations. In high uncertainty avoidance cultures, members try to avoid uncertainty and ambiguity because these situations are uncomfortable. To prevent high uncertainty situations from occurring, and to cope with them when they do occur, high anxiety avoidance cultures establish formal rules, seek consensus, rely on authority figures, and are less tolerant of deviant ideas and behaviors. Members of low uncertainty avoidance cultures are more comfortable with unfamiliar, new, and unstructured situations. They are more tolerant of unusual and nonconforming behavior, have fewer rules governing social behavior, dislike hierarchies and rigid social structures, and are more willing to take risks.

Hofstede et al. (2010) identified Greece, Portugal, Guatemala, and Uruguay as high uncertainty avoidance countries (do not like uncertainty), and Singapore, Jamaica, Denmark, and Sweden as low uncertainty avoidance countries (do not feel uncomfortable with uncertainty). The United States ranked 43 out of 53 countries (the higher the rank, the lower anxiety avoidance).

These cultural dimensions were identified by Hofstede and his colleagues in a series of studies beginning in 1967, the most recent in 2010. [. . .]

HALL'S HIGH- AND LOW-CONTEXT CULTURES

According to Hall (1981), intercultural communication can be analyzed by considering how much emphasis is placed on the context of information and how much emphasis is placed on the explicit message. The context of communication is the physical environment in which communication takes place, including its setting (e.g., formal board room or informal wine bar); the status and social positions of the participants; and nonverbal signs, such as gestures and facial expressions. In high-context cultures, most of the meanings exchanged among participants depend more on context and less on the explicit verbal message. High-context participants often come from homogeneous cultures in which tradition and past experience have taught them what behaviors are expected in social relationships and how to respond to messages from others. Much of the exchange of explicit verbal messages is ritualistic and formal. The real meaning of the interaction is in its context—roles, nonverbal signs, and other situational cues. Communication is often indirect to promote harmony and to avoid public expressions of discord.

In contrast, members of low-context cultures place more emphasis on the explicit verbal message. "Tell me what you think, and put it in writing" is a common expectation. Low-context people have difficulty reading meanings from the context of communication. They expect that meanings will be expressed in explicit verbal messages. Communication is direct, and people are expected to express themselves.

Some high-context cultures, according to Hall (1981) are Japanese, Chinese, and Korean. Examples of low-context cultures are German, Scandinavian, and North American. [. . .]

KLUCKHOHN AND STRODTBECK'S CULTURAL DIMENSIONS

According to Kluckohn and Strodtbeck (1961), culture is best understood by analyzing how people respond to human problems. The solutions to these problems, which could be caused by environmental stresses like drought and earthquakes or by human conflicts like war, depend on values held by members of a group or community. They define a value as "a conception, explicit or implicit, … of the desirable which influences the selection from available modes, means and ends of action," a definition they borrowed from Kluckhohn (1951, p. 395). Therefore, values are deeply held beliefs about what is important in life (goals), what are the best means to achieving these goals, and what are the important results (ends). In a group, community, or society (an aggregate of many communities), members will share a few values that guide the selection of solutions to problems and which are manifestations of the group's, community's, or society's culture. Kluckhohn and Strodtbeck (1961) identified five problems confronted by human societies with different possible strategies for finding solutions. The preferred strategies are based on cultural values. Here are the societal problems, posed as questions, and possible strategies for solving them (Hills, 2002):

- *Time*: Should we focus on the past, present, or future?
- *Humans and the natural environment*: Should we master the environment? Live in harmony with it? Submit to it?
- *Relations with other people*: Should we relate to others hierarchically (*lineal*)? As equals (*collateral*)? According to individual merit?
- *Motivation for human behavior*: Is the prime motivation to express one's self, to grow, or to achieve?
- *Human nature*: Are humans naturally good, bad, or a mixture?

The possible answers to these questions indicate a society's values, which, in turn, reflect that society's culture. The preferred solutions help us understand how people in the culture respond to common problems. Here is a summary adapted from Hills (2002, p. 5):
- Time
    - Past: Focus on the time before now—or the past—and on preserving and maintaining traditional teachings and beliefs.
    - Present: Focus on what is now—the present—and on accommodating changes in beliefs and traditions.
    - Future: Focus on the time to come—the future—and on planning ahead and seeking new ways to replace the old.

- Natural environment
  - Mastery: Can and should exercise total control over nature.
  - Harmonious: Can and should exercise partial, but not total, control by living in balance with nature.
  - Submissive: Cannot and should not exercise control over nature; subject to the "higher power" of these forces.
- Relating to other people
  - Hierarchical (lineal): Deferring to higher authorities within the group.
  - As equals (collateral): Seeking consensus within the group as equal members.
  - Individualistic: Making decisions independently from others in the group.
- Motive for individual actions
  - To express oneself: Emphasizes activity valued by the individual but not necessarily by others in the group.
  - To grow: Emphasizes growth in abilities that are valued by the individual, but not necessarily by others.
  - To achieve: Emphasizes activity valued by the individual and approved by others.

As you can see, each of these values leads to a particular response that might be used in solving a problem. According to Kluckhohn and Strodtbeck (1961), these values are indicative of a group's culture, and agreement on which values are important can be found within many groups. They began their research to determine how much agreement can be found within cultural groups by interviewing Navahos, Mexican Americans, Texan homesteaders, Mormon villagers, and Zuni pueblo dwellers in the American Southwest. They developed scenarios to describe real-life situations that all five cultural groups would find realistic and relevant. They then asked their participants how they would respond to the situations, and assigned the participants, based on responses, to a value orientation category (e.g., past, present, or future time orientation). They drew value orientation profiles of each group, showing how much agreement there was within the groups, and how similar or different the groups were from each other. These profiles described the cultures of each group based on their value orientations.

Other researchers have used Kluckhohn and Strodtbeck's value orientation model to describe and compare cultures in different contexts and geographical regions. Russo (2000) and Russo, Hills et al. (1984) analyzed the value orientations of the Lumni, an indigenous community in Washington state. Hills (1977) and Hills & Goneyali 1980) studied generational changes in values between young people and their parents as a result of migration. They looked at samples of migrants to New Zealand from Samoa, Fiji, and the Cook Islands. Using Kluckhohn and Strodtbeck's value orientations, they interviewed young people ages 16 to 18 and their parents, using tape-recorded questions in the respondent's native language. Here are some examples of the interview questions (from Hills, 2002, p. 8):

I will ask you 25 questions. There are three possible answers to each question. Please listen carefully to each question and then each of the three suggested answers to that question. I can play them again if you would like to listen to them again. We do not want your name. There are no right or wrong answers to these questions—we want to know how you feel about them. Take as much time as you need to answer them.
Here is the first one.

When our group sends a delegate to a meeting I think it's best—
Relational
1 To let everyone discuss it until everyone agrees on the person.
   Collateral
2 To let the important leaders decide. They have more experience than us.
   Lineal
3 For a vote to be taken and the one with the most votes goes, even if some people disagree.
   Individualistic

Now please tell me the answer which comes closest to the way you feel.
Now tell me the answer which is your second choice.
Thanks. Here's the next one.

When I get sick I believe:
Humanity and Nature
1 Doctors will be able to find a way to cure it.
   Mastery
2 I should live properly so I don't get sick.
   Harmony
3 I cannot do much about it and just have to accept it.
   Subjugation

Here's the third …

When I send money for use overseas, I think it should be spent to:
Time
1 Make a better life for the future.
   Future
2 Make a better life now.
   Present
3 Keep the old ways and customs alive.
   Past

Using this interview protocol, Hills (1977) and Hills and Goneyali (1980) showed changes in value orientations between young immigrants and their parents, which he attributed to migration. Young people showed more agreement with the predominant values of the new environment (New Zealand) than did their parents.

Kluckhohn and Strodtbeck (1961) provide us with a useful tool for differentiating between cultures. However, we should be aware of two possible weaknesses in their theory. First, the definitions of values are heavily influenced by the researchers' perceptions of how cultures might differ from each other. The starting point is their theory, which they then test in different cultures. An alternative strategy is to first ask people to describe their cultures and then build a theory based on the responses. Thus, theory is developed from the ground up, respondents to researcher, rather than from the top, researcher to respondents. Second, the theory does not adequately provide for the possibility that respondents may use different values as a basis for solving a problem, depending on context. These values are not necessarily mutually exclusive. For example, on the relational value orientation, I may be individualistic at work but lineal in my family.

Nonetheless, Kluckhohn and Strodtbeck's values orientation theory has provided researchers with a useful tool for differentiating between cultures. These weaknesses are not unique to their theory, but are weaknesses of most of the other cultural dimension theories as well. The common problem is how do we generalize from individual data or information obtained from the individual through interviews and questionnaires to the entire group, and how do we account for individual differences within the group? Researchers continue to grapple with this problem with varying degrees of success.

TROMPENAARS AND HAMPDEN-TURNER'S SEVEN DIMENSIONS OF CULTURE

According to Trompenaars and Hampden-Turner (1997), culture has seven dimensions, which they identified from surveys of 40,000 teenagers in 40 countries. These dimensions are as follows:

1. *Universalism (rules) versus particularism (relationships)*: People with a universalism point of view place a high value on laws, rules, and obligations; rules come before relationships. People who are particularistic place relationships

above rules; their actions are determined by the situation and who is involved, rather than by rules and laws.

2. *Individualism (the individual) versus communitarianism (the group)*: Individualistic people value personal freedom and achievement, and believe that the individual should make his or her own decisions. People who value communitarianism believe that the group is more important than the individual, the group provides help and safety in exchange for loyalty, and the group always comes before the individual.

3. *Specific versus diffuse relationships at work*: People with a specific perspective believe that personal relationships are separate from work and that people can work together without having a good relationship. People with a diffuse relationship believe that good relationships are important at work and are necessary for success at work.

4. *Neutral versus emotional*: Neutral people control their emotions. They believe more in reason than in emotions. They keep their emotions to themselves. Emotional people express how they feel more openly; their behaviors are influenced by emotions.

5. *Achievement versus ascription*: People who value ascription believe that a person's worth should be based on performance, what a person does. People who subscribe to ascription believe that a person's worth is based on status, power, title, and position.

6. *Sequential time versus synchronous time*: People who value sequential time believe that time is valuable and that events should happen in order, in a linear fashion. They value punctuality, planning, and sticking to a schedule. To people who value synchronous time, the past, present and future are interchangeable and related. Therefore, time is not linear, but circular. It's more important to complete many tasks and projects rather than sticking to a schedule to finish one task.

7. *Internal direction (internal locus of control) versus outer direction (external locus of control)*: People who are internally directed believe that they can control their environment to achieve goals. People who are externally directed believe that their environment controls them; therefore, they must work within the constraints of what is around them, including other people.

The dimensions of culture defined above give the end points of a scale, meaning that they are bipolar extremes. A culture could be assigned to any point between these extreme anchors based on responses to a questionnaire by individuals within the culture. Again, we are faced with the problem of generalizing from individuals to the group and accounting for individual differences.

The cultural dimensions I have discussed are a convenient way of describing and categorizing cultures based on their worldviews and values. And, as you can see, there is quite a bit of commonality among these dimensions. [. . .] I discuss how the cultures of several countries have been placed along several of these dimensions. I also suggest communication strategies that might be appropriate and effective in several cultures based on their placement on the continuum. A word of caution, though: these dimensions are generalizations, so we should take care to first know whether the individual we are interacting with fits into the cultural mode we have assigned to him or her. There is no substitute [. . .] to treating people as individuals first before we consider their culture.

HOW DO WE LEARN CULTURE?

So far, we have looked at several dimensions on which culture can be described. These dimensions do not exhaust all the possible manifestations of culture, but they are the ones that are most relevant to intercultural communication. Remember that culture is learned and transmitted from one generation to the next. Further, culture is patterned, meaning that the dimensions are all related to and consistent with each other and they, taken together, provide a general guide for making sense of and acting within a person's environment in the context of membership in a group. How then is such a complex pattern of accepted norms for action and believing learned within a group?

A number of theories from anthropology, sociology, education, and social psychology explain how culture is learned. In this section, I focus on those theories that assign an important role to communication.

MOTIVATION TO LEARN A CULTURE: SOCIAL IDENTITY THEORY

Why should a person be motivated to learn a culture? Tajfel and Turner's (1986) social identity theory gives us a clue. First, group membership provides us with a source of identity, a sense of who we are. Research has shown that, indeed, our sense of who we are is determined by groups we strongly identify with—for example, student organizations, work organizations, ethnic and racial groups, religious groups, countries, or nationalities. Not all of these groups will be salient or will influence our actions, perceptions, and beliefs at all times; group influence on the individual is situational rather than general. For example, organizational culture may influence my behavior at work (e.g., I work 12-hour days because everybody else seems to do so) while national or country culture (e.g., "American") may influence my behavior when travelling abroad. In intercultural communication, much of the emphasis has been on national cultures. We ask, how does culture at this level affect communication interactions? We are also interested in how co-cultures, defined as smaller group cultures within a nation, such as the cultures of racial and ethnic groups, interact with each other. The basic premises of social identity theory hold regardless of the level of analysis from small to large groups for two reasons. First, group membership is a source of self-identity. Second, the stronger the individual's identification with the group, the greater the motivation to learn its culture.

Another motivation for learning a group's culture is self-preservation, meaning that the individual needs the group to survive and thrive in the natural and social environment. The group provides the resources needed by the individual to function effectively in interactions with other groups and with nature. At the national level, consider social security, laws, disaster relief, health insurance, and the military. These resources are available to us because we identify as "Americans" and are members of this national group.

THE PROCESS OF LEARNING CULTURE: ENCULTURATION AND SOCIALIZATION

Learning a culture continues over time from childhood to adulthood. Although most of the research emphasis has been on children and adolescents, attention has also been given to how immigrants, sojourners (temporary visitors to a country), and adults in new environments learn cultures.

Two general and related theories explain the process of learning culture. *Enculturation* is defined by Kottak (2011) as:

> the process where the culture that is currently established teaches an individual the accepted norms and values of the culture or society where the individual lives. The individual can become an accepted member and fulfill the needed functions and roles of the group.

Most importantly the individual knows and establishes a context of boundaries and accepted behavior that dictates what is acceptable and not acceptable within the framework of that society. It teaches the individual their role within society as well as what is accepted behavior within that society and lifestyle.

Socialization is a similar concept, defined as:

1. A lifelong process of learning the norms, customs and ideologies of a society that are needed for participation, functioning, and continued membership (Macionis, 2010);

2. A learning process influenced by agents such as the family (Macionis & Gerber, 2011); peers (other members of the group who are important to the learner, sometimes referred to as "significant others") (Macionis & Gerber, 2011); teachers and schools (Macionis & Gerber, 2011); and the media, new and traditional (McQuail, 2005).

These definitions help us understand what is learned and who the teachers might be, but gives little information on how culture is learned. The next two theories tell us about the learning process.

SOCIAL COGNITIVE THEORY

Most theories of how behaviors, beliefs, values, and other dimensions of culture are learned include two processes: learning by direct experience and by purposive teaching. Traditional learning theories, for example, explain that learning occurs by actually performing the behavior and then experiencing its consequences. Learning is facilitated by reinforcement, or the extent to which the behavior is rewarded or punished. People will learn culture by acting out its components and then repeating the actions if they are rewarded. They learn these behaviors from information and instruction given to them by parents, peers, and teachers. For example, how does a child learn that in American culture he or she is supposed to act independently and not depend too much on a group? The child may be instructed to do so by parents or teachers; then he or she does a class assignment independently of a group; parents or teachers show approval; and consequently, this behavior, acting independently, becomes part of the child's pattern of responses to the environment.

Unlike traditional learning theories, *social cognitive theory* (SCT) explains how behaviors are learned from observation. The opportunity to learn and practice or enact behaviors from direct instruction is present in most cultures, particularly in classrooms and the home. However, there is also a great deal of opportunity to learn indirectly from observation without direct instruction—for example, children observing their parents' interaction with people in the mall; actions of their favorite characters in television and the movies, and the consequences of these actions; and the behavior of classmates in the playground. Developed by Albert Bandura (1986, 2002), SCT explains how we learn by observation. This theory is particularly relevant to intercultural communication because many of the behaviors we can learn, such as those included in cultural dimensions, are presented in new and traditional media, including television and the movies.

According to SCT (Bandura 1985, 2002), learning by observation occurs in sequential steps:

1. The learner, such as a child being socialized into a culture, is motivated to acquire knowledge about a behavior. Motivation will depend on the child' sense of self-efficacy, the ability to learn and repeat the observed behavior, and on perceived rewards from performing the behavior, such as parental approval: the higher the sense of self-efficacy, the greater the motivation; also, the greater the expectation that the behavior will be rewarded, the greater the motivation to learn it.

2. The behavior to be learned is presented in a medium that reaches the learner. Children watch television. They play video games on their electronic devices. Behaviors and values demonstrated or implied in these media can be observed by children and potentially learned.

3. The learner pays attention to the behavior presented in a medium. Attention is facilitated by repetition; portrayals of characters that the observer identifies with because they have similar characteristics ("They are just like me"); portrayals of situations that the learner identifies with because of experience (e.g., "I have been there") or relevance (e.g., "This applies to me"); distinctiveness (portrayals that stand out); simple (easy to understand and follow); and positive emotional arousal ("This makes me feel good," "This is funny," "The good people won").

4. The learner remembers the behavior learned, stores it using symbolic codes (language and visually), and rehearses it mentally. Retention is facilitated by simplicity of the act and its prevalence or repetition in the environment.

5. When the occasion arises, the remembered behavior is enacted or produced, such as child preferring to work alone rather than in a group. Enactment will be consistent and repeated when the behavior is rewarded, as when a child is praised by parents and teachers.

SCT, as you can see, is a powerful model for explaining how *deliberate* learning occurs by observation. The learner actively processes information from observed events and reenactment occurs consciously and with purpose. Because much of a culture's values and behavioral norms are indeed reenacted by socialized members repeatedly in everyday life and in the media, the opportunity for deliberate observational learning is not only present, but inviting to the novice learner. But what about unconscious learning?

CULTIVATION THEORY

Not all learning is deliberate and conscious. We also learn cultural beliefs and behaviors unconsciously. That is, we are learning them but we do not actively exert effort to learn them. And we are not consciously aware of having learned these behaviors until we enact them. Bias and prejudice [. . .] are examples of cultural behaviors that many of us learn unconsciously.

So how do we learn culture unconsciously? *Cultivation theory* (CT) provides an explanation of unconscious learning from the mass media. Developed by George Gerbner and Larry Gross more than 30 years ago, CT continues to be an influential theory about how we learn from television (e.g., Morgan & Shanahan, 2010). The basic premise of CT is that heavy viewers of television learn to believe the social realities portrayed in television. And most of us, especially children, are heavy viewers. This learning is cumulative, happens over time after repeated exposure, and is unconscious and not deliberate. We learn from constant exposure; we do not deliberately seek out behaviors and norms that will help us adapt and function in a culture.

Gerbner and his colleagues propose the following propositions about television's effects on culture:

1. Television is "the source of the most broadly shared images and messages in history. Television cultivates from infancy the very predispositions that used to be acquired from other primary sources. The repetitive pattern of television's mass produced messages and images forms the mainstream of a common symbolic environment" (Gerbner, Gross & Signorielli, 1986). Further, Gerbner et al. (1986) propose that "the substance of consciousness cultivated by television is not so much specific attitudes and opinions as more basic assumptions about the facts of life and standards of judgment on which conclusions are based."

    In other words, television has supplanted parents, peers, and the school as the primary agents of cultural socialization because of its ubiquity (especially today, with availability in a variety of platforms); the effects of television are not on specific attitudes, but on a person's worldview (dimensions of culture in our previous discussion); and these effects are cumulative and happen over time.

2. Television presents a reality that supports existing institutions, power structures, and cultural norms. Television's reality does not always (one might say rarely) coincide with realities in our natural environment. For example, more violence is portrayed in television than actually happens in the real world. Although Gerbner's cultural indicators project, which maps out television realities through content analysis, does not address most of the cultural dimensions I discussed earlier, several themes related to culture have been identified. These include gender roles; racial and ethnic representation and status; fear of crime; police presence and effectiveness; mistrust of people; and, the television reality that has attracted the most attention from researchers, violence in the real world.

3. Heavy viewers of television have accepted television realities as their own and natural realities. For example, research has found that heavy viewers in comparison to light viewers:

   a. Are more afraid of being victims of crime;
   b. Believe that there are more police officers in the real world and that police are more effective in solving crimes than they are in the real world;
   c. Have a greater mistrust of people.

There is, therefore, evidence that television "cultivates" in heavy viewers some indicators of a culture and that this cultivation can be found across co-cultures, such as racial groups within a society, thereby resulting in a common outlook, at least on some cultural indicators, a process Gerbner calls "mainstreaming." Further research can confirm our expectation that television might be able to similarly influence viewer adaptations of other cultural dimensions discussed earlier in this chapter.

DOES CULTURE CHANGE?

The short answer is "yes." Learned patterns of behavior and beliefs can be unlearned and replaced with new ones when human needs change or when external pressures support change (Rochon, 1998). Although resistant to change, considering that its many dimensions are imbedded in group members over a long period of time, culture can change in response to the following forces (Rochon, 1998):

1. *Discovery and invention.* Discovery is "addition to knowledge" and invention is "new application of knowledge" (Linton, 1955). To lead to cultural change, an invention or discovery would first have to be understood and accepted and then used regularly. Acceptance comes after the invention or discovery is shown to be beneficial to the individual and society. Examples in the United States are technological inventions such as the automobile, new energy sources, and new digital technologies, all of which have affected how Americans view the world and related behaviors.

2. *Internal changes within a society, such as changes in political and economic structures.* Much has been written in the media about changes in some values and related behaviors, particularly among young people, in some Middle Eastern countries and China because of changes in political and economic conditions. Whether and to what extent the cultural dimensions discussed earlier in this chapter have changed in these countries is a matter for empirical research.

3. *Influence from foreign countries.* Powerful countries and cultures such as the United States have the potential to change cultures in less powerful countries. This process is called *acculturation*, the replacement of native cultures with foreign cultures. This process can take many forms: conquest through war; economic domination; and, most relevant to intercultural communication, influence through the media. Many scholars have expanded on the original notion that "the media are American" (Tunstall, 1977; Scotton and Hatchen, 2008), showing that American media, particularly movies and television, have indeed influenced young people around the world to adopt the American cultural realities portrayed (accurately or not), from the more superficial manifestations in dress, music, and food to values emphasizing consumption and hedonism.

4. *Influence of a new culture.* To be accepted, an immigrant is expected to adapt the values and behavioral norms of the new culture. When this change occurs, the process is called *transculturation*. The extent to which total transculturation is functional for the immigrant and the new culture continues to be subject of debate, especially as migration increases around the world, significantly changing the demographics in host societies, including the United States. One view says that complete transculturation is necessary to preserve the culture of the host country. Another view says that the diversity in cultures brought by immigrants adds to the richness of the host culture. Others say that diverse values, worldviews, and behavioral norms indeed add to the host culture and should be accepted and respected, but that certain fundamental values, such as those identified in the host country's constitution, should be upheld. (In the United States these values include freedom and equality.)

REFERENCES

Bandura, A. (1985). *Social foundations of thought and action*. Englewood Cliffs, NJ: Prentice Hall.

Bandura, A. (2002). Social cognitive theory in cultural context. *Applied Psychology, 51*(2), 269–290.

Gerbner, G., Gross, L., Morgan, M., & Signorielli, N. (1986). Living with television: The dynamics of the cultivation process. In J. Bryant and D. Zillman (Eds.), *Perspectives on media effects* (pp. 17–40). Hillsdale, NJ: Lawrence Erlbaum Associates.

Hall, E. (1981). *Beyond culture*. New York, NY: Anchor Books.

Hills, M. D. (2002). Kluckhohn and Strodtbeck's values orientation theory. *Online Readings in Psychology and Culture, 4*(4). Retrieved from http://dx.doi.org/10.9707/2307-0919.1040.

Hills, M.D. (1977). *Values in the South Pacific*. Paper presented at the Annual Conference of the New Zealand Psychological Society, Auckland, New Zealand.

Hills, M. D., & Goneyali, E. (1980). *Values in Fijan families* (Monograph). Hamilton, New Zealand: University of Waikato, Dept. of Psychology.

Hofstede, G. (1984). *Culture's consequences: International differences in work-related values*. Beverly Hills, CA: Sage.

Hofstede, G. (2001). *Culture's consequences: Comparing, values, behaviors, institutions, and organizations across nations*. Beverly Hills, CA: Sage.

Hofstede, G., Hofstede, G. J., & Minkov, M. (2010). *Cultures and organizations: Software of the mind*. New York, NY: McGraw-Hill.

Kluckhohn, C. K. (1951). Values and value orientations in the theory of action. In T. Parsons and E. A. Shils (Eds.), *Toward a general theory of action*. Cambridge, MA: Harvard University Press.

Kluckhohn, F. R., & Strodtbeck, F. L. (1961). *Variations in value orientations*. Evanston, IL: Row, Peterson.

Kottak, C. P. (2011). *Window on humanity: A concise introduction to Anthropology*. New York: McGraw-Hill.

Linton, R. (1955). *The tree of culture*. New York, NY: Alfred Knopf.

Macionis, J. (2010). *Sociology*. New York, NY: Pearson Education.

Macionis, J., & Gerber, L. (2011) *Sociology*. New York, NY: Pearson Education.

McQuail, D. (2005). *McQuail's mass communication theory*. Beverly Hills, CA: Sage.

Morgan, M., & Shanahan, J. (2010). The state of cultivation research. *Journal of Broadcasting & Electronic Media, 54*(2), 337–355.

Rochon, T. (1998). *Culture moves: Ideas, activism, and changing values*. Princeton, NJ: Princeton University Press.

Russo, K. W. (Ed.). (2000). *Finding the middle ground: Insights and applications of the value orientations method*. Yarmouth, ME: Intercultural Press.

Russo, K., Hills, M.D. et al. (1984). *Value orientations in the Lumni Indian community and their commercial associates*. Report to the Lumni Indian Council. Bellingham, WA.

Schwartz, S. (Ed.). (1994). *Beyond individualism/collectivism: New cultural dimension of values*. Thousand Oaks, CA: Sage.

Scotton, J., & Hachten, W. (2008). *New media for a new China*. New York, NY: Wiley.

Tajfel H., & Turner, J.C. (1986). The social identity theory of intergroup behavior. In S. Worchel & W.G. Austin (Eds.). *Psychology of intergroup relations* (pp. 7–24). Chicago, IL: Nelson-Hall.

Trompenaars, F., & Hampden-Turner, C. (1997). *Riding the waves of culture: Understanding diversity in global business*. (3rd ed.). New York, NY: McGraw-Hill.

Tunstall, J. (1977). *The media are American*. New York, NY: Columbia University Press.

ADAPTING TO THE U.S. ACADEMIC CULTURE

PART II

CHAPTER 4
CROSS-CULTURAL ADAPTATION TO THE UNITED STATES

THEORIES OF INTERCULTURAL COMMUNICATION

BY ALEXIS TAN

Intercultural communication occurs in different contexts, some of which are the following:

- One-time initial encounters, such as when visiting another country and asking for directions.
- Repeated encounters over a very short term, such as when negotiating a business deal in a day or two.
- Repeated encounters for a short and temporary period of time, such as when studying abroad for a semester.
- Repeated encounters over an extended period of time, usually of a permanent nature, such as when an immigrant relocates to another country.

Most theories of intercultural communication explain what happens when participants interact face-to-face or interpersonally and, more recently, via social media in the Internet. In intercultural communication, the participants come from different cultures. They bring different and sometimes contradictory worldviews to the interaction. To be effective in intercultural communication we should identify the conditions that result in success and the conditions that result in failure. Failure to do so can be costly to the participants. The immediate consequence of failure is that the source and receiver do not achieve their goals. A more serious consequence, arising when there is prolonged and repeated contact between a

Alexis Tan, "Theories of Intercultural Communication," *The Intercultural Communication Guidebook: Research-based Strategies for Successful Interactions*, pp. 63-92. Copyright © 2016 by Cognella, Inc. Reprinted with permission.

newcomer or out-group member and members of another culture, in-group, or host culture is culture shock.

Culture shock is severe discomfort felt by a newcomer when interacting with people from another culture, usually in the latter's territory and over an extended period of time. It is manifested in "washing hands excessively, being overly concerned with food and drinking, fearing people, being absent-minded, refusing to learn the host country's language and customs, and worrying about being robbed, cheated or injured" (Chen, 1992, p. 63). In extreme cases, when the newcomer has no choice but to continue living in the new culture, culture shock can lead to paranoia, schizophrenia, and lack of confidence (Yeh, Chu, Klein, Alexander & Miller, 1981). Culture shock, therefore, is the newcomer's failure to adapt to a new cultural environment where signs, symbols, customs, beliefs, and behaviors are different from what he or she is used to. This failure has serious negative consequences for both the newcomer and members of the host culture. Culture shock is brought about by unpleasant and unfamiliar international and co-cultural experiences. The newcomer finds difficulty understanding the new environment because it lacks familiar social cues and contextual signs that guided him or her at home. Behaviors and beliefs in the host culture seem "strange," and some may be offensive or simply difficult to comprehend. The newcomer is lost and feels helpless; common responses are anger toward the host culture and glorification of the home culture. In extreme cases, the newcomer avoids the host culture altogether ("sticking to ourselves") or may abruptly leave. Culture shock is more likely to occur when the host and home cultures are significantly different from each other; that is, they differ in values, worldviews, and behavioral norms. These differences may derive from religion (e.g., Muslim and Christian) or world geography (e.g., East and West), resulting in differences in one or more cultural dimensions (e.g., individualism/collectivism, power distance). For example, an American is more likely to experience culture shock in China than in Ireland; the Chinese are more likely to experience culture shock in the United States than in Japan. Also, the severity of culture shock depends on the duration of stay in the host country. A tourist may be able to shake off the effects of culture shock by staying with the tourist group (and reinforcing evaluations of the host culture as "strange"). However, a student studying abroad for several months or an expatriate living and working abroad will have to cope with culture shock if he or she is to interact effectively in the host culture.

In general, then, cultural differences lead to culture shock. But what everyday behaviors trigger culture shock? A study in Oman provides some answers. Rajasekar and Renand (2013) interviewed 110 expatriates living in Oman and Omanis who had travelled abroad, asking them to relate "one main event" they had experienced (expatriates in Oman, Omanis in another country) that "shocked" or seriously surprised them. The study included expatriates from several Western and Asian countries, and Omanis who had visited several Western and Asian countries. Here are some results for Americans in Oman and Omanis who had lived in the United States. Americans, in general, have been characterized as individualist and low power distance; Omanis as collectivist and high power distance (Hofstede, Hofstede, & Minton, 2010). Also, Oman is predominantly Muslim; the United States is predominantly Christian. Therefore, this comparison highlights differences in behavioral norms (what is accepted behavior) that might trigger culture shock.

"Main events" leading to culture shock, experienced or observed by Americans in Oman (from Rajasekar & Renand, 2013, p. 154):

- Men kissing each other and touching each other nose to nose
- Having a boyfriend not being acceptable
- The shopkeeper being angry when asked for beer
- Being told that smoking and drinking are forbidden but seeing Omanis smoking
- Woman refusing to shake hands with her male colleague
- The weekend being Thursday and Friday
- Politeness of Omani students
- People eating from the same plate with their hands
- Eating with their hand and sitting on the ground
- Omani women wearing black Abaya
- Daughter's friends never establishing eye contact

"Main events" leading to culture shock, experienced or observed by Omanis in the United States (from Rajasekar & Renand, 2013, p. 155):

- Nobody caring about a naked man's presence in the station
- Being confused by people using the word "bathroom" instead of "toilet"
- Christian friends singing and dancing inside the church
- People asking why Omanis do not eat pork, why women cover up, and why only men marry four wives
- A friend living alone because his parents asked him to leave home

As you can see, most of these possible culture shock triggers are rather mundane, everyday behaviors. But they can make a newcomer uncomfortable, because they appear "strange" and "not right." These behaviors derive from deeply held cultural traditions and beliefs, and they are shocking or surprising because they are unfamiliar. The key to coping with and reducing culture shock is knowledge; understanding that some behaviors acceptable in the home country may be rejected in the host country; and understanding that some behaviors considered offensive in the home country may be acceptable in the host country (Black & Gregersen, 1991).

Theories of intercultural communication have focused on identifying communication competencies that can reduce culture shock, or, in general, reduce failures in adapting to new cultures. Here are a few theories that assign a central role to communication and that explain how communication can lead to effective intercultural interactions. I group these theories into three categories based on the stage in the communication process that is their focus: predispositions and initial interactions, ongoing interactions in single encounters, and long-term and repeated interactions. I discuss a fourth category, new digital media theories of intercultural communication. These theories have the following elements in common: (1) they are concerned with individual traits, group characteristics, and situational conditions leading to effective communication; (2) the units of analysis are individuals engaged in face-to-face or internet mediated interactions; and (3) the outcomes are communication competence, effective communication, and adaptation in brief or prolonged cultural encounters.

PREDISPOSITIONS AND INITIAL ENCOUNTERS

What individual traits and group characteristics predict successful initial intercultural interactions? What obstacles to effective communication are encountered by the participants at the onset or beginning of an intercultural encounter? The two theories I review below provide some answers to these questions.

ANXIETY/UNCERTAINTY MANAGEMENT THEORY

William Gudykunst (2005) developed anxiety/uncertainty management theory to explain how anxiety and uncertainty can lead to ineffective intercultural communication between newcomers or strangers and members of a host culture. He assumes that at least one participant in an intercultural interaction is a "stranger" to the new and different culture and will therefore be unfamiliar with the host culture's worldviews, values, behaviors, and norms. An example would be an American exchange student attending college for a year in China on the first day in her host college. Gudykunst's theory takes the perspective of the stranger, providing a number of propositions to guide successful and mutually satisfying initial encounters. The key concepts are communication effectiveness, anxiety and uncertainty, anxiety and uncertainty management, and the causes of anxiety and uncertainty. These concepts are shown in causal order in Figure 4.1.

In the model shown in Figure 4.1, the desired result or outcome of the intercultural interaction is effective communication, defined by Gudykunst (2005) as "the extent that a person interpreting the message attaches a meaning to the message that is relatively similar to what was intended by the person transmitting it." This definition is quite similar to the "mutual understanding" goal of communication in the transactional model [. . .]. Effective communication is the means by which the stranger and host culture members learn adaptive behaviors so that a mutually satisfying relationship can develop. Examples of adaptive behaviors are accommodation of different worldviews and mutual respect. For example, in my visits to Middle Eastern countries, I will make sure that I do not shake hands with my female professional associates. I learn about appropriate behaviors from communication with my hosts; effective communication is achieved when my hosts and I have a mutual understanding of what the appropriate behaviors are for specific situations. They tell me how to act; I understand what they are telling me; I accept their advice; they understand and appreciate that I will act appropriately.

Figure 4.1 A Model of the Anxiety/Uncertainty Management Theory

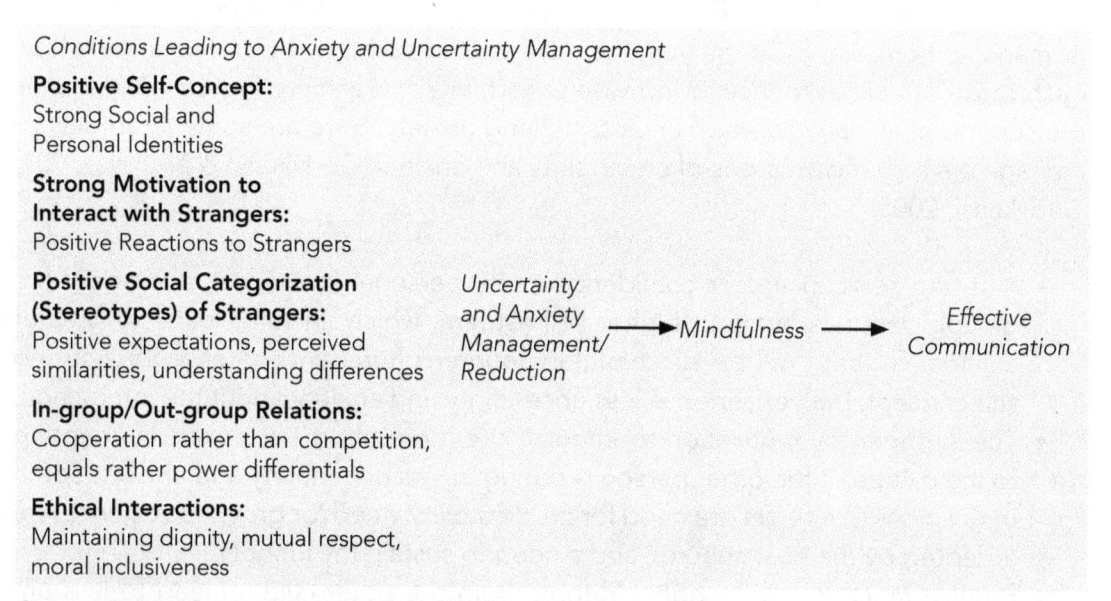

Conditions Leading to Anxiety and Uncertainty Management

Positive Self-Concept:
Strong Social and Personal Identities

Strong Motivation to Interact with Strangers:
Positive Reactions to Strangers

Positive Social Categorization (Stereotypes) of Strangers:
Positive expectations, perceived similarities, understanding differences

In-group/Out-group Relations:
Cooperation rather than competition, equals rather power differentials

Ethical Interactions:
Maintaining dignity, mutual respect, moral inclusiveness

Uncertainty and Anxiety Management/Reduction → Mindfulness → Effective Communication

Source: Copyright © Kaolincash (CC BY-SA 3.0) at http://commons.wikimedia.org/wiki/File:Anxiety-Uncertainty_Management_Theory_-_Graphical_Representation.svg

According to Gudykunst (2005), two barriers to effective communication are uncertainty and anxiety, normal responses of people to a new environment, such as when strangers interact with people from another culture. *Uncertainty* includes our doubts about how to act in an intercultural encounter, about what behavior is appropriate, and doubts about the consequences of the interaction. We bring these uncertain thoughts with us to the encounter. Even when we are provided with information about the host culture, such as information provided in orientation workshops, we can still be unsure of whether we have truly learned the appropriate behaviors, whether we have remembered all of them, whether we are capable of performing them, and how our hosts will react. For example, I still experience uncertainty when I am in the Middle East even after repeated visits. A new environment elicits uncertainty particularly when the new environment is very different from what we are used to; the greater the difference, the more the resulting uncertainty. Uncertainty leads to discomfort and stress which are barriers to effective communication.

Conditions leading to high anxiety and uncertainty include negative self-concept, weak personal and social identities, weak motivation to interact, negative reactions to strangers, negative social categorization of strangers, competition and power differential with strangers, absence of mutual respect and dignity, and moral exclusiveness.

While uncertainty is a thought, anxiety is an emotion. Anxiety is "the feeling of being uneasy, tense, worried or apprehensive about what might happen" in an intercultural interaction (Gudykunst, 2005). Uncertainty and anxiety are twin threats to communication effectiveness. To be effective in communication, we must learn how to control or manage them, first by identifying their causes and secondly by understanding how each cause can either reduce or increase uncertainty and anxiety. Figure 4.1 identifies the superficial (initial) causes of uncertainty and anxiety. Here are some strategies to manage the superficial causes of uncertainty and anxiety (Gudykunst & Nishida, 2001; Gudykunst, 2005):

- A strong self-concept or confidence in my personal (individual) and social (in-group) identities leads to higher self-esteem, which, in turn, leads to greater confidence that I will be successful in an intercultural encounter. With a strong self-concept, I will experience less uncertainty and anxiety about the interaction.
- The stronger my motivation to interact, the more effort I will exert in adapting to the culture of the other person resulting in less uncertainty and anxiety. Some motivations to interact are need for predictability, need for group inclusion (to be accepted by the host culture), and a need to sustain my identity.
- Positive reactions to strangers (people from the other culture) lead to less uncertainty and anxiety. Positive reactions are facilitated by empathy (an ability to

place myself in the other person's position), a high tolerance for ambiguity, and less rigid adherence to in-group's attitudes.
- Positive social categorization of strangers can reduce uncertainty and ambiguity. I would have positive expectations of the interaction (i.e., expect success rather than failure), focus on similarities rather than differences, and try harder to understand differences.
- Some processes in the situation affect outcomes of the interaction. Anxiety and uncertainty are reduced when I perceive my counterpart to be an equal rather than a subordinate, when we are engaged in cooperative rather than competitive tasks, and when I feel that I am not being overwhelmed by the sheer number of host culture (in-group) members.
- How I connect with members of the host culture (strangers) can also affect the outcomes of the interaction. Anxiety and uncertainty can be reduced when I am attracted to strangers, when we are interdependent (i.e., depend upon each other for the completion of a task), and when our contact is repeated and long enough to give us the opportunity to know each other.
- Anxiety and uncertainty can be reduced when the interactions are "ethical," meaning that both parties maintain dignity, that neither party makes moral judgments about the other's culture, and when mutual respect is shown.

Gudykunst (2005) offers 47 axioms or rules that provide specific predictions regarding the reduction of anxiety and uncertainty in intercultural interactions. Here are a few of them, as reported by Griffin, (2012):

- An increase in our self-esteem when interacting with strangers will produce a decrease in our anxiety and an increase in our ability to predict their behavior accurately.
- An increase in confidence in our ability to predict strangers' behavior will produce a decrease in anxiety; a decrease in anxiety will produce an increase in our confidence in predicting strangers' behavior.
- An increase in our ability to process complex information about strangers will produce a decrease in anxiety and an increase in our ability to predict their behavior accurately.
- An increase in our tolerance for ambiguity will produce a decrease in anxiety.
- An increase in the personal similarities we perceive between ourselves and strangers will produce a decrease in anxiety and an increase in our ability to accurately predict their behavior.
- An increase in perceiving that we share superordinate in-group identities based on a larger group that includes both in-group and out-group (such as "Asians,"

rather than Japanese or Chinese) will produce a decrease in our anxiety and an increase in our ability to accurately predict their behavior.

These are predictions about how anxiety and uncertainty can be reduced or managed, leading to "mindfulness," the next step toward communication effectiveness (Figure 4.1). *Mindfulness*, according to Gudykunst (2005), is thinking about how we are communicating while we are communicating (while the process is ongoing) and continually working to change and adapt to become more effective. As a mindful communicator, I will make an effort to understand your point of view or your frames of reference; your motives, values, and worldviews. I will then adjust my communication behavior such as use of language, nonverbal signs and gestures, expectations, and goals to meet you halfway. All of this happens while we are engaged in communication.

Anxiety/uncertainty management theory focuses on two common obstacles to intercultural communication effectiveness that we might experience at the start of the interaction. We might experience anxiety and uncertainty at the mere thought of interacting with people from another culture even before the actual interaction. The theory also tells us what individual and group characteristics might lead to more effective communication.

INTERCULTURAL COMMUNICATION COMPETENCE

Ruben (1976) defines *communication competence* as "the ability to function in a manner that is perceived to be relatively consistent with the needs, goals, and expectations of the individuals in one's environment while satisfying one's own needs, capacities, goals and expectations" (p. 336). Does this sound familiar? It is very similar to our definition of effective communication from the transactional model [. . .] What the intercultural communication competence theory adds to the transactional model is the identification of individual traits and behaviors that lead to competence. According to Ruben (1976), communication competence is facilitated by the following individual traits and behaviors:

- *Display of respect* is "the ability to express respect and positive regard for another person" (p. 339). It is demonstrated in nonverbal cues such as eye contact, body posture, voice tone, and pitch. We should be cautious in generalizing from Western cultures what we know about these cues and respect. In general, White

Americans, for example, consider direct eye contact and a lean forward posture to be signs of interest in and respect for the other person. This is not so in other cultures, where direct eye contact is disrespectful and close physical proximity can be misinterpreted. [. . .]. In displaying respect a competent communicator "responds to others in a descriptive, non-evaluating and non-judgmental way" (p. 340).

- *Orientation to knowledge* is recognition that knowledge of others is "individual in nature" (p. 340). A competent communicator evaluates each person as an individual first rather than as a group member, and refrains from using group stereotypes as bases for behaviors toward the other. A competent communicator also demonstrates *empathy*, the ability to imagine what it's like to be the other person, by expressing interest in and understanding of the other's position and circumstances. Of course, there is a risk in overly demonstrating empathy, particularly if there is a real or imagined power differential between the participants. This "over-accommodation," as some scholars call it, can lead to the opposite effect—a show of disrespect. For an extreme example, Bill Gates wouldn't tell a gathering of homeless people that he knows what it's like to be poor. Or, a Peace Corps volunteer wouldn't tell villagers in a poor country that she understands what it's like not to have running water. The competent communicator surveys the situation, and will adjust his or her show of empathy accordingly. The key principle is to evaluate people as individuals first and as group members secondarily.
- *Role behaviors flexibility* is the ability to adjust roles in groups according to the needs of the group rather than to satisfy his or her own interests. These role behaviors are demonstrated by a competent communicator in interactions within a group. They include:
  o Requesting information, seeking clarification, consulting others; collaborating with rather than directing others;
  o Willingness to compromise at the expense of a personal agenda, promoting harmony and mediation by setting an example;
  o Openness to ideas from others; participation in group activities; refrain from manipulating the group and calling attention to himself/herself.
- *Interaction management* is "taking turns in discussion and initiating and terminating interaction based on a reasonably accurate assessment of the needs and desires of others" (p. 341). A competent communicator considers "the interests, tolerances, and orientations of others who are party to the discussions" (p. 350).
- *Tolerance of ambiguity* is the ability to "react to new and ambiguous situations with little visible discomfort" (p. 341). A competent communicator adapts to new

situations quickly without "noticeable personal, interpersonal, or group consequences" (p. 352).

Ruben's (1976) model of intercultural communication competence presents principles that apply in general cross-cultural interactions; that is, they work regardless of the cultures involved. Other scholars have proposed similar and general (not culture-specific) models. According to Brislin (1981), intercultural competence consists of the following skills: (1) knowledge of the subject matter; (2) language; (3) communication skills; (4) positive orientations to opportunities; and (5) traits such as tolerance, problem-solving ability, and task orientation. These models have in common four general attributes of intercultural competence:

- Motivation to interact effectively
- Knowledge of the other's culture
- Personality traits such as display of respect and tolerance of ambiguity
- Behavioral skills such as interaction management

These attributes provide general guidelines, regardless of the cultures involved in the interaction. More recently, scholars have placed greater emphasis on culture-specific attributes and skill sets, suggesting that what may work in one culture may not work in another (Lustig & Koester, 2012). Therefore, the competent intercultural communicator will be aware of culture-specific behaviors, such as the importance of showing respect and deference to authority in Japan, the importance of speaking out in the United States, and the virtues of silence in Thailand. The keys to culture-specific intercultural competence, as the general models suggest (e.g., Ruben, 1976), are knowledge, the ability and motivation to demonstrate knowledge in actions (efficacy), and behavioral flexibility (interaction management in Ruben's model).

Intercultural communication competence is facilitated by several personality traits and variables that are predictive of self-perceived and observed competence: empathy (ability to put self in the other's situation), positive attitudes towards people from other cultures, cultural awareness and understanding, open-mindedness, nonjudgmental attitudes, experience with other cultures, motivation, active listening, accuracy in recognizing nonverbal gestures in different cultures, and low ethnocentrism (Arasaratnam, 2013).

These personality traits, motivational variables, knowledge, and skill sets identified by the models above predict success in intercultural interactions. Research shows that they minimize the stress, anxiety, and uncertainty that can result from intercultural encounters. They also predict high satisfaction, high psychological adjustment, and less culture shock in intercultural interactions (Chen, 1992).

ONGOING INTERACTIONS

The anxiety/uncertainty management and intercultural competence theories tell us about the individual and group traits that lead to effective communication and how to manage stress at the onset of intercultural interactions. What happens after we get over the initial anxiety and uncertainty, and how we do use strategies we've learned to be more effective *during* the interaction? The following theories discuss the adjustments competent communicators make while engaged in intercultural interactions.

COMMUNICATION ACCOMMODATION THEORY

What could happen when I am engaged in conversation with a person from another culture whose first language is not English, we are speaking in English, and the other person has an accent? Or, I am in France, speaking in French with an accent, and the other person is a native speaker of French? These are quite common encounters in intercultural communication: participants conversing in one language, one person is a native speaker, the other person speaks with an accent and "imperfectly." These encounters will naturally produce some stress since differential capabilities with the language will be an impediment to common understanding of the topic of communication and the development of a mutually satisfying relationship. But we can no longer avoid these encounters, given the changing demographics in our own countries; the proximity of other countries via travel and the Internet; and the growth in global commerce, education, and politics [. . .]. So, if we cannot avoid encounters with people whose first language is not the same as ours, and if, in fact, we seek these encounters to attain communication and other goals, what are we to do? I do not assume that we will always be speaking in English; it could very well be that we will be speaking in a language other than English with a native speaker, and therefore we will be the "strangers," assuming, of course, that more Americans will be learning a foreign language.

Communication accommodation theory (CAT), developed by Giles (2008), explains the processes leading to either success or failure in intercultural encounters, more specifically, in intercultural conversations. There is more stress, anxiety, and uncertainty in these encounters because the participants do not share experiences or a culture that might lead to common understanding of symbols and their meanings, including language and nonverbal signs. At the onset of a communication encounter, CAT says that we will make a judgment as to whether the other participants share our culture.

According to one study (Ellingsworth, 1988), this judgment is made in approximately 30 to 60 seconds, and is based on external cues like accent in speaking, skin color, physical characteristics, and behavior. CAT is mainly concerned with initial categorization of the other person as a "stranger" (i.e., from a different culture) based on accent when speaking in a nonnative language, and from the perspective of the other participant (the native speaker). When the native speaker is motivated to continue the interaction, he or she will adapt the communication style to achieve effective communication. This adaptation or accommodation happens early in the interaction, to preempt failure. The necessary conditions for accommodation are first, the perception that the other participant is a stranger (as indicated by external cues like accent), and second, motivation to succeed in the interaction. Motivation is primarily driven by the desire to achieve valued goals or end states, which could simply be acceptance and approval by the other participant. Other goals—as laid out in the transactional communication model [. . .]—include the acquisition of knowledge, learning of a new skill, assistance in making a decision, or to feel good and be entertained. Effective communication results in the achievement of goals by both participants and a mutually satisfying relationship, based on a common understanding of the topics of communication. Communication accommodation facilitates this common understanding.

CAT says there are at least two courses of action in intercultural conversations involving strangers. The first is mutual accommodation by the participants of the disparity in language skills. CAT calls this *convergence*, which can be defined as the process through which an individual adjusts speech patterns in the conversation to more closely resemble the speech patterns of the other person. These speech patterns include "pronunciation, pause and utterance lengths, vocal intensities, non-verbal behaviors and intimacy of self-disclosures" (Giles & Smith, 1979, p. 46). Other accommodations are speech rate (speaking slowly), repetition, decreasing the variety of vocabulary (using simple words), simplifying syntax (an extreme is "baby talk"), and selecting conversational topics and examples that are familiar to the other participant (Cai & Rodriguez, 1996–97; Berger & diBattista, 1993). In accommodating a stranger in conversation, most of us will first use those strategies that require less effort, such as speech rate, vocal intensity, and repetition rather than those strategies requiring more effort, such as altering message content, adjusting structure of the message, and using examples that are familiar to the other participant (Berger & diBattista, 1993). If the easy strategies don't work, then we go on to the more difficult strategies, providing that the motivation to achieve effective communication persists.

A second option in intercultural conversations is *divergence*, which can be defined as the process through which an individual emphasizes differences in speech patterns between the participants. Convergence leads to some degree of integration, whereas divergence leads to greater separation of the participants. CAT explains the situational and individual trait predictors of convergence and divergence. But first, let's take a look at the assumptions of CAT (Giles, 2008):

1. All conversations will have speech and nonverbal behavioral similarities and dissimilarities that are determined by the cultures of the participants. Examples are accents, gestures, and facial expressions.

2. Our perceptions of the speech and nonverbal behaviors of the other person will guide our evaluation of the conversation independently of content. In joining a conversation, we first make initial evaluations of the other participants based on their speech and other behaviors. We then use these evaluations to decide whether we will join the conversation, how we should join in, and whether we will make any adjustments while participating.

3. Language and nonverbal behaviors in the conversation signal social status and group identification of the participants. For example, the language used in the conversation will often be the language of the person with "higher" status by virtue of authority, control of resources, home territory, or other social standards.

4. Group norms direct the appropriateness of the accommodation strategies we use in striving for convergence. Groups will have explicit or implicit rules regarding what is acceptable. For example, speaking loudly is acceptable in some cultures but not in others. Also, accommodation can be overdone, as when behaviors and language are exaggerated to conform to behaviors and language of the other person. CAT calls this *over-accommodation*, which can be perceived by the other participants as patronizing and demeaning. Examples are my speaking very slowly and loudly when speaking to an elderly person or to my students from China. The appropriate convergence strategies will depend and vary according to group norms, so it's important to know what those norms are before using them.

Given these assumptions, CAT makes some predictions regarding the initiation of convergence or divergence in intercultural conversations:

1. The more attractive (such as being perceived to have similar goals and interests) the other participant is, the greater the need of the other person to be liked or approved, and the more likely accommodation will occur.

2. The less effort required, the more likely accommodation will occur.

3. The greater the rewards, the more likely accommodation will occur.

4   The greater the need to establish and differentiate a distinct group identity, the more likely divergence will occur.

CAT gives us some insight into how we can adjust our use of language and nonverbal behaviors during intercultural conversations to facilitate effective communication. As with other models of communication competence, strategies should consider the culture, group norms, and needs of the other participant.

FACE NEGOTIATION THEORY

What do we bring to an intercultural communication encounter? We might have goals—what do we want to accomplish? But we also bring our identities, our sense of who we are as an individual and as a group member, perhaps not always consciously, but nonetheless, our identities are there. These identities define the public image that we would like to project not only in intercultural encounters but in our public behaviors as well. We also bring to these encounters a sense or awareness of the identities of the persons we are interacting with—who they are, what groups they belong to, what their status is in comparison to mine—in other words, their identities. The identities that we bring are situational, meaning that the salience or importance of a particular identity depends on the situation. Which identities we bring to an interaction also will depend on the situation. These identities, our own as well as those of the other participants, affect how we communicate and interact in intercultural encounters. To illustrate:

When I present a research paper at a conference of academics (university faculty) in the Middle East, the relevant and important personal identity is that of a university professor and researcher, and my group identity is that I am a member of the faculty of an American university. I would think that I am a capable researcher with a good reputation and that my university is likewise well-regarded. I would communicate and interact with my hosts and other conference participants to project and preserve these individual and group identities. If I am successful, my private (personal) and group (university) identities would match my public image. At the same time, my hosts and colleagues will have a sense and awareness of who I am and the reputation of my university. The ideal situation is when all three perceptions or images match—my personal identities (individual and group), the public image I project, and the image my hosts and colleagues have of me. I will use communication to achieve as much symmetry as possible in these perceptions in a particular situation—an academic conference.

On the other hand, if I am visiting Egypt to see the pyramids as a tourist with my family, my personal identity will be that of a father and husband; my group identity will be that of an American, or perhaps, more specifically, as a Filipino American. So my interactions and communication behaviors with members of the host culture will be very different than when I am in an academic conference. I will not be projecting an image as a professor and academic; instead I will be the attentive family member, and the "good" American, displaying behaviors to dispel the negative perception that some people abroad have of Americans in general.

Personal and group identities and the communication behaviors we use to maintain them are the key components of face negotiation theory, developed by Ting-Toomey (2005) and Ting-Toomey & Kurogi, 1998). Our identities define the "faces" we bring with us to interactions with other people. According to Ting-Toomey (2005), faces are our personal and group images based on identities that are influenced by group memberships, culture, and experiences. By the time we are adults we have a good sense of these identities (although some research shows that identities are developed in children as early as age 3 years or younger). We are protective of these identities; when they are questioned, challenged, or threatened, we engage in behaviors, including communication, to maintain or enhance them. At the same time, the other participants may also be concerned about maintaining my face because of cultural norms ("don't want to embarrass anybody") or because doing so can facilitate a mutually satisfying relationship and therefore the attainment of communication goals. Face negotiation theory explains the processes involved to maintain face. These maintenance strategies are called *facework* (Ting-Toomey, 2005; Ting-Toomey & Kurogi, 1998).

The first principle of the theory is that maintenance of face is important in all cultures, although the relative importance of personal and group faces and the resulting communication strategies to maintain face depend on the culture, such as whether the culture is individualistic or collectivist [. . .]. Facework strategies, conceptualized by Ting-Toomey, to apply to conflict resolution when face is threatened include:

- *Dominating strategies*, where a participant reinforces his or her face to attain communication goals even at the cost of the other participant's goals. This then is a "win" for one participant. For example, if the validity of a study I was presenting at an academic conference was questioned by another attendee, I could emphasize, in my response, my credentials ("I have published 10 other studies on the topic with similar results; these studies have been cited by 50 other scholars") and the credibility of the study being questioned ("This study will soon be published by Journal X, the leading research journal in our field"). By doing so, I am dominating the conversation without going into the merits of the challenging question.

- *Avoidance strategies*, where a participant sidesteps the conflict and deals with it indirectly. In my example, I could tell my challenger that the answer is too complicated and would take too much time, and so could she e-mail me the

question and I will respond. (Most likely, in these situations, I would never receive the e-mail, and if I did, I most likely won't answer it.)
- *Integrating strategies*, where the participant addresses the conflict, establishes understanding of the issues, and attempts to arrive at a mutually satisfying resolution so that the relationship is maintained. In the example I've given, I would listen closely to my challenger; say that she raises some good points; I might agree with some of them but I don't agree with all of them; I would look into the issues raised. In doing so, I would have addressed her concerns about the study and, hopefully, maintain a positive relationship (she won't hate me and won't tell her colleagues that I am a pompous snob).

A second principle of face negotiation theory is that the motivation to maintain face varies by situation, depending on the following variables:

- Strength of the self (individual) and group identities determines the importance of maintaining face; the stronger the identification, the more important it is to maintain face.
- Cultural norms determine the importance of maintaining face. In individualistic cultures (such as the United States), it's more important to maintain personal face; in collectivist cultures (such as Japan), it's more important to maintain group face.
- The power structure, perceived or real, in the interaction influences the motivation to manage face. Generally, the more powerful participant will be more motivated to preserve face than the participant with less power.
- The importance of the topic of conversation influences face maintenance; the more important the topic, the more likely it is that faces will be negotiated, a precursor to the attainment of mutual goals.
- Distance between the cultures will result in different face maintenance strategies; the greater the distance, the more difficult it will be to negotiate face.

FACE-NEGOTIATION AND CONFLICT

Face negotiation theory also has been applied to the analysis of conflict management styles (e.g., Ting-Toomey et al., 2000). In particular, this analysis says that the self-image (face) we bring to a conflict situation determines the conflict management style we will use. Oetzel and Ting-Toomey (2003) tested this general proposition in a cross-cultural study of college students from individualist and collectivist countries. They measured and analyzed the following variables:

- *Conflict*: "the perceived and/or actual incompatibility of values, expectations, processes or outcomes between two or more parties over substantive and/or relational issues" (Ting-Toomey, 1994, p. 360). In their study, Oetzel and Ting-Toomey (2003) asked their research participants to recall a conflict with a person of the same gender and ethnic group.
- *National culture individualism/collectivism*: Based on Hofstede et al. (2010), student participants from China and Japan were identified as collectivist; students from Germany and the United States as individualist. National culture was measured in the study by asking, "What is your country of permanent residence?"
- *Self-construal*: Self-image of an independent self (a unique individual who acts on his or her own) or an interdependent self (an individual who emphasizes his or her group and relationships over individual actions), measured by five-point agree/disagree Likert scales. Examples of independent self-construal items were:
  o I preferred to be self-reliant rather than depend on others.
  o I tried not to depend on others.
  Examples of interdependent self-construal items were:
- My relationship with the other person is more important than winning the conflict.
- I sacrificed my self-interest for the benefits of our relationship.
- *Face concerns* consisted of self-face, defined as concern for one's image, and other-face, concern for another's image. In general, people from individualist cultures are more concerned with self-face compared to people from collectivist cultures who are more concerned with other-face. Measures of other-face in the Oetzel and Ting-Toomey (2003) study included:
  o I tried to be sensitive to the other person's self-worth.
  Examples of self-face measures were:
  o I was concerned with not appearing weak in front of the other person.
  o I was concerned with protecting my self-image.
- *Conflict negotiation styles* consisted of three strategies (defined earlier in this chapter): avoiding, dominating, and integrating strategies. Here are examples of measures of avoiding strategies:
  o I tried to avoid the conflict and behaved as if nothing happened.
  o I tried to pretend that the conflict didn't happen.
  Examples of dominating strategies were:
  o I tried to persuade the other person that my way was the best way.
  o I insisted my position be accepted during the conflict.
  Examples of integrating strategies were:
  o I tried to meet the other person halfway.
  o I tried to use "give and take" so that a compromise could be made.

To collect data, Oetzel and Ting-Toomey (2003) asked 768 college students from Japan, China, Germany, and the United States to recall a recent conflict, and then to answer a questionnaire with items (examples above) measuring self-construal, face concern, and conflict management behavior. They were interested in analyzing relationships between these variables, particularly which variables would predict conflict negotiation styles. Here are some of their results:

- Cultural individualism/collectivism predicted self-construal, face concern, and conflict management style. Students from collectivist cultures (Japan and China) preferred an interdependent self-image, another-face concern in the interaction, and an avoiding conflict style. Conversely, students from individualist cultures (Germany and the United States) preferred an independent self-image, a self-face concern in the interaction, and an integrating conflict style.
- Independent self-image led to self-face concern in the interaction whereas interdependent self-image led to other-face concern in the interaction.
- Self-face led to dominating conflict styles; other-face led to avoiding and integrating conflict styles.

This study tells us how a critical cultural dimension—individualism/collectivism—and resulting face concerns might affect conflict negotiation styles. When these negotiation styles clash, the potential for a breakdown in communication is heightened, as well as the importance of cultural competency in the participants.

Face negotiation theory explains a process of maintaining face in intercultural interactions. The principles and resulting strategies for effective communication apply to initial and ongoing interactions, primarily in face-to-face communication and conflict negotiation. Recognition and understanding of the face concerns and face maintenance strategies of the other participant are an important component of intercultural competence.

LONG-TERM AND REPEATED INTERACTIONS

So far we have looked at theories that explain processes of communication at the onset of and during intercultural interactions. With worldwide migrations and increased numbers of racial and ethnic minorities in countries around the world, including the

United States, prolonged and repeated contact between people of different cultures is increasingly happening. What happens in communication interactions in these contexts is the subject of our next set of theories, those that focus on long-term and repeated intercultural interactions.

CO-CULTURAL THEORY

In the United States and other countries, dominant groups (sometimes called *mainstream groups*) exert overt or implicit authority over other groups (sometimes referred to as *minorities*, and, more recently, *co-cultures*). Both dominant groups and co-cultures have distinct cultures of their own although they share a superordinate culture because of membership in a larger, encompassing super group, such as a citizens in a country. Dominance may be based on sheer numbers (a majority) or the control of resources leading to economic, political, and social power. Social power is exercised by controlling the signs and symbols of the mainstream culture, including those in the mass media. How co-cultures interact and communicate with the dominant groups to achieve their own goals is the subject of co-cultural theory.

Developed by Orbe (1998), co-cultural theory explains how co-cultures in the United States communicate in everyday life with the dominant cultures to achieve their goals. These cocultures are defined by Orbe (1998) as "traditionally marginalized in societal structures," meaning that they have less power, share in less of society's resources and benefits, and are under the influence in almost all spheres of life by the dominant groups. Co-cultures share many cultural dimensions with the dominant group. However, they also are distinctively different on some cultural dimensions. Co-cultures themselves may have different cultures; what they have in common is a "similar positioning that renders them marginalized within society" (Orbe, 1998). Examples of co-cultures in the United States are racial and ethnic minorities, women, persons with disabilities, gays/lesbians/bisexuals, and poor people. Examples of dominant cultures are European Americans, men, able-bodied persons, heterosexuals, and wealthy people. Members of co-cultures and dominant cultures, because they share the larger community (the United States) and occupy the same space, will interact on a daily basis. According to Orbe (1998), cocultures, to attain desired outcomes, will use specific communication strategies depending on the situation, what outcome is desired, and the power position of the other participants. From the perspective of the co-culture groups, possible outcomes of interactions between dominant and co-culture groups include:

- Assimilation, which is fitting in, adopting the cultural norms of the dominant culture, and minimizing cultural differences and distinctions between groups.
- Accommodation, which is developing appreciation of the dominant culture while maintaining the co-culture; changing social relationships and structural constraints to make this happen.
- Separation, which is maintaining a group identity separate from the dominant culture; rejecting identification with the dominant culture.

According to Orbe (1998), co-cultures will choose communication strategies in everyday interactions that facilitate the attainment of a preferred outcome. He identifies the following communication strategies or orientations:

- Nonassertive communication is being nonconfrontational and inhibited; people place the needs of others before their own.
- Assertive communication is "expressive behavior that considers both self and other needs equally" (Lapinski & Orbe, 2007).
- Aggressive communication is overly expressive, confrontational, and attacking.

According to Orbe (1998), the preferred outcomes and communication styles of co-cultures will be demonstrated in degrees measurable in continuous scales. For example, aggressive communication could be observed from an intensity of 1 (low) to 5 (high). Also, the communication style used will be determined by preferred outcomes, although this relationship is based on situational goals and motivations. Lapinski and Orbe (2007) provide some evidence of a general relationship between preferred outcomes and communication style. They found, for example, that co-cultural members who preferred assimilation as an outcome used nonassertive communication; those who preferred separation used assertive and aggressive communication. These results support the theory's general prediction that the desirable end states of a co-culture regarding its place in society (preferred outcomes) will influence its choice of communication style in interacting with the dominant culture in everyday interactions.

ACCULTURATION THEORIES

When I was 18 years old, I immigrated to the United States from the Philippines. Although the Philippines has been an American colony and English is a second language, Filipino culture is distinctly different from American culture. For example, in Hofstede's et al. (2010) taxonomy, Filipinos are "collectivist" (i.e., more centered on the group than the individual), whereas Americans (mainstream White America, in particular) are individualists (more centered on the individual than the group). So there I was in a strange land, my new home. How did I adapt? Or, perhaps the first question, what did "adapting" mean? These are the issues that acculturation theories seek to answer.

At least 50 definitions of acculturation can be found in the literature (e.g., Boruhis, Mosie, Perreault, & Senecal, 1997); many of them consider the process to be linear (change from original culture to complete adoption of the new culture, often referred to as *assimilation*) and from the perspective of the new member (how an immigrant or "stranger," the new member, adjusts to the new culture). An example of a linear model is the unidimensional assimilation model (Gordon, 1964), which says that across a life span, immigrants, the new members, move along a continuum from maintenance of the original culture to total adoption of the host culture. *Biculturalism*, defined as adoption of some cultural elements from the host culture while maintaining elements from the original culture, is the midpoint. The end result in this model is assimilation, or adoption of the host culture at the expense of the original culture.

Other definitions of acculturation describe interactive and nonlinear processes of cultural adaptation. The interactive processes assume reciprocal influence between the new member and members of the "host" culture, meaning that both participants are affected by the interaction. Nonlinear models provide for the possibility of other results from the acculturation process besides complete adoption of the host culture by the new member. Here is an example of an interactive and nonlinear definition:

> Those phenomena which result when groups or individuals having different cultures come into continuous first-hand contact, with subsequent changes in the original cultural patterns of either or both groups ... under this definition acculturation is to be distinguished from assimilation, which is at times a phase of acculturation. (Redfield, Linton, & Herskovits, 1936, p. 149)

According to this definition, acculturation occurs when the following conditions are met:

- Firsthand contact occurs, meaning face-to-face contact. The new member lives in the host culture and interacts on a daily basis with members of the host culture. Although there has been some interest in acculturation from vicarious contact via the mass media and the Internet, traditional acculturation theories assume that contact is face-to-face.

- Contact is continuous, resulting in repeated interactions over a period of time, such as is the case with immigrants to a new country. Acculturation does not happen spontaneously or over a temporary stay, such as is the case with tourists or "sojourners" or temporary residents.
- Change is reciprocal; the new member and members of the host culture may change as a result of the interaction.

Acculturation is concerned with several dimensions of change:

- How much change and the direction of change (e.g., from one culture to another)
- What dimensions of culture change—food, dress, behaviors, values, worldviews
- Effects of acculturation on the new member—stress, psychological adjustments, social adjustment
- Effects of acculturation on the host members—stress, psychological adjustments, social adjustments

A BIDIMENSIONAL MODEL OF IMMIGRANT ACCULTURATION

The bidimensional model, developed by Berry (1980, 1984), says that acculturation resulting from face-to-face interaction over a period of time can have several outcomes depending on what the new member, such as an immigrant, values in the new environment. The process is not linear because assimilation is only one of four possible outcomes. Which outcome happens depends on whether the immigrant values maintenance of his or her original culture and/or maintaining relationships with members of the host culture, as shown in Figure 4.2.

Figure 4.2 A Bidimensional Model of Immigrant Acculturation

	Dimension 1: Is it considered to be of value to maintain immigrant's cultural identity and characteristics?	
Dimension 2: Is it considered to be of value to maintain relationships with other groups?	YES	NO
YES	Integration	Assimilation
NO	Separation	Marginalization

Sources: Adapted from: J.W. Berry, "A Bi-dimensional Model of Immigrant Acculturation," *Groups in Contact*. Copyright © 1984 by Academic Press.

In this model, integration indicates the immigrant's desire to maintain his or her native culture while adopting key features of the host culture. With assimilation, the immigrant gives up his or her native culture and identity and completely adopts the culture and identity of the host culture. Separation indicates the rejection of the host culture and maintenance of the native culture. In marginalization, the immigrant rejects both the host and native cultures in the new environment.

According to Berry, these four orientations can be shown by members of the same immigrant group depending on education, income, age, and other demographics. For example, younger members may prefer integration while older members may prefer assimilation. Also, the preferred outcomes will vary by immigrant group. Some groups may prefer integration while others may prefer assimilation depending on factors such as cultural similarity to the host culture and whether immigration is voluntary or compulsory. An example of compulsory immigration is when refugees are forced by war to relocate. Studies have shown that immigrants in a variety of contexts have preferred integration, followed by either assimilation or separation. Some examples are Portuguese, Hungarians, and Koreans in Canada (Berry et al., 1989); Lebanese in Canada (Sayegh & Lasry, 1993); and Indian immigrants in the United States (Berry & Krishnan, 1992).

Bourhis et al. (1997) refined the Berry model to more clearly identify the behaviors of immigrants and to refine the concept of marginalization by replacing it with two related subconcepts. The revised model is shown in Figure 4.3.

Figure 4.3 Revised Bidimensional Model

	Dimension 1: Is it considered to be of value to maintain immigrant cultural identity?	
Dimension 2: Is it considered to be of value to adopt the cultural identity of the host community?	YES	NO
YES	Integration	Assimilation
NO	Separation	Anomie
		Individualism

Source: Adapted from: Richard Bourhis, Lena Celine Moise, Stephane Perreault, & Sacha Senecal, "[image]: Revised Bi-Dimensional Model," International Journal of Psychology, 32(6). Copyright © 1997 by Taylor & Francis.

In the revised model, the questions more clearly indicate the behaviors being evaluated. Also, marginalization has been replaced with two subconcepts, anomie and individualism. Anomie is alienation from both cultures resulting from a lack of identification with either. Individualism is rejection of group identities and a preference to treat others as individuals rather than group members. These orientations—anomie and individualism—are observed in immigrants who do not value the native and host cultures.

THE INTERACTIVE ACCULTURATION MODEL

The interactive acculturation model (IAM) developed by Bourhis et al. (1997) conceptualizes acculturation as an interactive process involving both the immigrant's and host's cultures. Outcomes depend both on immigrant and host culture orientations. The model begins with a specification of acculturation orientations preferred by the host community, as shown in Figure 4.4.

Figure 4.4 Bidimensional Model of Host Community Acculturation Orientations

	Dimension 1: Do you find it acceptable that immigrants maintain their cultural identity?	
Dimension 2: Do you accept that immigrants adopt the cultural identity of the host community?	YES	NO
YES	Integration	Assimilation
NO	Segregation	Exclusion
		Individualization

Source: Adapted from: Richard Bourhis, Lena Celine Moise, Stephane Perreault, & Sacha Senecal, "A Bi-dimensional Model of Host Community Acculturation Orientations," *International Journal of Psychology*, 32(6). Copyright © 1997 by Taylor & Francis.

As Figure 4.4 shows, the outcomes of acculturation depend on the host community's approval or disapproval of cultural orientations:

- Integration results when the host community approves of the immigrant maintaining his or her cultural identity while at the same time adopting the host's cultural identity.
- Assimilation is the outcome when the host community disapproves of the immigrant maintaining his or her cultural identity but approves of the immigrant adopting the host's cultural identity.
- Segregation results when the host community approves of the immigrant maintaining his or her culture but disapproves of the immigrant adopting the host's cultural identity.
- Exclusion and individualism are the outcomes when the host community disapproves of both cultural orientations.

The preferred cultural orientations—acceptance of immigrant cultural maintenance and/or acceptance of host culture adoption—will vary according to characteristics of the immigrant group. Similarity in cultures, for example, can lead to host community acceptance of native culture maintenance and host culture adoption.

The IAM combines the outcomes from host and immigrant acculturation orientations and shows the resulting relational outcomes (Figure 4.5).

Figure 4.5 The Interactive Acculturation Model

Host Community: low-medium high vitality group	Immigrant Community: low, medium vitality groups				
	Integration	Assimilation	Separation	Anomie	Individualism
Integration	Consensual	Problematic	Conflictual	Problematic	Problematic
Assimilation	Problematic	Consensual	Conflictual	Problematic	Problematic
Segregation	Conflictual	Conflictual	Conflictual	Conflictual	Conflictual
Exclusion	Conflictual	Conflictual	Conflictual	Conflictual	Conflictual
Individualism	Problematic	Problematic	Problematic	Problematic	Consensual

Source: Adapted from: Richard Bourhis, Lena Celine Moise, Stephane Perreault, & Sacha Senecal, "The Interactive Acculturation Model," International Journal of Psychology, 32 (6). Copyright © 1997 by Taylor & Francis.

The IAM shown in Figure 4.5 tells us what happens when immigrants join a host community. The model assumes that immigrants and hosts will bring to the interactions different levels of "vitality," defined as relative strength and weaknesses, status, power, and authority (Giles, Bourhis, & Taylor, 1977). Vitality, which is usually ascribed to the group but which may also be assigned to an individual, is determined by:

- Demographic variables, such as the immigrant's age, education, and income
- The extent to which the immigrant group has gained access to political and economic power, as indicated by representation in government, business, the media, and other social institutions
- Status, which depends on the prestige of the immigrant group's language and culture in the host community and globally

Considering these indicators, most immigrant groups will have lower vitality compared to the host culture, which will have more members, generally higher education and income levels, and more institutional control. The IAM assumes that host cultural orientations will have greater influence than immigrant orientations on the relational outcomes of their interactions.

Immigrants will have their own cultural orientations—whether they value maintaining their cultural identity and/or whether they value the adoption of the host culture. The hosts will also have their cultural orientations—whether they accept maintenance of the immigrants' culture and/or whether they accept adoption of the host culture by immigrants. These cultural orientations will lead to desired outcomes. For immigrants, these outcomes are integration, assimilation, separation, anomie, and individualism (Figure 4.3); for the host culture the outcomes are integration, assimilation, segregation, exclusion, and individualism (Figure 4.4). The IAM (Figure 4.5) shows the interpersonal relational outcomes that result from the interaction of host and immigrant cultural orientations.

According to Bourhis et al. (1997), relational outcomes can be either concordant or discordant. *Concordant* relations result when the host and immigrant communities agree on cultural orientations, such as when both value integration or when both agree that assimilation is a desirable outcome. In contrast, *discordant* relations occur when hosts and immigrants disagree on cultural orientations, such as when immigrants favor assimilation and hosts favor segregation. Concordance and discordance are bipolar opposites, from total agreement to total disagreement between the two groups. The degree of concordance/discordance predicts the valence (whether positive or negative) of the resulting relational outcomes, with concordance at the positive end and discordance at the negative end of the continuum.

According to the IAM, relational outcomes are the patterns of interactions between immigrants and hosts, including verbal and nonverbal face-to-face communication; intergroup attitudes, stereotypes, prejudice, and discrimination; intergroup tension; and acculturative stress. These intergroup relations can be consensual, problematic, or conflictual (Figure 5-5). Consensual relations are characterized by mutually supportive interactions such as positive and effective verbal and nonverbal communication; mutually positive intergroup attitudes and stereotypes; little or no discrimination; low intergroup tension; and low acculturative stress. In other words, immigrants and hosts are getting along beautifully. Consensual relations occur when both groups share and value the integration and consensual acculturation outcomes, meaning that immigrants and hosts both want the immigrants to integrate, or to assimilate.

Problematic relations, according to the IAM, occur when there is partial disagreement between hosts and immigrants on acculturation outcomes, and the preferred outcomes are not significantly different from each other. For example, the hosts favor assimilation and immigrants favor integration. In this case, relations between the two groups will be less than ideal. Examples are a breakdown in communication, negative stereotyping, some discriminatory behaviors, and moderate levels of stress and intergroup tensions.

Conflictual relations, the most dysfunctional and destructive to all participants, result when hosts and immigrants favor substantially different acculturation orientations, such as when hosts favor separation and immigrants favor integration or when immigrants favor separation and hosts favor integration. Conflictual relations lead to intergroup conflict characterized by miscommunication or a lack of communication; extremely negative stereotyping; prejudice; discrimination in housing, health care, education, the workplace, and in everyday social interactions; and, in severe cases, racist attacks against immigrants, as in hate crimes.

The IAM demonstrates how interactions between immigrants and hosts lead to positive or negative relational outcomes. Interactions, including communication between immigrants and hosts, are affected by acculturation orientations and relational outcomes. Whether these interactions are positive or negative depends on whether hosts and immigrants agree or disagree on the value of distinct cultural orientations. But what about communication as a *cause* of acculturation?

COMMUNICATION AND ACCULTURATION

Gudykunst and Kim (1984) assign a central role to communication as a necessary condition for successful cultural adaptation:

> At the heart of the interactive acculturation process lies the communication process linking strangers to the host cultural milieu. Acquisition of communicative competence by strangers is not only instrumental to all aspects of cultural adaptation but also indicative of the strangers' accomplished acculturation. (p. 220)

Communication competence is both a cause and effect of successful acculturation, which could be assimilation or integration, according to the Gudykunst and Kim (1984) model. The key indicator of communication competence is fluency in the host's verbal and nonverbal language; that is, the ability to code and decode messages in a way that would be understood in the host community. Communication is both a necessary condition for successful adaptation as well as a measure of success.

Other models of acculturation and communication, notably in the field of mass communication, have looked at the mass media and interpersonal communication as causes of acculturation (Tan, Nelson, Dong, & Tan, 1997; Tan, Tan, & Gibson, 2003; Tan, Tan, & Tan, 1987). Some results of studies based on these models are the following:

- Use of American television, movies, newspapers, and magazines at the exclusion of ethnic media leads to adoption of mainstream American values and worldviews, and therefore assimilation.
- Use of ethnic media at the exclusion of American media leads to separation.
- Use of American and ethnic media leads to integration.
- Positive and frequent personal contact (as equals, in pursuit of similar goals, noncompetitive) leads to assimilation or integration.

Widely considered to be the first to focus on communication in the acculturation process, the Gudykunst and Kim (1984) model has been criticized by some scholars for its linearity; that is, its emphasis on immigrants, while paying less attention to the communication competency of hosts (Kramer, 2012). As suggested by the interactive acculturation model (Bourhis et al., 1997), acculturation is an interactive process between hosts and immigrants. The hosts, according to this model, must also develop communication competencies, such as fluencies in the immigrant's verbal and nonverbal language, so relational outcomes could be mutually satisfying. This criticism has also been directed at acculturation models developed to explain the role of the mass media in acculturation. Typically, these models address only the competencies and cultural orientations of immigrants.

For the most part, the communication and acculturation models discussed in this section conceptualize communication as face-to-face, with participants sharing the same space and time. But what about communication that transcends geographical boundaries, such as new digital media on the Internet?

NEW MEDIA AND ACCULTURATION

Consider the widespread and worldwide use of computer-mediated communication, social network sites, mobile phones, and other new media. Consider also that most of the intercultural communication theories we have discussed study face-to-face communication with participants sharing the same space at a particular point in time. Do these theories apply to the new digital media?

To answer this question, Robert Shuter (2012) analyzed results from a number of recent studies that looked at the influence of new digital media on acculturation, particularly on cultural identity, international dialogue, and intercultural competence. Here's what he concluded:

- *Cultural identity*: Virtual communities, those created by diverse people and cultures not grounded in time or space but bound together by common attendance to a technology, are theoretically possible if the technology is value free and independent of a monopolistic power. In reality, these diverse virtual communities do not occur very often because, according to Chen and Dai (2012), "the hardware, software, web design, and new/social media—appear to privilege the West" (p. 223). Therefore, a virtual culture without domination by one group, that is color-blind, and in which cultural identity and status differences are minimized, is hard to come by. One indication of cultural dominance is the use of English in many multicultural Internet encounters when English-speaking Westerners are participants (Chen, 2012). When members of the virtual communities are homogeneous (from the same marginalized co-culture, for example), new digital media can strengthen and reinforce the cultural identities of the participants. There is evidence that many cultural minorities and co-cultures (e.g., African Americans, Latinos, Native Americans, and Vietnamese) use social media to reinforce their subcultures and identities. Examples are Facebook profiles that accentuate their cultural origins.

- *Intercultural dialogue*: In the real world, intercultural dialogue promotes mutual understanding by emphasizing openness, empathy, and the acceptance of differences. The goal of mutual understanding is facilitated by the give-and-take, reciprocal behaviors with verbal and nonverbal feedback in face-to-face interactions. At the same time, effective intercultural dialogue in the real world is constrained by stereotypes, prejudice, group identification and loyalties, and preexisting social networks. Given these findings from the real world, will we find the same to be true of intercultural dialogue in virtual communities that are not bound by space and time limitations? We can draw the following conclusions from numerous recent studies (Shuter, 2012). First, the obstacles to effective intercultural dialogue in the real world operate in much the same way in virtual communities. Stereotypes, cultural loyalties and identities, and preexisting social networks hinder effective virtual intercultural dialogue. Second, empathy and understanding of cultural differences are difficult to achieve in virtual communities. Virtual intercultural dialogue, particularly collaboration, is also difficult to achieve. Third, intercultural dialogue is more likely to happen when participants use multiple new media technologies, such as Facebook and other Web 2.0 applications.
- *Acculturation*: In the real (physical) world, the adaptation of new members to a host community is facilitated by positive or mutually satisfying and reinforcing face-to-face communication and by the development of intercultural competence. Similar processes have been observed in virtual communities. Here are some results of recent studies (Shuter, 2012). First, online ethnic support groups composed of people from the same culture provide emotional support resulting in less acculturative stress. However, even these support groups do not provide the learning skills or competence to be successful in the new culture. Second, increased use of

homogeneous, ethnic social networking sites from the same culture are an obstacle to acculturation, reinforcing, instead, separate ethnic identities. Third, online interactions between people from different cultures can help acculturation and the development of intercultural competence including language acquisition.

The theories I reviewed in this section provide general principles on how to be effective in intercultural communication. In the next three chapters, I discuss specific principles, beginning with "Know Ourselves."

REFERENCES

Arasaratnam, L. (2013). Ten years of research in intercultural communication competence (2003–2013): A retrospective. *Journal of Intercultural Communication, 35*(5), 5–18.

Berger, C. R., & diBattista, P. (1993). Communication failure and plan adaptation: If at first you don't succeed, say it louder and slower. *Communication Monographs, 60*(3), 220–238.

Berry, J. W. (1980). Acculturation as varieties of adaptation. In A. Padilla (Ed.), *Acculturation; theory, models and some new findings*. Colorado, CO: Westview Press.

Berry, J. W. (1984). Cultural relations in plural societies: Alternatives to segregation and their socio-psychological implications. In N. Miller & M. Brewer (Eds.), *Groups in contact*. New York, NY: Academic Press.

Berry, J. W., Kim, U., Power, S., Young, M., & Bujaki, M. (1989). Acculturation attitudes in plural societies. *Applied Psychology: An International Review, 38*, 185–206.

Berry, J. W., & Krishnan, A. (1992). Acculturative stress and acculturation attitudes among Indian immigrants to the United States. *Psychology and Developing Societies, 4*, 187–212.

Black, J. S., & Gregerson, H. B. (1991). The other half of the picture: Antecedents of spouse cross-cultural adjustment. *Journal of International Business Studies, 22*(3), 461–477.

Bourhis, R. Y., Moise, L. C., Perreault, S., & Senecal, S. (1997). Toward an interactive acculturation model: A social psychological approach. *International Journal of Psychology, 32*(6), 369–386.

Brislin, R. W. (1981). *Cross-cultural encounters, face-to-face interaction*. New York, NY: Pergamon Press.

Cai, D., & Rodrigues, J. (1996–97). Adjusting to cultural differences: The intercultural adaptation model. *Intercultural Communication Studies, VI*(2).

Chen, G. (1992). A test of intercultural communication competence. *Intercultural Communication Studies, II*(2), 63–82.

Chen, G. (2012). The impact of new media on intercultural communication in global context. *China Media Research, 8*(2), 1–10.

Chen, G., & Dai, X. D. (2012). New media and asymmetry in cultural identity negotiation. In P. H. Cheong, J. N. Martin, & L. Macfadyen (Eds.), *New media and intercultural communication: Identity, community and politics* (pp. 123–138). New York, NY: Peter Lang.

Ellingsworth, H. W. (1988). A theory of adaptation intercultural dyads. In Y. Y. Kim & W. B. Gudykunst (Eds.), *Theories in intercultural communication* (pp. 19–27). Newbury Park, CA: Sage.

Giles, H. (2008). Communication accommodation theory. In L. Baxter & D. Braithewaite (Eds.), *Engaging theories in interpersonal communication: Multiple perspectives* (pp. 161–173). Thousand Oaks: Sage.

Giles, H., Bourhis, T. Y., & Taylor, D. M. (1977). Toward a theory of language in ethnic group relations. In H. Giles (Ed.), *Language, ethnicity and intergroup relations* (pp. 307–348). New York, NY: Academic Press.

Giles, H., & Smith, P. (1979). Accommodation theory: Optimal levels of convergence. In H. Giles & R. St. Clair (Eds.), *Language and social psychology* (pp. 45–65). Baltimore, MD: Basil Blackwell.

Gordon, M. M. (1964). *Assimilation in American life*. New York, NY: Oxford University Press.

Griffin, Em. (2012). *A first look at communication theory*. New York, NY: McGraw-Hill.

Gudykunst, W. (2005). An anxiety/uncertainty management (AUM) theory of effective communication: Making the mesh of the net finer. In W. Gudykunst (Ed.), *Theorizing about intercultural communication* (pp. 281–332). Thousand Oaks, CA: Sage.

Gudykunst, W., & Kim, Y. Y. (1984). *Communicating with strangers: An approach to intercultural communication*. New York, NY: Random House.

Gudykunst, W., & Nishida, T. (2001). Anxiety, uncertainty, and perceived effectiveness of communication across relationships and cultures. *International Journal of Intercultural relations, 25*, 55–71.

Hofstede, G., Hofstede, G. J., & Minkov, M. (2010). *Cultures and organizations: Software of the mind*. New York, NY: McGraw-Hill.

Kramer, E. M. (2012). Dimensional accrual and dissociation: An introduction. In J. Grace (Ed.), *Comparative cultures and civilizations* (Vol. 3, pp. 123–184). Cresskil, NJ: Hampton.

Lapinsky, M. K., & Orbe, M. (2007). Evidence of the construct validity and reliability of the co-cultural theory scales. *Communication Methods and Measures, 1*(2), 137–164.

Lustig, M., & Koester, J. (2012). *Intercultural competence*. (7th ed.). New York, NY: Pearson.

Oetzel, J. G., & Ting-Toomey, S. (2003). Face concerns in interpersonal conflict: A cross-cultural empirical test of the face negotiation theory. *Communication Research, 30*(6), 599–624.

Orbe, M. (1998). *Constructing co-cultural theory: An explication of culture, power and communication*. Thousand Oaks, CA: Sage.

Rajasekar, J., & Renand, F. (2013). Culture shock in a global world: Factors affecting culture shock experienced by expatriates in Oman and Omani expatriates abroad. *International Journal of Business and Management, 8*(13), 144–160.

Redfield, R., Linton, R., & Herskovits, M. J. (1936). Memorandum for the study of acculturation. *American Anthropologist, 38*, 149–152.

Ruben, B. (1976). Assessing communication competency for intercultural adaptation. *Group Organization Management, 1*(3), 334–354.

Sayegh, L. & Lasry, J. C. (1993). Immigrants' adaptation in Canada: Assimilation, acculturation, and orthogonal cultural identification. *Canadian Psychology, 34*, 98–109.

Shuter, R. (2012). Intercultural new media studies: The next frontier in intercultural communication. *Journal of Intercultural Communication Research, 41*(3), 219–237.

Tan, A., Nelson, L., Dong, Q., & Tan, G. (1997). Value acceptance in adolescent socialization: A test of a cognitive-functional theory of television effects. *Communication Monographs, 64*.

Tan, A., Tan, G., & Gibson, T. (2003). Socialization effects of American television on international audiences. In M. Elasmer (Ed.), *The impact of international television* (pp. 29–38). Mahwah, NJ: Lawrence Erlbaum.

Tan, A., Tan, G., & Tan, A. (1987). American TV in the Philippines: A test of cultural impact. *Journalism Quarterly, 64*, 648–654.

Ting-Toomey, S. (1994). Managing intercultural conflicts effectively. In L. Samovar & R. Porter (Eds.), *Intercultural communication: A reader* (7th ed., pp. 360–372). Belmont, CA: Wadsworth.

Ting-Toomey, S. (2005). The matrix of face: An updated face-negotiation theory. In W. Gudykunst (Ed.), *Theorizing about intercultural communication* (pp. 71–92), Thousand Oaks, CA: Sage.

Ting-Toomey, S., & Kurogi, A. (1998). Facework competence in intercultural conflict: An updated face-negotiation theory. *International Journal of Intercultural Relations, 22*(2), 187–225.

Ting-Toomey, S., Yee-Jung, S., Shapiro, R., Garcia, W., Wright, T., & Oetzel, J. (2000). Ethnic/cultural identity salience and conflict styles in four U.S. ethnic groups. *International Journal of Intercultural Relations, 24*(1), 47–81.

Yeh, E., Chu, H., Klein, M. H., Alexander, A. A., & Miller, M. H. (1981). Psychiatric implications of cross-cultural education: Chinese students in the United States. In S. Bochner (Ed.), *The mediating person: Bridges between cultures* (pp. 136–168). Cambridge, MA: Schenkman.

CHAPTER 5
HOW TO INTERACT WITH AMERICAN PROFESSORS

INTERACTING WITH PROFESSORS

BY ANDREW ROBERTS

My colleagues and I are continually surprised not only by how few students seek out personal contact with us, but by how poorly they behave when they do contact us. Even when they do show up at our office hours, students often show themselves to be rude, uncurious, and nakedly self-interested, the three biggest turnoffs for professors. You will get the best results from your professors by being courteous, curious, and not focusing on grades.

TIP 53 BE RESPECTFUL

It shocks me that I have to mention this, but showing common courtesy when interacting with professors is a basic floor you should not fall below. Most professors tend not to be impressed when students show up in their flip-flops and pajamas or worse. Or take cell phone calls in the middle of a conversation. Or want to discuss material that they have forgotten at home or haven't studied in the first place. Or fail to take notes on what they are being told. Or use vulgarities or informal forms of address. (Unless your professor specifies otherwise, referring to him or her as "professor" is most appropriate; never use a first name unless explicitly prompted to do so.) No, we are not shrinking violets, and you will not offend our delicate sensibilities by doing these things.

Andrew Roberts, "Interacting with Professors," *The Thinking Student's Guide to College: 75 Tips for Getting a Better Education*, pp. 112-126. Copyright © 2010 by University of Chicago Press. Reprinted with permission.

What you will do is single yourself out as a person who does not deserve serious attention. Our time is limited, and we have to decide who deserves more of it. Most student visits to us involve a request for some sort of help or advice. If you want our fullest attention, most sincere help, and best advice, then make it clear that it is important to you. That means showing up in a reasonable degree of organization and focused on the discussion at hand. If you give the impression that you don't care, then we will assume that you don't and adjust our advice accordingly.

So besides being courteous, show up to a professor's office hours with your course material—notes, readings, etc. Have pointed questions ready that you would like to discuss. Focus your attention on the topic at hand. And make sure to have paper and pencil in order to write down the professor's responses. When students don't write down what I am telling them, they almost always forget it, and because I know they will forget it, I give less thorough advice.

TIP 54   BE CURIOUS ABOUT THE SUBJECT

The fundamental thing to know about interacting with professors is that they genuinely care about their field. This is what they have devoted their lives to. Most of their nonteaching time is spent reading or writing about their field. They could literally talk for hours on end about their specialty without any notes. But aside from a handful of colleagues who work on the same topic, few people are interested in hearing their hard-earned opinions. Even their spouses have gotten sick and tired of their spouting off.

You should see this as an opportunity. Professors want to talk, and you want to learn. Make yourself their interlocutor. To do this, all you have to do is show genuine interest in their subject. Tell them how much you enjoy it and ask questions about it. It is easy to get professors chatting about their field of research because they know a lot that does not make it into their lectures.

Try to move beyond the course material in these discussions. Professors can go into a distracted, teaching mode when you ask specifically about their classes, which, truth be told, probably bore them a little. Ask them instead how the material sheds light on a current events issue or another book or article you have read recently. Or try to see the big picture or the meaning behind it all. Or ask about a subject not covered in class but related to it. Many professors will take this as an opportunity to be creative and witty, all to your benefit.

INTERACTING WITH FEMALE PROFESSORS

Male and female professors have identical job responsibilities—to teach, do research, and advise students. A colleague of mine, the sociologist Eszter Hargittai, however, has noted that students tend to treat them in different ways that can be both demeaning to and demanding for female professors. I include her reflections so that students—who perhaps are not aware of this—act more responsibly in their dealings with female professors.*

> Anyone who thinks male and female professors are treated equally by students is clueless. Just recently I came across a couple of examples that are very illustrative of this point. A friend of mine told me that her undergraduate advisees gave her a photo of themselves in a picture frame that says: "I love my Mommy" ...
>
> I can see the comments already: "If female profs are more caring then what's wrong with students expressing their appreciation for that?"
>
> First of all, students demand much more emotional work from female professors than they do of male profs. If the women don't provide it, they are often viewed as cold bitchy profs that don't care about students. Although I don't know of any systematic studies of what types of topics students bring up during interactions with professors by gender, I have heard plenty of anecdotal evidence suggesting that female profs get approached much more by students wanting to talk about life issues than male profs.
>
> Second, there are plenty of ways to express appreciation that don't involve putting the female prof in a mothering role, a role that certainly isn't emphasizing her academic strengths and credentials. As my friend noted, a gift of this sort makes her feel as though her only contribution to the students' success was in shepherding them through their projects and not in

* See Eszter Hargittai, "Herr Professor Daddy? I didn't think so," www.crookedtimber.org.

> providing intellectual stimulation, helping them professionally, or contributing to the creation of new well-trained researchers. Maybe, just maybe, she'd like to be recognized for her intellectual contributions and the part of mentoring that involves the research aspects of her job. And while it would be neat if mothering was equated with all of those things, don't kid yourself. Of course there is nothing wrong with being compassionate and caring, but it's not what tends to be rewarded professionally in academia.

TIP 55 VISIT ALL YOUR PROFESSORS DURING OFFICE HOURS AT LEAST ONCE

Every university requires professors to hold office hours at least once a week, usually for two or three hours.[1] While you might think that we would have long lines outside of our offices during these hours, there is usually only a trickle of students (except the week before an exam). I still haven't figured out why this is. The economist Brad DeLong found that even putting out cookies didn't help.

This is an incredible opportunity for you. You can go and chat with one of the most knowledgeable people in the world on the subject that they know best. You can ask them not only about issues you are having trouble with in class, but also about potential research ideas, your academic career, interesting things to read, or other classes that are worth taking. While you shouldn't view office hours simply as an opportunity to chew the fat—unless the professor leads you in that direction—you do have a good bit of freedom in the kind of issues you can discuss. I would recommend going in with an agenda—a set of questions that you wish to ask about the class or the field—and then see where things lead.

---

[1] Consistently not showing up for office hours is one of the few infractions for which professors will be reprimanded. Few professors will go to the lengths of the Slovenian philosopher Slavoj Žižek. As a profile of him explains, "Žižek says that he deals with student inquiries in a similar spirit. 'I understand I have to take questions during my lectures, since this is America and everybody is allowed to talk about everything. But when it comes to office hours, I have perfected a whole set of strategies for how to block this,' he says with a smirk. 'The real trick, however, is to minimize their access to me and simultaneously appear to be even more democratic!' Initially, Žižek scheduled office hours immediately before class so that students could not run on indefinitely. Then he came up with the idea of requiring them to submit a written question in advance, on the assumption that most would be too lazy to do it (they were). Žižek reserves what he calls 'the nasty strategy' for large lecture classes in which the students often don't know one another. 'I divide the time into six twenty-minute periods and then fill in the slots with invented names. That way the students think that all the hours are full and I can disappear,' he explains." See Robert T. Boynton, "Enjoy Your Žižek," *Lingua Franca*, October 1998.

You should do this at least once in every class you take. While not all of your encounters will be great successes, some will be, and all of them will mark you as a serious student to your professor. This leads to the next tip.

TIP 56   GET TO KNOW AT LEAST ONE PROFESSOR WELL

I hope that you leave university having made at least one personal bond with a professor. Even if teaching undergraduates is not always at the center of our mental worlds, we are people too and like to have as acquaintances smart and ambitious young people. What professors would be turned off by eager students who want to learn what they have to teach? Students also provide us with a connection to the real world that is often lacking in our lives, and we are genuinely curious to see how our students' lives turn out.

Such connections can be meaningful to you as well. Not only because you have made a new friend, but because I think we have something to offer. Perhaps it is as simple as advice on courses or careers. Maybe it is help in learning who you are and what you believe. Besides their families, young people have few non-self-interested adults in their lives who they can turn to with their dilemmas. While we are not equipped to deal with intimate or psychological problems—we are advised by our universities to refer you to counseling centers at the university—we can often give you some perspective on moral dilemmas or worries about your future. More practically, getting to know at least a couple of professors well is essential for obtaining good letters of recommendation (see Tip 61).

Some hard evidence backs me up in this advice. A recent survey showed that students who reported that a professor took a special interest in their work ended up being more satisfied with their university experience.[2] Another study noted that "frequent interaction with faculty is more strongly related to satisfaction with a college … than any other type of involvement."[3] In a series of interviews with recent graduates,

---

2 Charles T. Clotfelter, "Alumni Giving to Elite Private Colleges and Universities," *Economics of Education Review* 22, no. 2 (April 2003): 109–20.
3 Study Group on the Conditions of Excellence in American Higher Education, *Involvement in Learning: Realizing the Potential of American Higher Education* (Washington, DC: National Institute of Education, U.S. Department of Education, 1984), p. 18.

Richard Light found that students named close relations with a particular professor as among their most significant experiences in college.[4]

How do you get to know a professor well? Mostly by doing the things I have recommended in other rules: visiting office hours, taking small seminars and upper-division classes, writing a senior thesis, and becoming an RA. Most professors are glad to get to know students who are clever, ambitious, and curious. Show us that you possess these abilities and we will generally meet you halfway.

I would add in passing a neat trick to get to know professors better and find out the inside dope on a department and its classes. Get a job as a work-study in the department you are interested in. Departments often hire students to do simple secretarial jobs like answering the phone or photocopying course packets. While the work itself is not inspiring—though it may be intermittent enough to let you study while you work—it does plant you in the department for long stretches of time. You will thus get to know many of the professors—they will ask you to do jobs for them or will simply know your face—and you will hear scuttlebutt that will help you to become a more discerning student.

TIP 57   FIND OUT WHAT YOUR PROFESSORS RESEARCH

Few students realize that the intellectual center of their professors' lives is research. This ignorance may be natural. Students have few direct or indirect encounters with this side of the university. But since this is the focus of our mental lives, we are quite flattered when students bring it up. Your best ticket to impressing a professor is to mention his or her research.

You can find at least some basic information about what your professors are working on by looking at their departmental Web site or their personal homepage where they typically post a short biography and a list of recently published works. Many professors contribute to blogs or have Facebook sites where you can learn more about them. If you want to be the one in a thousand case, actually check one of their books out of the library or download one of their articles. Mention how much you enjoyed it and ask questions about it: how difficult was it to write, where did they get the idea, and what extensions would they like to see? Few students ask these questions, and professors are generally eager to answer them. In short, we are much easier to flatter than you might expect.

---

[4] Richard J. Light, *Making the Most of College: Students Speak Their Minds* (Cambridge, MA: Harvard University Press, 2001), pp. 81–87.

"TENURED RADICALS"

Despite occasional denials, it is true that university professors tend to be more liberal than the public at large.* They are considerably more likely to vote Democratic than Republican and to hold political beliefs that are on to the left side of the political spectrum. The question is what this means for your education.

In the first place, I'd note that lots of groups in American society differ from the "average" American. Businessmen, for example, are more conservative than the rest of society. And there is no conspiracy to keep universities on the left. The hiring process focuses almost entirely on a professor's research rather than his or her political beliefs. Even if universities wished to institute an affirmative action program for right-wing professors, they would have a hard time filling the positions. Conservatives seem to prefer other professions, and liberals seem to be attracted to universities.†

While many commentators have made hay out of this disparity, arguing that these "tenured radicals" are indoctrinating future generations, I am skeptical about whether this is true.‡ Though there are certainly cases of professors turning the classroom into a political forum, there is a strong ethic among most of us not to bring our own politics into our teaching. Most of the time it just isn't relevant—a discussion of *Jane Eyre* is not the time or place to talk about George Bush—and the rest of the time we see our function as challenging whatever preconceptions students have rather than inculcating our own. I view my own role as being a devil's advocate for unpopular ideas rather than pushing a particular political line.

Insofar as our politics does come out, I don't think the influence is as pernicious as most would have it and may even be beneficial. In the first place, even if some professors are advocates for their own views, I think it unlikely that students will take their word for it. Most professors only wish they had as much influence as critics attribute to them. Students usually don't learn the subject matter and forget it even faster; why should the professor's political opinions exert a greater hold over their minds? Second, I think there is arguably a conservative bias in society at large, a bias toward the tried and true, the status quo, the traditional. Given

---

* See Scott Jaschik, "The Liberal (and Moderating) Professoriate," *Inside Higher Ed*, October 8, 2007.
† Matthew Woessner and April Kelly-Woessner, "Left Pipeline: Why Conservatives Don't Get Doctorates," American Enterprise Institute, 2007.
‡ Roger Kimball, *Tenured Radicals: How Politics Has Corrupted Our Higher Education* (New York: Harper & Row, 1990).

that, it may be a useful thing for there to be a place where this bias is challenged constantly and in depth. What other organization pays people to think subversive thoughts? Most of these ideas won't pan out, but some will and become the conventional wisdom for future generations.

Finally, for the true conservative students out there, I believe that you will get a better education than your liberal counterparts. As I've mentioned several times, one of the most important parts of your education is challenging your established beliefs. What better way to do this than sit through classes that do nothing but. For the conservatively inclined, university is the perfect place to sharpen your debating skills and hone your ideas. It would probably be better if universities were more diverse politically, if there were more true conservatives and even reactionaries in the professoriate.§ Then students could test their ideas against a wider range of foils. But in the current environment at least conservative students get this benefit.

§ If you are curious, the humanities and social sciences are the most liberal fields, business and the health sciences the most conservative, while computer science and engineering contain the highest proportion of moderates. Interestingly, younger professors are more moderate and less liberal than their elders. See Neil Gross and Solon Simmons, "The Social and Political Views of American Professors," Working Paper, September 2007.

TIP 58 SEND E-MAILS JUDICIOUSLY, ANSWER E-MAILS PROMPTLY

It used to be that to contact professors, you had to catch them in their offices or risk disturbing them by telephone. With the advent of e-mail, this is no longer the case. Sending an e-mail is a simple and seemingly unobtrusive way of communicating with a professor. After all, professors are free to answer at their leisure; you're not interrupting their work or their dinner.

Nevertheless, I would urge you to treat e-mail with caution (see text box "Writing an Effective E-mail"). You should not e-mail professors to ask for information that has already been distributed: the due date of an assignment or the required reading. Consider your professor a last resort for obtaining information that has been made publicly available. Turn first to a fellow student or TA. For serious matters, by contrast, e-mail is usually not enough. If you want an extension on a paper or have a complaint about a grade, you will be better off visiting in person. Our suspicion meter rises when someone doesn't look us in the eye.

On the other hand, if you receive an e-mail from a professor, it is best to answer immediately. Not only might you forget about it as it drops down your e-mail queue, but you are potentially annoying a professor who has taken the time to think of you personally. Often students put off answering because they wish to change the state of affairs that has prompted the e-mail. If the professor is asking about a late assignment, students think that if they delay answering until they have finished, then they can honestly answer that it is done. This tactic fools no one. Better to come clean right away and say that you will hand in the assignment tomorrow or the next day.

WRITING AN EFFECTIVE E-MAIL

Many of your professors won't tolerate the casual e-mail conventions that you may be used to with your friends or family—the informality, the ubiquitous abbreviations, the grammatical looseness. Writing an e-mail with these characteristics will at best mildly annoy them and at worst threaten your standing in their eyes. Unless you are explicitly advised otherwise, you should write e-mails that resemble formal letters. This means they should include:

- An informative subject line like "Question about the final exam"
- A respectful salutation: best is "Dear Professor"; even if a professor signs his/her e-mails with a first name, this is not an invitation to respond in kind unless the professor explicitly says, "Call me Andrew."
- A clear, concise explanation of your problem or request written in grammatical English without abbreviations. If you are following up on a previous discussion, it is good to reference that discussion, for example, "As we talked about after class on Thursday …" If you wish to meet with a professor, specify exact times when you can come (and then be on time); their posted office hours are your best bet.
- A definite closing: appropriate ones are "Best," "Best regards," and "Thanks."

Here is an example:

Dear Professor Roberts,
I wanted to follow up on the discussion we had during your office hours last week. You mentioned that for my final paper on Clinton's healthcare plan, I should submit a revised bibliography. I have attached it to this email. I look forward to your comments.
Thanks for your help,
Lisa

TIP 59 AVOID COMPLAINTS ABOUT GRADES

There is nothing that professors dislike more than complaints about grades. It is probably even worse than grading itself, which is one of our least favorite things. Most professors put rules in place to prevent such complaints—they might require you to bring them up first with TAs or to submit complaints in writing. Nevertheless, complaints get to us no matter what we do, and it seems like with increasing frequency.

The main problem with complaints about grades is that they immediately signal to us that you are less interested in the subject of the course than in your grade. You show that you are person who is not interested in genuine learning but in credentials and symbols. You mark yourself as a grade grubber—yes, we use this term too—rather than a scholar.

A second annoyance is that most complaints are baseless. Professors produce their grades with the experience of hundreds or thousands of different exams and essays that they have graded in this course or others. If they think your exam was not up to snuff, it is because it did not measure up to all of these others that you naturally have not seen. This is not to say that grading is a science—far from it—only that it usually takes into account most of a student's objections.

The substance of most complaints moreover ends up being things that professors warn you about repeatedly before exams like remembering to read the entire question and producing a clear and well-organized answer. Many students bring in their exams to show us how much they wrote for a specific question or that bits and pieces of the answer are scattered around their essay. This is not a convincing complaint. A good answer to an essay or exam question is not a hidden code that needs to be deciphered; it is a clear and organized answer to the question. If you have not produced that, you should not be complaining. And this is not to mention the weakest claim of them all: the plea that your grade is especially important because you are applying to law school or medical school or because it is your major. This one carries zero (and perhaps negative) weight.

I would finally point out that even if your complaint is successful, it will have almost zero influence on your collegiate grade point average. Consider the standard request for an A− instead of a B+. The difference between these two grades is .33 grade points (3.67 versus 3.33). During your undergraduate career, you receive maybe thirty-two grades. The increase in your GPA as a result of a successful complaint is .33/32 or .01 grade points, which is not very different from zero.

Given all of this, what are your odds of getting the professor to change your grade? Will you be able to roll him or her? I don't know of any research on this, but my experience is that your chances are slim. You may have success with TAs—who lack the will to stand up to pesky students—but they usually have to intervene with the professor who is likely to reject your claim.

And what do you lose in exchange for the possible .01 increase in your GPA? If you view your relation with a professor as a one-shot encounter—meaning that you will never see him or her again—maybe nothing. But if you see any possibility of further encounters, whether classes, research assistantships, or letters of recommendation, you would be best advised to skip your complaint because the main impression you have left in the professor's head is of a student who cares more about grades than learning. And remember that professors talk with each other every day and enjoy stories about annoying or outrageous behavior by students. Your reputation will quickly spread around the department.

I don't want to overemphasize this advice (and there is a certain amount of self-interest in my perspective). There may be situations where professors or TAs have made a careless mistake, and it will not be held against you to alert them to it.[5] On matters of interpretation, you are on thinner ice. I suggest that if you really feel aggrieved you approach professors in the following manner. Tell them that you would like to do better in the class because you enjoy it a lot, but that you were discouraged by your performance on the exam or paper. Then show them the exam and ask how they think you could improve. This way, you get them to take a second look at the exam and mark yourself not as a complainer but as a student who cares about the subject and wishes to do better.

TIP 60 BECOME A RESEARCH ASSISTANT

I noted earlier that research is the most intense and probably the most natural type of learning that there is (see Tip 43). Besides writing a senior thesis, one of the best ways to get involved in research is to work for a professor as a research assistant (or RA). Particularly at larger universities, many professors have received large grants that they can use to hire students to assist with their research. RA work is an excellent way not

---

[5] I read about the following incident in my college's alumni review. A former student recalled how an elderly professor had throughout the semester confused him with another student and in the end given him the C that the other student deserved rather than the A that he had earned. When he asked another professor what he should do, the professor advised him to let it be because it would become a great cocktail party story for him in later years. Although the student in question heeded the professor's advice, you do not have to go that far.

just to earn money, but to learn more about a particular subject and to form a more personal bond with one of your professors.

What do RAs do? Their tasks vary widely by discipline and professor. In virtually all fields, there is a certain amount of secretarial work—tracking down articles, photocopying, and data entry. This is the least rewarding part of RA work. But doing it well will encourage a professor to trust you with more interesting tasks. Most professors are initially suspicious of undergraduates' abilities to do good and conscientious work, a suspicion born of past disappointments. If you do the simple tasks well, you will dispel some of this suspicion. Even in these simple tasks, however, you get a glimpse into how your professor conducts research—what sort of questions they ask, how they look for answers, and how they organize their work—all things that will help you in your own research.[6]

The interesting tasks are more diverse. In the sciences or psychology you may be asked to help conduct experiments—whether setting up the materials, administering tests or surveys, or even combining chemicals in beakers and flasks. In any field you may be asked to produce a literature review—that is, tracking down the latest articles or books in a given field and writing a summary of the major findings. Depending on your skills you might be asked to run statistical analyses or translate foreign texts. The more fortunate may be sent on trips to archives or to conduct interviews. The only limits to the kind of tasks you are assigned are your own abilities.

Indeed, talented undergraduates sometimes even end up as coauthors on their professor's published work, a nice notch to add to your résumé. RA work is also an excellent springboard to a senior thesis (see Tip 43). You will discover spin-off questions that your professor doesn't have time for answering. You will also develop the skills to answer these questions more effectively.

How do you find RA work? Some professors advertise for RAs whether on their office door or in the school newspaper. Some departments and institutes hire RAs to serve a group of professors. You may also write to specific professors or departments offering your services. Don't be shy about asking professors you know well if they are looking for an RA. The more practical skills you have, the better your chances of getting hired. Those with skills in statistics, computer programming, and foreign languages tend to be in high demand.[7] Being conscientious and hardworking top most skills.

---

[6] For a fascinating account of how one professor goes about doing research, see Paul Krugman, "How I Work," www.princeton.edu/~pkrugman/howiwork.

[7] Note, however, the political scientist Jacob Levy's advice on putting together a résumé: "Under no circumstances is 'Microsoft Word' a skill worth listing on your [résumé]. Neither is Power Point or Excel. Unless you're a certified [system administrator], under no circumstances is any version of Windows or a Mac operating system a skill worth listing on your [résumé]; it means 'I know how to turn my computer on.' And—really, truly—under no circumstances is your ability to e-mail or to operate a web browser a skill worth listing on your [résumé]. These things aren't just weighted at zero. They make you look ridiculous." See Jacob Levy, "The Unlicensed CV Doctor," jacobtlevy.blogspot.com.

TIP 61 ASK FOR RECOMMENDATION LETTERS FROM PROFESSORS WHO KNOW YOU WELL

Most professors are happy to write recommendations for students they know and like. They view this as part of their job and typically do it conscientiously. For this reason, be solicitous in your requests from them. In the first place, you need to come to their office hours with a set of future plans and materials about yourself. You might write to the professors in advance, so that they know to expect you and tell you what materials they would like to see. A list of programs you are applying to (with addresses and dates when the recommendation is due) along with a résumé and your application essay is a minimum.

Remember that you want a professor to write a recommendation that is both positive and detailed. For the positive part, you need to find a professor for whom you performed well and who enjoyed your company. But readers of recommendations will discount a positive recommendation if it is not backed up by detailed knowledge of your work. For the detailed part, you want to choose a professor who knows something about you. If you were one of a hundred students in a lecture class, don't expect much. If a professor never addressed you by name or wrote detailed comments on your papers, then they probably can't say much about you. In short, put yourself in your professors' shoes and think about what they could possibly say about you. We don't have a magical formula for turning chance encounters into effective recommendations.

The best recommendations are thus from professors who taught you in multiple classes, particularly in small, upper-division seminars where they could observe you up close engaging in challenging tasks. Better still would be a professor who advised you on a senior thesis or independent study and thus had sustained personal interactions with you.

Even when you have this sort of relationship, you still need to meet the professor halfway. We teach several hundred students a year and cannot remember very much (if anything) about all of them. You thus need to supply some of the details of your academic career. You may recall that you wrote a paper arguing X or Y, that you focused on this particular subject, or that you had certain extracurricular experiences. If you can come up with a list of bullet points about why you want the position and why you are qualified, this would be helpful. The more details you can fill in, the better the recommendation a professor can write.

Ideally you would take these steps somewhat but not too far in advance of the due date for the recommendation. While writing a recommendation probably only takes an hour or so of a professor's time, they may be particularly busy at certain times whether due to grading or research commitments. Two months in advance is a reasonable amount of time and less than two weeks is pushing things. Once you've done this, it is not considered offensive to check up with the professor to see whether they have actually sent off the recommendation. We do deserve our reputation for absent-mindedness, and recommendations are the sort of random tasks that may slip out of our schedule. A thank you note a week or two before the recommendation is due may be one unobtrusive way of sending a reminder.

One final note: you should consider it worrisome if the professor asks you to draft the recommendation letter yourself. Not only is it ethically dubious, but as the economist Tyler Cowen points out,

> Most people, especially undergraduates, do not know how to write a very good recommendation letter. They fail to realize that such letters, to be effective, should offer very specific and pointed comparisons. Those few students who understand this fact are probably too shy to call themselves "comparable to [the famous economist] Greg Mankiw as an undergraduate." … So if a professor asks the student to write the letter, the professor does not care about the letter or student very much. The resulting letter is likely to be very generic and thus not very effective. In addition, the professor probably has a hard time saying much about the student. This again suggests the letter will be less than overwhelming, no matter who writes it.[8]

I would add that much of the advice in this book is intended to forestall such situations. As you get to know more professors personally, you will have more possible recommenders who can describe your qualities in depth.

---

8   See Tyler Cowen, "Letters of Recommendation," www.marginalrevolution.com.

HOW AMERICAN STUDENTS PREPARE FOR COLLEGE

CHAPTER 6

BE AN ADULT

BY SAN BOLKAN

I know that at times you may not feel like you are an adult, but your professors consider you to be one and they hope that you act like one. Follow the advice in this chapter to discover what professors expect from you in college based on your newly discovered and special adult status.

One of the most important things to know when you walk into your college classrooms is that your professors consider you to be professional, adult students. They expect you to put school first and approach your studies in a mature fashion. That's right, in addition to class you may have a job, you may have a family, and you may have a significant other … but for your professors these other considerations are just that, other considerations.

Remember, while college might seem like a fun and exciting four-year buffer between high school and a full-time job, the reality is that college is the first step in your lifelong career. Therefore, your job in college is to be a professional student and you should approach your studies in the same way that professionals approach their careers. You are among the lucky ones, you are not working in a coal mine for a living, you are not fishing for crabmeat on the show *Deadliest Catch*, and you are not at Wal-Mart greeting old people as they walk/hobble into the store. No, you are in college and this job is a lot better than the alternatives presented above.

San Bolkan, "Be an Adult," *So, You Are Going to College?! Things You Wish You Knew before Heading to Class*, pp. 39-56, 134-136. Copyright © 2011 by Cognella, Inc. Reprinted with permission.

Unfortunately, most students do not think of school as a first step in their careers and instead they think of it as a four-year social event. They think of it as a time to hang out, have fun, go to parties, and then post pictures of themselves on Facebook doing keg stands while drunk dudes cheer them on. Sure, all of these things are fun and, as a matter of fact, your professors know that your social experiences in college *are* valuable to you. However, the problems start when students begin to prioritize their fun ahead of their educations. Most professors don't really care about your specific social events outside of class and most will probably never know whether you do keg stands or not. But they will know if you come to class, they will know if you do your work, and they will know how well you complete your assignments.

Although professors are not worried about your extracurricular activities, they are concerned about whether you learn the material in their courses. And if you do not master the material, you will not earn a passing grade. So, since the government considers you to be an adult at age eighteen, I suggest that you do the same. The next few pages will outline how to do this. Being an adult in college means that you need to treat school like it is your full-time job. Specifically, this means that you need to show up to class, come to class on time, take responsibility for your actions, respect your professors, and master the basics.

SHOW UP TO CLASS!

Are you kidding me? Writing this in a book for adult students makes me feel terrible. Yet, I think many of you need the information. That or you need a kick in the pants. Maybe you need both. Studies consistently show that an important predictor of success for college students is classroom attendance.[1] No, Einstein did not conduct these studies. But despite their commonsensical advice, the idea of attending class eludes many college students. I can confidently say that the majority of students who do poorly in my courses are the ones who do not show up. They miss instructions for class, they miss class notes, they miss quizzes, they miss participation points, they miss opportunities to turn in assignments, and they miss face time with me, the professor. I do not understand why students do not come to class. I mean, I know that people understand cause-and-effect relationships: you punch a bear in the face and it's going to bite you. So I find it strange that people don't come to class but still expect to do well in school.

Now, don't get me wrong. On occasion a person is going to miss class. You may have a medical emergency, you may have a friend who is getting married, or the surf may be up. However, if you miss class, the reason for missing it should be a good one and you should understand your professor's policies when it comes to making it up. That is, some excuses will be OK and will allow you to make up assignments and others will not.

If you decide to miss class for something fun (e.g., the surf's up, it is national dog bite prevention week, a homeless man pays you to play catch in the park) then it is up to you to be an adult and simply live with your decision. Do not ask for an extension of a deadline, do not ask for participation points to be made up, and do not ask for any special favors. Part of being an adult means that you take responsibility for your behaviors and that you accept the consequences of your actions. If that means missing a five-point quiz because the surf was up then great, I hope it was worth it. If it wasn't, then don't go surfing during class.

For absences that are excused (check your university's policies regarding what types of excuses allow for class content to be made up) be sure to make the process of making up the work easy for you and your professors. That is, bring them the necessary paperwork if the reason for your absence needs to be documented, be sure to stay in contact with your professors while you are gone, and be sure to send them an e-mail (at the very least) to let them know *ahead of time* (or as soon as possible) that you cannot make it to class.

In fact, letting your professors know that you cannot make it to class, ahead of time, is important despite the reason for missing class. So, do it when you are not going to be there. Now, you may be asking why it is important to let professors know that you cannot make class ahead of time. This is important for two reasons. First, when you cannot make it to class and you communicate this to your professors, they will make arrangements to accommodate your emergency. They can help you formulate a plan for turning in assignments and they can set up special appointments to take care of other things (such as tests and participation points) as well. Second, they will think of you as a thoughtful individual; you took the time to alert them of your impending absence and they will appreciate your consideration. However, if you simply do not show up to class you leave it up to your professor's imaginations to determine why you are not present. When no explanation is given, research suggests that there is a tendency for people to attribute the negative actions of others to stable, personal dispositions such as irresponsibility and selfishness.[2] On the other hand, if you can provide information that would discount these negative perceptions, your professors may be less likely to form them.[3] To do this you need to provide an appropriate explanation. To be appropriate, the explanation needs to be provided ahead of time.

Moreover, regardless of your reasons for missing a day, if you cannot make it to class it is still your responsibility to turn in your assignments on time and to get the day's material you missed *on your own*. At the very least, arrange for a classmate to turn in assignments that are due and arrange to get lecture notes from somebody else. I suggest that the first day you go to class you make a friend and have a buddy system for notes. If you miss a day then you can stay caught up and the same will be true if your friend needs the help. You may not know this but professors have lives too. In addition to working really hard as teachers we do a lot of writing and research. Furthermore, we are on a variety of committees (that help run the university) which require a lot of work. On top of that we also have social lives. The last thing we want to do when you miss class is spend our time lecturing twice or answering e-mails that ask, "Hey professor, what did I miss in class? Did we do anything important?" My response to messages like this is always the same: "Dear A**hole, figure it out. Love, Dad."

DO NOT COME TO CLASS LATE!

Let me ask you a question, what do you think would happen if you came late to work on multiple occasions? I am sure most of you know the answer to this one. If you do not, try showing up late to your job on a regular basis and report back to me with the results. Coming late to work is unprofessional and shows a lack of concern for your employer. If it becomes a habit your boss is going to think less of you and eventually you are going to be let go. The same process that happens at work happens in the classroom as well. That is, if you come to class late on multiple occasions your professors are going to think less of you and your tardiness will start to affect your grade.

Now, admittedly, things happen. I know that a person can't always help being late. But when it happens on multiple instances it starts to reflect negatively upon you. Think about it, do you love getting dressed for a night out and then waiting on your friends to finish getting ready? Do you enjoy arriving on time to an event and then waiting for others to show up? Do you like it when people tell you they will pick you up at seven o'clock and then show up at eight? I bet you find this behavior annoying and, although you would let it slide on the odd occasion, if these types of things happened on a regular basis you would start to get upset. You may not think that your tardiness affects the way your classes are run or that it shows disrespect to your professors, but the truth is it doesn't matter what you think. In fact, it doesn't matter what the truth is! People do not act based on the truth. Instead, they act based on their perceptions of the truth. And when you arrive to class late on multiple occasions you will be perceived as an uncaring individual. You do not want your professors to think that you do not care about their classes. When it comes to benefit of the doubt time (e.g., at the end of the semester when you are on the cusp of one grade or another), your professors will look at these types of things to help them make their decisions about your grade.

OK, so sometimes the bus comes late and I know that this can be a bummer for you ☹. But as far as I'm concerned, this shouldn't matter. I mean, why are you catching the latest bus possible anyway? My father is never late to work. You know why? Because he shows up every day at six in the morning. Sure, his work doesn't start until eight but he shows up early to guarantee that no matter what may go wrong on his commute he has time to take care of it before it comes time to clock in. And guess what? My dad is the director of a major research corporation in Northern California. He is the head honcho for a number of reasons and those include his responsibility, his attention to detail, and his dedication to doing things the right way.

Although this example is admittedly extreme, you should apply the same principle in your lives as well. If you are a student of mine, never tell me that you were late to class because your bus was late. My response is usually "so what?" I am not responsible for getting the bus on schedule and neither are you. But you *are* responsible for being to class on time. Accordingly, do not cut your timing so close that you depend on others for your success. You are better than that. Being on time is up to you, it is not up to Joe the bus driver. And while it may be Joe's fault that you are late, ultimately it is your problem.

The same is true for turning in assignments for class. You are sorely mistaken if you think that your professors care that your printer wasn't working or that the library's printers were on the fritz the morning that you were supposed to turn in an assignment. Instead of thinking that the problem is "sad" for you, your professors are more likely to be thinking, "Why are you printing your assignment at the last minute in the first place?" Remember Murphy's Law: if things can go wrong, they will. Take the time to make sure that all of your assignments are completed *at least* a few hours early and then print them so nothing goes awry. If something does, you will have time to correct the issue.

TAKE RESPONSIBILITY FOR YOUR EDUCATION

Some people have what scientists call an internal locus of control.[4] Generally speaking, these people believe they have the ability to influence the world around them. People with an internal locus of control believe that they have a say in their fates. Other people have an external locus of control and believe, for the most part, that the outside world affects their lives. This is what I call the "Uncle Rico Effect." You know what I'm talking about. In the movie *Napoleon Dynamite*, Uncle Rico was convinced that if Coach had only put him in the game during the fourth quarter they would have won the game and been state champs. Uncle Rico would have gone pro, he would have made millions, and he would have met his soul mate ... things would have been different! As a student you need to adopt an internal locus of control for your academic affairs. Adopting an internal locus of control will help you with your studies in at least two ways.

For one, if you did not do well on a test, instead of blaming the circumstances an internal locus of control will help you look at what *you* did (or did not do) to prepare for the test and discover why this may be the case. Doing this will allow you to correct the issue for your next exam. For instance, perhaps you did not study in a manner that helped you do well on the exam, perhaps you did not study long enough, or perhaps you simply did not understand the material. With an internal locus of control you will realize that these explanations are more likely an accurate reflection of your grade than is the professor's desire to "get you." Professors do not do the "No A's Dance" at the end of the semester, and contrary to the beliefs of some people they actually want you to do well in school. Therefore, when you do poorly on an exam, it is important to do some introspection to discover what happened. With an internal locus of control you will most likely discover that the best way to correct the problem for the next time is not to get your professor to stop being a jerk; instead, it may be to study both harder and smarter.

Second, an internal locus of control will help you create a positive impression with your professors. People develop expectations about the communication behavior of others based both on their relationships and on the context of their interactions.[5] And negative violations of these expectations often lead to negative results. For example, some of my own research points to the notion that people have expectations for companies following a failure.[6] One of these expectations is that companies take responsibility when things go wrong.[7] I discovered that because people expect businesses to take responsibility for their actions when there is a mistake, *not doing so* leads to negative impressions of the company. The same is true for students. Professors expect students to take responsibility for their own educations. Therefore, if you fail to take responsibility for your education your professors are likely to ascribe negative qualities to you. An internal locus of control will help you to prevent this from occurring.

So how can you take responsibility for your actions? Easy, by realizing that in college it is up to you to learn. Understand that one of the fundamental differences between high school and college is that in college learning is self-directed. That means you should not need a professor to breathe down your neck to get you to learn the material. YOU need to keep up with the readings on the course schedules, YOU need to remember when assignments are due as they are stated on the syllabi, and YOU need to make sure that you learn the material in your courses. Professors simply expect you to do these things. Your professors are not going to call your parents or even contact you to let you know they are concerned if you do not show up for class, if you turn in low-quality work, or if you do poorly on an exam. Most of them are just going to assign you a failing grade. Believe it.

RESPECT YOUR PROFESSORS

Conflict occurs in a variety of relationships and at some point it is bound to occur between you and your professors as well. You may disagree with a course policy, you may have questions about a grade on an assignment, or you may need to change the date of an exam. In any case, you will eventually have conflict with your professors and when you do you need to handle it appropriately. Although the word "conflict" typically has a negative connotation, know that it is normal, it is to be expected in your relationships, and it may lead to positive outcomes.[8] Consequently, when interacting with others it's important to remember that conflict is not a bad thing. Instead, how you handle the conflict determines the positivity or negativity of the relational outcome.[9]

OK, if handling conflict is so important then you may be wondering how you can do it correctly. You can handle conflict well by doing three things: first, by bringing up conflict when it is important to you; second, by doing so at an appropriate time; and third, by working through conflict respectfully. Let's begin with the first idea. Do not avoid bringing up a topic to your professors if it is significant to you. Despite the fact that professors are very, very powerful, our powers do not include mind reading. Most professors I know are happy to work through problems with students. To do so, however, the problems must first come to our attention. Realize that professors are flexible people that are willing to listen to your point of view. Also, realize that most professors appreciate their students and want them to do well. With that in mind, instead of complaining to your fellow classmates when you have issues with your classes or with your professors, consider talking to your professors themselves. Most of them will be glad for the opportunity to rectify the situation. If you turn away from conflict you may never work out your problems, you may never be able to discover why things are the way they are, and ultimately your relationships with your professors may suffer.

Second, when you decide to bring up conflict, you need to do so appropriately. To help you remember this in the future I want you to memorize this simple rule: there is a time and place for everything. That said, some times and some places are better for discussing conflict than others. When you have conflict with your professors do not approach them at the beginning of class—when other students may be around and your professors are getting ready for their lectures. And do not approach them at the end of class—when they are scrambling to get to their next classroom. Instead, if you have any type of conflict, even if you just need to ask your professors for a special request, you need to make sure you bring up the issue with them when they can devote the appropriate resources to the problem (a good time may be during office hours).

You also need to make sure that you bring up the conflict in private. *In private*. The matter is between you and the professor and it should never involve the entire class. Now why should you bring up the matter in private? I'll tell you why. Research suggests that conflict in relationships is usually about one of four things: content, you may have conflict over a grade; relationships, you may have conflict over your role or status in a relationship; identities, you may have a conflict over how you are portrayed or thought of by others; and processes, you may have conflict over how your conflict is being handled.[10] When you bring up matters in front of other people you change the nature of the situation. Instead of being about the content only, you are likely to bring other conflict dimensions into the conversation. And if you change the nature of the conflict you may also unwittingly change the possibility of obtaining the outcome you are expecting.

Let me give you an example. Sometimes I have students who need to reschedule an exam for certain reasons (a content conflict). If they ask me in front of the class, I *have to* say no. I cannot be seen as playing favorites or bending the rules (this creates an identity conflict because it challenges the type of person that I said I was in class) and I do not want to do that. On the other hand, if I am asked in private to accommodate a student's schedule then I am going to be more willing to entertain the possibility of rescheduling the exam. Doing so only entails working out the logistics of meeting to administer the test and does not involve me re-negotiating my identity with the entire class.

In addition to bringing up conflict, and doing so at an appropriate time and in a private setting, the third way to handle conflict well when interacting with others is to make sure that you respect them and the way they see themselves. Why? Because our egos are intertwined with our basic human needs which include a) autonomy, b) relatedness, and c) competence[11] and a failure to help a person fulfill these needs may bring about self-protective mechanisms. As illustrated in the example above, these self-protective mechanisms may not have anything to do with the conflict at hand. And importantly, when others enact this type of behavior their actions may be detrimental to your final goal. You need to know that if you upset people based on the way you treat them, they are prone to fight you at any cost; not because they think they are right, but because they want you to be wrong. Therefore, in your interactions with others in general, and when you have conflict with your professors in specific, be sure to help people feel a) that they are free to do what they want, b) that they are liked, and c) that they are intelligent. By doing these things you may find that people react to you more fairly than if you had treated them otherwise.

Ultimately, I advise that when you have conflict with others, and expect any type of change, you bring the problem up to them. In addition, you need to bring up the conflict when they are in a position to deal with your concerns appropriately. Finally, when you bring up your conflict, you have to be careful not to upset people based on their identities, the way you frame the relationship, or the way you approach the conflict. People may not always remember the content of your conversations but they will always remember how you treated them and how you made them feel. The same is true for professors.

MASTER THE BASICS

Before I conclude this section I want to mention one last important component of being an adult at college. That is, you need to master the basics. In college, mastering the basics means knowing your professors' class policies, knowing your university's policies, and keeping information related to your studies organized. It may seem simple, but if you take the time to master the basics your life on campus will be a lot easier than if you do not.

To begin, let's talk about knowing your professors' policies. Knowing the policies means that when your professors pass out their syllabi on the first day of class you *actually* need to read them. Yes, this *is* important. Your professors use their syllabi to lay out their course guidelines and to let you know exactly what they expect from you throughout the semester. Reading your syllabi will help you figure out what you are getting yourself into and will also help you figure out what you need to do to be successful in your classes. Reading your syllabi is something that your professors assume you will do and it is your responsibility to make sure you understand the rules of your classes as designated by your teachers. Do it.

In addition to knowing your professors' policies, the second thing I want to talk about is knowing your university's policies. Knowing these is an important step toward your success on campus. For example, important policies include the process for adding and dropping courses, the time frame for withdrawing from a course without penalty, and the ability to retake classes without the first grade affecting your cumulative grade point average. Other important policies may include figuring out how to register for classes, when to register for classes, and what classes you need to take (and in what order) if you want to graduate in a certain period of time.

Determining these policies may simply be a matter of searching for information on your university's Web site. Alternatively, you may need to set up meetings with professors, department chairs, or deans to determine what is needed from you to succeed. In any case, make it a point to take the time to get to know the policies at your institution. I promise that doing so will save you some major headaches down the road.

The third thing I want to address concerning your knowledge of the basics is staying organized. What would happen if you went to the library to find a book and instead of having a catalog of books on different floors and shelves the library simply had all of its volumes stored in a gigantic pile in the middle of a poorly lit room? What would happen is that you would never go to the library again. Why would you go if you could never find anything you needed? Libraries can have the greatest books in the world but if you can't access them those books might as well not exist. Because going to a library and not finding what you need can be frustrating, librarians make sure that their collections are organized and easy to access. The same should be true of your personal information. Think about the feeling that accompanies losing important documents, and think about how you feel when you know that you have something you need but cannot find it. The feeling you get when something like this occurs is probably that of anxious frustration. You don't want that sort of negativity in your life. Being organized will help save you time and will also serve as a blessing for your professional well-being.

If you want to be organized then I suggest you start with your computer. Instead of having a million documents displayed all over your desktop, create appropriately labeled folders to keep your information segregated. For example, whenever you start a new semester in school you can create a folder (to do this simply right-click, select "new" and then "folder"; if you are working on a Mac, simply press control and click, then select "new folder") on your desktop labeled by the semester. Then, once you click on that folder and open it you can create new folders for every class you are taking. If you have five classes that means you will have five folders. Within each class folder you should create other folders that help organize your information even further. For instance, you can create a folder labeled "class documents" for the syllabus and course schedule, you can create a folder called "assignments" for the work you do throughout the semester, and you can create a folder called "notes" for the PowerPoint slides and notes you take in class. Once you are done with each semester you can create a master folder for the academic year and then drag and drop each semester into this space.

I know that when you first create a file and place it somewhere on your computer it seems as if you will always remember its name and location. However, this is just not the case. Weeks and even just days later you may be surprised to learn that when you log onto your computer to access a certain file you have a hard time doing so because you cannot find it. Because you do not want this to happen you need to take the time to create folders, place them consistently on your computer (e.g., on the desktop or on the C drive, etc.), and label them with enough information so that when you look for the files later you don't spend two hours searching for them without any luck.

In addition to your computer files, you also need to be organized with the physical components of your education. That is, you need to be sure that you have a system for cataloging your class notes, your graded assignments, and your completed tests. This is important should you ever need to use the information to help a friend study for the same course, help yourself in another course by accessing information you already learned, or help a teacher determine a final grade by having your exams ready in case there was a mistake in scoring. To be organized you need to create file folders just like you would on your computer. And you need to organize them in the same way. Create labeled folders of information that are segregated by topic so that when you store them you can put them in master folders, or hard-backed three-ring binders, that are labeled for easy access.

Being organized is part of what it means to be an adult and taking the time to have your work streamlined and easy to access will make you more efficient. Learning to create and use an organized system will help you beyond the classroom as well. When you are in the working world people will expect you to keep a variety of information on hand and they will want to keep detailed records of your work. If you are unorganized you will be in for a world of hurt when people ask you to retrieve something. This is a fact. So, practice now and reap the benefits of being an individual with a well-structured education.

SO WHAT?

There are many things that come with being an adult and I am positive that I did not cover all of them in this section. However, I did cover the notions of showing up to class, coming to class on time, taking responsibility for your education, respecting your professors, and mastering the basics. Despite the fact that I did not cover all of the situations in which acting like an adult will help you, if you keep the general idea in mind you can apply the rule in a variety of circumstances. So the next time you are in a situation and trying to figure out the proper behavior to employ, think about what an adult version of you would do and do that ;-). I am simply asking you to take responsibility for your actions. Although doing so might not necessarily be something you are used to, taking responsibility for your behaviors will help you tremendously in life. [...] it will also help you in your communication with others.

NOTES

1. Romer, D. "Do students go to class? Should they?" *Journal of Economic Perspectives* (1993) 7, 167–174.
   Van Blerkom, M. L. "Academic perseverance, class attendance, and performance in the college classroom." Paper presented at the annual Meeting of the American Psychological Association, Toronto, Ontario, Canada, 1996.
2. Jones, E. E., and Nisbett, R. E. "The actor observer: Divergent perceptions of the causes of behavior," in *Attribution: Perceiving the causes of behavior*, edited by E. E. Jones, D. E. Kanouse, H. H. Kelley, R. E. Nisbett, S. Valins, and B. Weiner (Morristown, NJ: General Learning Press, 1971), 79–94.
3. Kelley, H. H. "The process of causal attribution." *American Psychologist* (1973) 28, 107–128.
4. Lefcourt, H. M. 1976. *Locus of control: Current trends in theory and research*. Hillsdale, NJ: Erlbaum.
5. Rotter, J. B. 1954. *Social learning and clinical psychology*. New York: Prentice-Hall.
6. Burgoon, J. K., Dunbar, N. E., and Segrin, C. "Nonverbal influence," in *The persuasion handbook: Developments in theory and practice*, edited by J. P. Dillard and M. Pfau (Thousand Oaks, CA: Sage, 2002), 445–473.
7. Bolkan, S., and Daly, J. A. "Organizational responses to consumer complaints: A re-examination of the impact of organizational messages in response to service and product-based failures." *Journal of Consumer Satisfaction, Dissatisfaction & Complaining Behavior* (2008) 21, 1–22.
   Bolkan, S., and Daly, J. A. "Organizational responses to consumer complaints: An approach to understanding the effectiveness of remedial accounts." *Journal of Applied Communication Research* (2009) 37, 21–39.
7. Conlon, D. E., and Murray, N. M. "Customer perceptions of corporate responses to product complaints: The role of explanations." *Academy of Management Journal* (1996) 39, 1040–1056.
8. Coser, L. A. 1967. *Continuities in the study of social conflict*. New York: Free Press.
   Simmel, G. 1953. *Conflict and the web of group affiliations*. Translated by K. H. Wolff. New York: Free Press.
9. Galvin, K. M., Bylund, C. L., and Brommel, B. J. 2007. *Family communication: Cohesion and change*. Boston, MA: Allyn and Bacon.
10. Wilmot, W. W., and Hocker, J. L. 2005. *Interpersonal conflict*. Boston, MA: McGraw-Hill.

CHAPTER 7
EFFECTIVE STUDY STRATEGIES AND ACADEMIC HONESTY

CONCENTRATION AND STUDY ENVIRONMENT

BY ROBIN ROACH GILLEY

Thinking about a task, mental or physical, and focusing attention to that task leads to concentration.

People sometimes believe that concentration when studying comes easier for some people than others. This is true, but only true because they have mastered the **skill** of concentrating, of focusing. Research studies report that individuals do not have the ability to concentrate on tasks for hours at a time. It is a learned behavior.

If the task is a pleasant one or one that is interesting, concentration becomes MUCH easier. This is because we have motivation behind the thinking.

DUE	TABLE OF CONTENTS	TO DO	CHECK
	Concentration: What is it?	Written Assignment	
	External Study Distractions	Written Assignment	
	Internal Study Distractions	Written Assignment	
	Reduce Study Distractions	Written Assignment	
	Study-Period Concentration Analysis	Written Assignment	
	Concentration Trouble-Shooting	Written Assignment	

Robin Roach Gilley, "Concentration and Study Environment," *Effective Study Strategies: Practicing Academic Skills*, pp. 31-40. Copyright © 2015 by Cognella, Inc. Reprinted with permission.

ASSIGNMENT:
CONCENTRATION: WHAT IS IT?

Think about the following tasks
See if you find concentration during pleasant activities *easier* than during study periods.

My favorite TV show is

My favorite place to watch TV is

Some distractions that might occur during the show are

My favorite hobby is

The place where I conduct my hobby is

Some distractions that might occur during my hobby time are

I enjoy reading (describe the reading material):

My favorite place for reading is

I can usually read for _____ minutes; hours.

Some distractions that might occur during my reading enjoyment are

Now, make a list the distractions you identified.

1.

2.

3.

4.

5.

6.

7.

8.

9.

10.

ASSIGNMENT: EXTERNAL STUDY DISTRACTIONS

Lack of concentration comes from disturbances in the study area. Sometimes these disturbances are outside of your body and sometimes you feel them inside your body.

For example, your phone ringing is outside your body and it is called an **external** distraction.

However, when your stomach growls or feels as if it has butterflies in it, this is inside of you. This is an **internal** distraction.

This next assignment will deal with EXTERNAL distractions only.

Begin this exercise by listing as many EXTERNAL distractions you have encountered during a concentrated study time. List as many as you can think of:

After you have run out of ideas, ask a fellow student to read your list. Can he or she add to your list of EXTERNAL distractions? List any different distractions that your fellow student has shared.

ASSIGNMENT: INTERNAL STUDY DISTRACTIONS

Lack of concentration comes from disturbances in the study area. Sometimes these disturbances are outside of your body and sometimes you feel them inside your body. Your last assignment dealt with external distractions.

Now, you are going to be asked to think of **INTERNAL (inside)** distractions that occur when you study. Remember that an example of an internal distraction is when your stomach growls or feels as if it has butterflies in it; this is inside of you. This is an **INTERNAL** distraction. Other internal distractions might include headaches and worries.

This next assignment will deal with INTERNAL distractions only.

Begin this exercise by listing the INTERNAL distractions you have encountered during a concentrated study time. List as many as you can think of:

After you have run out of ideas, ask another student to read your list. Can he or she add to your list of INTERNAL distractions? List any different distractions that your fellow student has shared.

SUGGESTIONS FOR REDUCING STUDY DISTRACTIONS

EXTERNAL DISTRACTIONS	INTERNAL DISTRACTIONS
Turn off all electronic devices that are not NECESSARY for study.	If you are hungry, eat something!
Pretend you have blinders on. Perhaps some of you have seen them on racehorses; these are used so the horse is not distracted as it runs. Visualize yourself having only room for concentrating on what is in the blinders field of vision.	If something is on your mind, write it on a scrap piece of paper. Tell yourself that you will deal with what is bothering you AFTER you finish your study time. The act of writing it down aids with commitment.
Create a study space: Only for studying.	Physical exercise and activity on a regular basis keep your mind alert and active. Thus, you have fewer distractions and less stress.
Make sure you have the proper amount of lighting so your eyes aren't strained.	
All necessary supplies should be within reaching distance.	
Make sure everyone you live with understands that you need quiet.	
Now list your ideas:	Now list your ideas:

* Your instructor may have you turn in the assignment, or discuss in a small group or as a class.

ASSIGNMENT: STUDY ENVIRONMENT

List three places where *you usually study* in the order you most use them.

(1st) A. _____ (2nd) B. _____

(3rd) C. _____

Now circle the word in each column that applies to the appropriate place.

DISTRACTIONS	PLACE A	PLACE B	PLACE C
1. Other people often interrupt me when I study here.	Yes No	Yes No	Yes No
2. Much of what I can see here reminds me of things that don't have anything to do with studying.	Yes No	Yes No	Yes No
3. I often hear music or the TV when I study here.	Yes No	Yes No	Yes No
4. My phone often interrupts me.	Yes No	Yes No	Yes No
5. I talk too much on the phone when I am here.	Yes No	Yes No	Yes No
6. I think I take too many breaks when I study here.	Yes No	Yes No	Yes No
7. The things I need to study are often somewhere else.	Yes No	Yes No	Yes No
8. My breaks tend to be too long when I study here.	Yes No	Yes No	Yes No
9. I tend to look out a window or door.	Yes No	Yes No	Yes No
10. I hear other people talking here.	Yes No	Yes No	Yes No
11. I tend to daydream.	Yes No	Yes No	Yes No
12. The temperature here is not very good for studying.	Yes No	Yes No	Yes No
13. The ventilation here is not very good for studying.	Yes No	Yes No	Yes No
14. Chair, desk, and lighting arrangements here are not very helpful for studying.	Yes No	Yes No	Yes No
15. When I study here, I often people-watch.	Yes No	Yes No	Yes No
16. I can use this study place for things other than studying.	Yes No	Yes No	Yes No

Now total the "yes" responses and total the "no" responses in each column. The column that has the most "yes" responses may be the poorest place to study.

My poorest place to study is_____

Based on the results of this study-distractions analysis, describe what you could do to improve your place(s) of study to make it more ideal for studying.

Given your recently acquired knowledge, describe your ideal study environment.

* Your instructor may have you turn in the assignment, or discuss in a small group or as a class.

ASSIGNMENT: STUDY PERIOD CONCENTRATION ANALYSIS

Sometimes a lack of concentration may come from distractions, disturbances in the study area, mental fatigue, or maybe just a lack of interest in the task at hand.

If you identify the problem, you have a better chance of overcoming poor concentration.

Try using the following method. During your study periods, each time you find you've lost concentration, mark the page. Then write the reason you lost concentration. In other words, list the cause.

At the end of the study period, look at the disturbances/causes and identify ways to reduce or eliminate them.

Date of study period:

Subject being studied:

Time spent:	How spent:
• Beginning time:	• Reading assignment
• Ending time:	• Writing assignment
Study break time:	Other:

Concentration Broken (+) (*) (#) (!)   Cause of Break

Describe possible ways to reduce or eliminate the cause of the problem.

ASSIGNMENT: CONCENTRATION TROUBLE SHOOTING

This is a collaborative activity.

Once your group is formed, select someone to be the group recorder. This individual will fill out the activity sheet for the whole group. Then select someone to be the group reporter. The group reporter will share your results with the class.

Collectively agree on four different distractors that affect your concentration. List the four in the first column. The distractors may be internal or external. Then name one technique that could be used to reduce or eliminate the distractor. Briefly explain how that technique could be a solution. In the last column, name one more technique and explain how it also could be used as a solution.

CONCENTRATION AND STUDY ENVIRONMENT | 133

DISTRACTOR	TECHNIQUE #1	TECHNIQUE #2

LISTENING IN CLASS
BY SAN BOLKAN

Listening as a skill can be hard to do. But experience should tell you that anything in life worth having is hard to get. (If your experience didn't tell you that, I just did … Booya!)

You know that when you walk into your college classrooms you are there to learn. However, you might not know that if you lack the skills needed to listen effectively you will never maximize your potential in the classroom. This chapter was written to help you understand what it takes to learn while in class. And no, just showing up isn't enough *insert frownie face*. Although many people think that listening simply involves sound entering their giant heads, they are wrong. In fact, there are six interrelated steps to listening as a skill and hearing sound is only the first step. There are five more that follow. I am going to tell you about them now!

As I just mentioned, the first step to listening as a skill is for a person to actually hear the sound that another person, or thing, is making. In addition, you must be able to see what people are doing in order to interpret their nonverbal communication. What I am talking about here is the simple ability to process information. So, the first step in listening as a skill is hearing or seeing. How can you use this information to help you in class? Simple, if you cannot see what is being written on the board, move closer. And if you cannot hear the lecture then you need to make arrangements to change this. For instance, when I was a student I sat in many classes where the professors left the door open. Often, other students would roam the

San Bolkan, "Listening in Class," *So, You Are Going to College?! Things You Wish You Knew before Heading to Class*, pp. 75-89, 137. Copyright © 2011 by Cognella, Inc. Reprinted with permission.

halls and sometimes they would talk on their phones. When I was in class I was there to learn, and if I heard Jack talking on his phone about how Jill was a nasty girlfriend then I always took it upon myself to ask my professors if they minded if I closed the door. You should do the same. Try to cut out all physical distractions from your learning environment and concentrate on making listening easy. If there is someone next to you who is talking then either move or ask that person to be quiet. If the person refuses then simply ask yourself, "What would Chuck Norris do?" You know what he would do? He would roundhouse kick their hearts out of their chests.

The second step in the process of listening as a skill is to attend to the sound. This means to pay attention to it. Often, sounds can become background noise that gets filtered out of our conscious experience (such as traffic or a clock ticking). If you have ever slept with the fan on and forgotten that it is making a sound when you are in the room with it then you know that without attending to a noise you will simply not listen to it. Accordingly, if you want to actually listen to a sound you have to focus your attention on it. The same thing is true in class. Although you will undoubtedly take interesting courses while in college, it is quite possible that you will still want to daydream when your professors are talking. In fact, it is quite easy to do this (more on that later). But what you need to do is catch yourself when daydreaming, focus on the lecture, and make sure you are paying attention to your professors when they are speaking. A major barrier to listening is a lack of motivation. Therefore, you need to take an active approach to listening if you want to do it well.

The third step to listening as a skill is understanding. If you are talking to a person who is speaking Spanish, for example, you will have a hard time understanding him or her if you cannot speak the language. If that person said to you, "Yo quiero tocar su pajaro," you would never know that the speaker wanted to touch your bird. To come to this conclusion you would have to ask the person to speak in English so that you might understand what is being said. The same goes for class—while listening to your professors speak it is important that you make sure you can follow the organization and the logic of their lectures. If you cannot, then you need to raise your hand and ask them to clarify. People often think that what they have said inherently makes sense to their listeners. Therefore, without the appropriate feedback your professors will never know that you are having a problem understanding the material.

The fourth step to listening as a skill is remembering. That is, you need to remember the material presented to you if you want to count it as listening. If I were Superman my kryptonite would be remembering people's names. Five minutes after meeting somebody for the first time I cannot, for the life of me, remember his or her name. Although I hear the name, I never remember it, and many people would suggest that I simply did not listen when the person introduced himself or herself to me. The same is true of lectures. If you cannot recall what your professor said then either a) you did not listen or b) you might as well not have listened.

Here's a trick I use to remember names: every time a person tells me their name, I quickly think of a person who has the same name. Then I match the new person to the old person in my mind. This association helps me recall a mental picture of the old person when I meet the new person on a different occasion. And though I have a hard time remembering new friends' names, I am pretty good at remembering old friends' names. By using this method I have become better at remembering people's names. A similar trick that people use to remember lectures is to paraphrase the material. Try it. In essence, when you hear information in your lectures simply try to repeat it back to yourself in your own words. If you can do this you may be more likely to remember the content because you will have learned it in a fashion that makes sense to you.

The fifth step in listening as a skill is evaluating. This involves putting the material you listened to into a framework that you are already familiar with. Scholars assert that we have schemas that help us organize data in our brains. Schemas are like filing cabinets that hold information according to various categories. For example, you have animal schemas that help you make sense of the animal world. The facts that a cat is furry, sweet, loving, and cute all involve your cat schema. If you can evaluate new information and place it into a schema with other information that you are already familiar with (in other words, if you can think about how examples from your lectures apply to experiences from your life), you may be more likely to recall the new information in the future.[1]

The sixth and last step in listening as a skill is responding. This means that to be considered a good listener you have to provide appropriate feedback (both verbal and nonverbal) to the person speaking. Although responding to someone makes perfect sense in the case of a conversation, students often forget to do this while in the classroom. If you ever have the chance to look at yourself while listening in a college classroom be sure to e-mail me and tell me what you observe. I can place a pretty safe bet that you are simply sitting in a chair, you are probably slouched, have your hands folded in front of you, and your face wears a blank expression that mumbles "blah … teach me." You have to realize that this type of behavior is a big turn-off for professors. When the energy in a classroom is low professors get down. You have the ability to fix that with the way you respond to us when you are listening in class. More on this next.

A TRANSACTIONAL MODEL OF HUMAN COMMUNICATION

If you asked me to draw a transactional model of human communication, the transactional model of communication would probably look something like this:

Now, I know you are wondering why I would draw a transactional model of human communication. You are probably also wondering how many times I can write the term "transactional model of human communication" in one paragraph. The answer to the latter question is four. The answer to the former question is that you may learn a little bit about your role as an effective listener by examining how the communication process works. Although there are a variety of things we could discuss with this model, in the pages that follow I am going to talk about three ideas in particular. These ideas include feedback, barriers to listening, and the problem with human communication.

What you might notice first about the transactional model of communication is that it includes lines going from one speaker to the other. These lines indicate that both people in the conversation are sending and receiving messages at the same time. This is called a feedback loop. The presence of feedback implies that, instead of being a passive listener when interacting with others, you are constantly communicating to the person you are speaking with. This should make sense in a conversation when you are taking turns talking back and forth, but it also applies when you are simply listening. This is because when you listen to people, even though you may not be saying anything explicitly through words, your nonverbal communication (e.g., your posture, eye contact, head nods, etc.) can convey a lot of meaning. You need to be aware of this fact so that when you communicate with others you only send messages you intend to. You also need to be aware of this fact because nonverbal communication is highly reciprocal. In other words, when one person does something in an interaction (e.g., speaks loudly, moves forward, smiles more), the other person will tend to mirror that behavior.

Here's why this is key in communication. The way you listen to others affects the way they speak to you. If you understand this concept then you know that by providing appropriate feedback you can help speakers communicate better. Don't believe me? The next time you are on the phone with a friend try to read a book at the same time. What you will notice is that your friend will have a hard time being expressive because your lack of attention to the conversation will indicate an inherent disinterest. If your conversational partner senses that you have become disinterested, he or she may start to feel unvalued and may likely terminate the conversation. So remember, you are constantly communicating with others when you are listening to them and this information influences their interactions with you. Therefore, it is important that you take responsibility for your feedback and recognize your role in healthy communication interactions.

OK, I know that you will not always feel like being an active listener in class and I know that you might not always feel like sending expert feedback to your professors. But consider this, there is an idea in science called the facial feedback hypothesis[2] which argues that, because physiological processes can influence the way you experience events, the act of smiling can actually make you feel happier. I think the same thing may be true for listening. Therefore, even if you do not feel like listening in class, try to pretend that you are a good listener. Sit up straight in your seat, look the teacher in the eyes, give appropriate feedback with your facial expressions, and take notes at important points in the lecture. What you may find is that the more you try to listen in class, the more you actually pay attention. And importantly, by looking like a good listener and providing appropriate feedback, you may also help your professors lecture better!

Moving on. After noticing feedback, what you might spot next in the model of communication are the two barriers to listening (these are the lightning bolt looking thingies I drew). These barriers make it hard to pay attention to others because they compete for your attention and make the already difficult task of listening even harder. By being aware of what these barriers are, however, you may be able to take the appropriate measures to get rid of them and listen successfully.

The first type of barrier is physical noise. This barrier includes anything that will physically disrupt your ability to listen. As I mentioned earlier in the book, if you want to listen well you have to make sure you do what it takes to proactively remove physical barriers to your hearing and you have to put yourself in a position to be able to listen to the best of your ability.

The second barrier to listening is psychological noise. Psychological noise is anything that goes on in your noodle that prevents you from being able to listen to the material presented in class. In essence, psychological noise blocks you from consciously attending to the message. How does this happen? It can happen in a variety of ways. Maybe you have a test next period that you are nervous about. Instead of listening to the lecture at hand, you worry about the exam. Or, perhaps you just got in a fight with your significant other. Instead of listening to the lecture, you are thinking about all of the great arguments you should have made but couldn't think of in the moment.

Or, maybe psychological noise creeps up on you. It is a known fact that your brain can process more information in a minute than most people can speak in a minute. This means that, while listening, your brain has a lot of space left over to process other information. Unfortunately, instead of using this space to their advantage, most students allow their brains to distract them. It happens simple enough … while listening to a lecture you notice that your professor has on a blue tie. Then out of nowhere you think, "Wow that tie is nice, I wonder where he bought it. Speaking of buying stuff, I need to buy a new shirt for the party this weekend. It is going to be an awesome party. Maybe if I buy a new shirt I can impress all of my new friends and they will see that I am a great guy and they will give me the duty, *nay* the honor, of being the party DJ. With my new shirt on I will play the heck out of Sisqo's "Thong Song" and I will spin only the finest in hip hop dance beats. Still this honor will be a blessing and a curse, for while I can play whatever songs I want, I will be stuck behind the turntables. Not a great spot to be if I cannot meet new people," blah, blah, blah … By the time you catch yourself in mid-thought you realize that you are thinking about nonsense when you should be listening to the professor. Not good.

The key to overcoming psychological noise in class is to notice when you stop listening to the lectures and actively refocus on the message. If you find yourself thinking about the test you have next period, or about how your significant other is a jerk, or about how you can't wait to dance to a song about thongs then you need to adjust your attention to fit the situation—you need to actively monitor the content of your thoughts and focus on the information being presented in class. And, if you are smart, instead of using the difference between a person's rate of speech and your rate of thinking to daydream about foolishness, you can use your brain's extra computing power to paraphrase the content of the lecture and think about how the material fits with other experiences you have had in your life.

The last thing I want you to notice about the transactional model of communication is that it is inherently flawed. I know, yikes! The problem is that in order to communicate the thoughts that are in our heads to other people we need to use symbols (i.e. words). Essentially, because you cannot throw the thoughts from your mind into the head of another person, you need to communicate using sounds (that can be transferred between people). One of the things you need to know about symbols is that they are not fundamentally tied to the objects they represent. Instead, they are arbitrary means of conveying a message to another person. That is, the word "cat" is simply a sound that we have agreed on to represent a fluffy, furry, lovable animal in our minds. We could have just as easily called a cat a "gato" (Spanish), a "chat" (French), or a "blortute" (my fun, make-believe language). As long as we all agree that a certain sound or word represents the animal, we can communicate.

The problem with this method of communication is that, unlike shooting an arrow into your head, I cannot shoot my meaning of a cat into your head. Instead, all I can do is hope to say a word that triggers a reaction for you. Here's the dilemma: because we have all had different experiences of cats, we are all going to think of different ones when I say the word. Don't believe me? Try it. Close your eyes and think of a cat. Got it? Think about what it looks like, what color it is, how big it is, what is it doing, and perhaps what you are doing to it. OK, ready? What did your cat look like? Was it a medium-sized cat with orange and gray fur and a big white chest? Was it sitting on a bench in Istanbul's Topkapi Palace with its eyes closed? Did it have white feet and skinny legs? Did it have really long whiskers? No? Well, what the heck? I wanted to communicate my thoughts about a cat to you so what happened?

What happened was that when you thought of a cat you probably thought of one based on an experience you have had with a cat. And, because we have all lived different lives, we have all had different experiences. What that means is that I can never communicate to you exactly what I mean by a "cat." Sure, I can communicate generally, but I can never hope to get you to think of a cat in the exact same way as I do. We can get close, but communication between people may never be perfect. Not only is your image of a cat likely to be different than mine, but your feelings about cats are sure to differ too—adding an extra problem to our potential for miscommunication. And think about this: if we cannot communicate clearly about a simple, tangible object like a cat, what happens when we communicate about complicated things such as "love," or what it means to be "free," or what it means to be "good parent"? Depending on who you speak with the meanings of each of these words are bound to be different. Human communication is inherently flawed and to expect that what you said directly translated into what someone else heard is potentially disastrous. Do not do it. The same is true for you as a listener. Do not assume that what you heard is what a speaker meant to say.

All right, if the communication process is flawed then how can you fix it? By using more communication! Hooray! To communicate with somebody effectively it is important that you provide feedback to the person you are speaking with to verify that you are both on the same page. Using a feedback mechanism is the only way to ensure that what you think you heard is actually what the person talking meant to say. Therefore, instead of relying on a single message for the foundation of your meaning, I recommend that you create loops of interaction to help you communicate with precision. There are a few ways to do this.

One way to make certain that what you heard is an accurate reflection of what someone meant to say is to tell that person your interpretation of their message and then ask him or her to report back to you regarding whether your understanding is correct. For example, in the transactional model of communication I drew, the smiley face on the right is trying to verify with the other smiley face whether the cat he is thinking of is the same cat as the one being described. By doing this, the smiley face on the right is trying to ensure that when he continues the conversation he and his conversational partner are talking about the same creature.

A second way to make sure that what you heard is an accurate reflection of what someone else meant to say is to ask for more information. For example, if a man is speaking to you and you think you hear him say he does not like your cooking (e.g., maybe he says "this pasta sauce tastes different") you may want to double-check his meaning by asking him what he meant by the word "different." You may discover that what you think he said was not his intention after all. That is, though he liked it, perhaps he was not expecting to taste a sweet and spicy sauce. Take a moment to think about how much trouble using feedback can save you in your personal life.

Take a moment to think about how much trouble using feedback can save you in your studies as well. Many of my students listen to my lectures and then simply assume that their notes are accurate and that they understand the theories we have discussed. Yet, when I ask for examples in class I sometimes discover that a few people have not understood all of the theories in the way that I meant to describe them. This is a problem of communication that I try to rectify by asking students to repeat the theories back to me using their personal experiences so I can check whether they are learning the information I have presented in the way that I intended. Although this tactic helps, many of your teachers will not do this. And even if they do, they might not ask you to personally repeat the theories back to them. Therefore, you need to make it a point to talk with your professors to ensure that you understand the ideas in their classes the way they intended for you to learn them. This is your job. Instead of relying on a single message to inform your education, you need to interact with your professors using loops of communication to make sure that what you are learning is accurate. I have had many students who thought they knew the information in my classes before a test only to find out from their low grade on an exam that, in fact, they did not know the content either fully or correctly. Don't be that person.

Did you think of this cat?

SO WHAT?

Listening as a skill contains six steps: hearing, attending, understanding, remembering, evaluating, and responding. However, because of the inherent flaws in communication, listening can be difficult. Still, despite the fact that listening is hard, I am positive that with work you can all (to quote the rapper LL Cool J) do it, and do it, and do it well.

Just remember, this will take effort—to listen well you will have to be motivated to do it and you will need to be an active participant in the process.

The better you get at listening the better you will be at recalling information and using it down the road (for example, on tests). In addition, by listening correctly you will help create the healthy learning atmosphere that your professors require to lecture well. However, even though listening well is an important component of your education, it won't help you master your coursework by itself. To do that you also need to study. We turn to that concept next.

NOTES

1. Brewer, W. F., and Treyens, J. C. "Role of schemata in memory for places." *Cognitive Psychology* (1981) 13, 207–230.
2. McIntosh, D. N. "Facial feedback hypothesis: Evidence, implications, and directions." *Motivation and Emotion* (1996) 20, 121–147.

NOTE-TAKING GUIDELINES AND FORMATS

BY ROBIN ROACH GILLEY

DUE	TABLE OF CONTENTS	TO DO	CHECK
	Note-Taking Guidelines with Rationale	Read and Study	
	Note-Taking Tips	Read and Study	
	The 5Rs Cornell Note-Taking Method	Read and Study	
	Two-Column Method	Read and Study	
	Outlining	Read and Study	
	Making Study Cards	Read and Study	
	Concept Map I	Written Assignment	
	Concept Map II	Written Assignment	
	Timeline	Read and Study	
	Your Timeline	Written Assignment	
	Active Reading and Note-Taking Application	Written Assignment	

Robin Roach Gilley, "Note-Taking Guidelines and Formats," *Effective Study Strategies: Practicing Academic Skills*, pp. 71-79. Copyright © 2015 by Cognella, Inc. Reprinted with permission.

NOTE-TAKING GUIDELINES WITH RATIONALE

Finish reading before writing!

The first time you read the information it all seems new to you.
Be extremely selective.
Get the main point.
Rationale or Why: Too many notes overload your memory.

Summarize the information in your own words.

Rationale or Why: Your own words help keep it in your memory better. Jot these at the bottom of your note page and they will trigger your memory later.

Write phrases, not the whole sentences.
Rationale or Why: Easier to use when you recite and review.

Organize facts and ideas under categories.
Rationale or Why: Items in categories are far easier to remember than random facts and ideas.

NOTE-TAKING TIPS

1. Taking notes on the introduction.
   a. key ideas
   b. ask yourself, did you capture them?

2. Leaving spaces between sections.
   a. Visually group what belongs together.

3. Using the headings.
   a. If there are no headings, create your own by looking for categories of information.

4. Writing summary words or phrases in your notes. This pulls together ideas and puts them in your own words.

5   Starring (*) important points in your notes that were emphasized by the teacher.

6   Placing question marks (?) next to confusing passages so you may get more information later.

7   Placing a "T" beside a possible test item.

8   Including graphs and charts in your notes.

9   Including a summary or conclusion—written in your own words.

THE 5 R'S OF THE CORNELL NOTE TAKING SYSTEM

The Cornell Note Taking system was developed by Cornell University Emeritus Professor Walter Pauk.

The system consists of five steps, which if followed, have proven to aid student comprehension of textbook notes as well as lecture notes. The unique feature of this system is the Recall column. Used properly, this column gives the student ample practice and feedback. The process reinforces self-testing.

1   First, purchase prepared notebook paper (8 1/2" × 11" is recommended) and draw a line or fold 2" to 3" from the left. Remember to use only one side of the paper. You will then be able to lay each page down on a large flat surface, and quiz yourself.

- **Record:** Use the right hand column to record your notes.
- **Reduce:** Create questions and/or key words to aid recall—these should be adjacent to the related information recorded in the notes
- **Recite:** After reducing your notes, cover the right side of your paper. Do this with your hand or use a blank sheet of paper. Try to recite the full notes aloud. Uncover the notes and check for accuracy. Repeat until you are confident that you have retained the correct information. Go to the next question/key word. Repeat procedure.
- **Reflect:** Ponder the information you have just learned. Note connections between the new knowledge and prior learning. Question and think critically about the material.

- **Review:** Do not end your study session until you have reviewed all of the notes you just finished, as well as the notes taken to date. Continual review will ensure that the information is fixed in your long term memory.

Record

    Reduce

        Recite

            Reflect

                Review

THE CORNELL NOTE TAKING SYSTEM EXAMPLE

FORMAT FOR CORNELL NOTES	Paper
	Purchase specially prepared notebook paper Draw a line or fold 2" to 3" from the left Use only one side of paper Loose-leaf paper is recommended
HOW TO TAKE NOTES	<u>Use area to right of line to write full notes</u> <u>Title of Chapter</u> <u>Introduction</u> <u>1. Important point</u> <u>2. Important point</u> <u>First Heading</u> <u>1.</u> <u>2.</u> <u>3.</u> <u>minor supporting detail</u> <u>minor supporting detail</u> <u>Second Heading</u> <u>See diagram on page #</u>
COMPLETING NOTES WITH CUES/QUESTIONS	After writing notes on the right side of the line, go back over your notes before eight hours have passed
	–Make illegible scribbles legible—do **not rewrite** notes –Underline or highlight key ideas –Discriminate between key ideas and examples/illustrations –Embellish and personalize

	Place cues or study questions written from your full notes on the left side of the line
STUDYING FROM NOTES	During studying, cover notes in the right column. Look at first cue/question in the left column. Try to recite full notes aloud. Uncover notes and check. Repeat until correct. Go to next cue/question. Repeat procedure.

TWO-COLUMN NOTE-TAKING SYSTEM

FORMAT	*Draw a line or fold your paper in half*
TOPICS	*Details*
HOW TO SURVEY A TEXTBOOK CHAPTER	1. **Read** the chapter title. 2. **Read** the chapter introduction. 3. Go to the back of the chapter, and **read** the summary. 4. Return to the front of the chapter and **read** the boldfaced headings and subheadings. 5. **Study** the visual material. Graphs, charts, pictures, etc. 6. **Circle** or box the words in boldface or italics.

OUTLINING

1. **Read the chapter title.**
   a. If the title tells you nothing, look up unfamiliar terms in the dictionary.
   b. You must understand the title before you continue.

2. **Read the chapter introduction.**
   a. The introduction highlights the main ideas of each chapter before you begin to read it.
   b. Look for a list of main points to be covered.

3. **Go to the back of the chapter and read the summary.**
   a. The summary restates the most important ideas in the chapter.
   b. If there is no summary or exercises, read the concluding paragraph to see which idea the author emphasizes.

4. **Return to the front of the chapter and read the boldfaced headings and subheadings.**
    a. The headings and subheadings give you the main ideas and their sequence.
    b. If there are no headings, read the first sentence in each paragraph to help you discover the main ideas in the chapter.
5. ***Study*** the visual material. Graphs, charts, pictures, etc.
6. **Circle** or box the words in boldface or italics.
    a. Identify them now and make them stand out from the text so that your eyes will not slide over them later as you read.
    b. These words are vocabulary you will need to master.

MAKING STUDY CARDS

The beauty of making up flashcards is that they help you to take advantage of short periods of time throughout your day because they can so easily be taken anywhere you go.

The easier you make it for yourself, the more likely you are to do it!

As you learn concepts and definitions, put those cards aside, and concentrate on the new or more difficult information. Then take out the "old cards" that contain information you know pretty well to refresh your memory.

Here are some hints for making flashcards:

- Choose the most important facts or concepts from each chapter you read or lecture you attend.
- Use your own words unless a specific definition is required.
- Label the cards with a subject heading and date so you'll be able to put them into categories for various types of quizzes and tests.

Example:

Front	Back
Preview	Anything that gives an advance idea or impression of something to come.

Put terms on one side with definitions and examples on the other side.

Place types of math problems on one side with examples on the other side.

Draw an illustration on one side with an arrow pointing to the part you need to know and place the answer on the other.

CONCEPT MAP

Below is an example of a concept map, sometimes known as a "mind map." The visual study tool is created to graphically illustrate relationships between ideas. The concept map shows relationships between levels of information. The topic is in the middle of the graphic and the branches are the main ideas. Topic = Level 1 information; Main Ideas = Level 2; Supporting Details Level 3.

ASSIGNMENT: CONCEPT MAP I

Fill in the 4 P's for writing goals. On each of the lines provided, define the Level 2 information, according to what you have learned about each step.

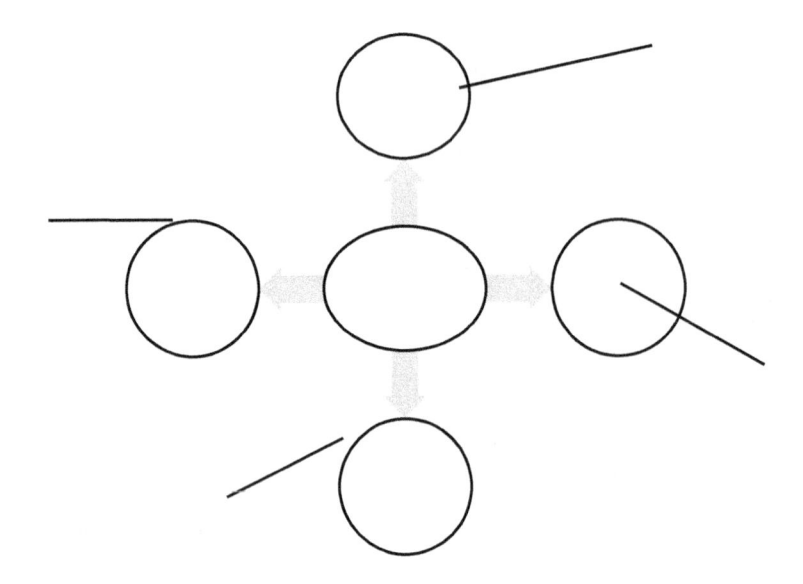

ASSIGNMENT: CONCEPT MAP II

Create your own concept map using material you have learned in this course. Remember to distinguish between levels of main ideas and supporting details. Expand this concept map to three levels of information. Your instructor may have you turn in the assignment, or discuss in a small group or as a class.

ASSIGNMENT: TIMELINE

A timeline lists events in chronological order. It is a long line or bar labelled with dates alongside itself. The points on the line indicate where and when the events happened. This note taking method is useful when you need to remember consecutive dates and/or events coinciding with related information. For example, in history class, sociology class, literature class.

See the illustration below

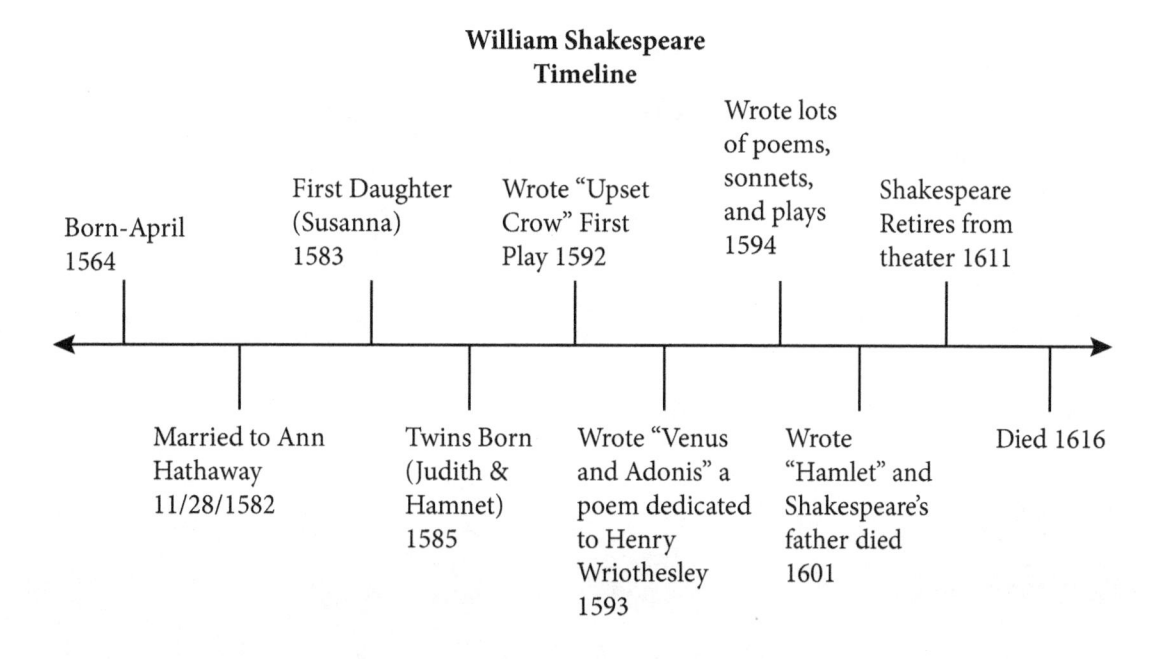

William Shakespeare Timeline

Above the line:
- Born-April 1564
- First Daughter (Susanna) 1583
- Wrote "Upset Crow" First Play 1592
- Wrote lots of poems, sonnets, and plays 1594
- Shakespeare Retires from theater 1611

Below the line:
- Married to Ann Hathaway 11/28/1582
- Twins Born (Judith & Hamnet) 1585
- Wrote "Venus and Adonis" a poem dedicated to Henry Wriothesley 1593
- Wrote "Hamlet" and Shakespeare's father died 1601
- Died 1616

ASSIGNMENT: YOUR TIMELINE

Begin by drawing a line across your paper, dividing the line into units of time and then labeling the timeline with dates and events. The dates and events are of your life. You will be creating a "your life" timeline. Personalize your time line with pictures that relate to the events.

ASSIGNMENT: ACTIVE READING AND NOTE-TAKING

APPLICATION

STEP ONE
- You will be using a short textbook chapter. You may use the chapter provided below or your instructor may assign a chapter they deem fitting.

STEP TWO
- Read the selection using the SQ3R process described in your textbook and in class.

STEP THREE
- On your own paper, develop a concept map of the chapter.

TURN IN:
- Reading notes
- Your concept map

ACADEMIC HONESTY AND PLAGIARISM

CHAPTER 8

PREVENTING PLAGIARISM

BY KATE L. TURABIAN, GREGORY G. COLOMB, AND JOSEPH M. WILLIAMS

1. Guard against Inadvertent Plagiarism
2. Take Good Notes
3. Signal Every Quotation, Even When You Cite Its Source
4. Don't Paraphrase Too Closely
5. (Almost Always) Cite a Source for Ideas Not Your Own
6. Don't Plead Ignorance, Misunderstanding, or Innocent Intentions
7. Guard against Inappropriate Assistance

1 GUARD AGAINST INADVERTENT PLAGIARISM

It will be as you draft that you risk making one of the worst mistakes you can make: you lead readers to think that you're trying to pass off the work of another writer as your own. Do that and you risk an accusation of plagiarism, a charge so serious that, if sustained, could mean a failing grade or, if you're in a college class, expulsion.

These days teachers are intensely concerned about plagiarism, because they believe the Internet makes it easier for students to cheat. So they are

Kate L. Turabian, Gregory G. Colomb, and Joseph M. Williams, "Preventing Plagiarism," Student's Guide to Writing College Papers, pp. 99-103. Copyright © 2010 by University of Chicago Press. Reprinted with permission.

especially vigilant for signs of plagiarism. Even if you don't mean to cheat, you may still have a problem if you fail to follow the rules for using and citing material from sources, because many teachers won't accept ignorance as an excuse. In any case, you do not help readers trust you or your argument if you fail on something as basic as properly citing everything you have used from a source.

Many instructors punish students for plagiarism but don't explain it, because they think it needs no explanation. And in some cases they are right: students don't need to be told that they cheat when they put their name on a paper they didn't write. Most also know they cheat when they pass off as their own work page after page downloaded from the web. But many students fail to realize that they risk a charge of plagiarism even when they are not intentionally dishonest, but only ignorant or careless.

Three Principles for Citing Sources

When you use any source in any way, readers expect you to follow three principles. You risk a charge of plagiarism if you ignore any one of them.

1. You must cite the source for any words, ideas, or methods that are not your own.

   Writers can avoid paraphrasing too closely if they focus on remembering what they understand from the original, not its actual words. One way to do this is simply to put the original aside as you write the paraphrase (Colomb and Williams, 92). But a better way is to imagine that you are explaining the idea to someone who hasn't read the original.

2. When you quote the exact words of a source, you must put those words in quotation marks or a block quotation, *even if you cite the source in your own text*. This would be plagiarism:

   According to Colomb and Williams, when you quote the exact words of a source, you must put those words in quotation marks or a block quotation, *even if you cite the source in your own text* (100).

3. When you paraphrase the words of a source, you must use your own sentences, not sentences so similar to the original that they are almost a quotation. This would be considered plagiarism by many teachers:

   According to Colomb and Williams, you risk being charged with plagiarism when you paraphrase a passage from a source not in your own words but in sentences so similar to it that you almost quote them, regardless of whether your own text cites the source (100).

Some students think that they don't have to cite all of the material freely circulated online. Not so. These principles apply to sources of any kind—printed, recorded, oral, *and* online—but teachers are most on the lookout for plagiarism of online sources. You risk a charge of plagiarism if you fail to cite *anything* you get from a source, *especially* if it's from a website, a database, a podcast, or other online source. A source is a source, and you must cite them all.

2 TAKE GOOD NOTES

We warned you about this earlier, in 4.2, but it is so important to take good notes that we will repeat ourselves. You cannot follow the rules in using and citing information from a source if you don't have the right information in your notes. So, long before you draft, you have to make sure that your notes do the following:

- Record all bibliographic data for each source.
- Clearly distinguish between your words and those of the source.
- Correctly transcribe each quotation, including punctuation.
- Record page numbers for each quotation and paraphrase in your notes.

3 SIGNAL EVERY QUOTATION, EVEN WHEN YOU CITE ITS SOURCE

Even if you cite your source, readers must know unambiguously which words are yours and which you quote. You risk a charge of plagiarism if you fail to use quotation marks to signal that you have copied as little as a single line.

It gets complicated, however, when you copy just a few words. Suppose you were writing about this passage from Jared Diamond:

> Because technology begets more technology, the importance of an invention's diffusion potentially exceeds the importance of the original invention. Technology's history exemplifies what is termed an autocatalytic process: that is, one that speeds up at a rate that increases with time, because the process catalyzes itself (Diamond, 301).

To write about Diamond's ideas, you would probably use some of his words, such as *the importance of an invention*. But you wouldn't put that short phrase in quotation marks, because it shows no originality of thought or expression. Two of his phrases, however, are so striking that they do need quotation marks: *technology begets more technology* and *autocatalytic process*. For example:

> The power of technology goes beyond individual inventions because technology "begets more technology." It is, as Diamond puts it, an "autocatalytic process" (301).

Once you cite those words, you can use them again without quotation marks or citation:

> So as one invention begets another to spark a self-sustaining catalysis, the effect spreads exponentially across all national boundaries.

This is a gray area: words that seem striking to some are commonplace to others. If you use quotation marks around too many common phrases, readers may think you're naive or insecure. But if you fail to use them when readers think you should, they may suspect you of plagiarism. It's better to seem naive than dishonest, especially early in your research career, so use quotation marks freely.

4 DON'T PARAPHRASE TOO CLOSELY

You paraphrase appropriately when you represent an idea in your own words more clearly or pointedly than the source does. But readers will think that you cross the line from fair paraphrase to plagiarism if they can match most of your words with those of your source. For example, unlike the paraphrase in 10.3, this one plagiarizes the original:

> **Original:**
> Because technology begets more technology, the importance of an invention's diffusion potentially exceeds the importance of the original invention. Technology's history exemplifies what is termed an autocatalytic process: that is, one that speeds up at a rate that increases with time, because the process catalyzes itself (Diamond, 301).

Paraphrase:
According to Diamond, technology gives birth to more technology. As a result, the importance of the spread of an invention may exceed the importance of the invention itself. The history of technology shows what is called an autocatalytic process through which the invention of new technologies speeds up at an increasing rate because the process of change catalyzes itself (301).

The writer of this version may think that she has used her own words: she changes some of Diamond's complex phrases into simpler ones: *begets* → *gives birth*, *diffusion* → *spread*, *exemplifies* → *shows*. But the paraphrase follows the original step-by-step, word by word. That, for most readers, is plagiarism.

> **QUICK TIP**
>
> **Safe Paraphrasing**
> To avoid unintentionally seeming to be guilty of plagiarism by paraphrase, don't read your source as you paraphrase it. Read the passage, look away, think about it for a moment. *Then still looking away*, restate it in your own words. Then check whether you can run your finger along your sentence and find the same ideas in the same order as in your source. If you can, so can your readers. Try again.

5 (ALMOST ALWAYS) CITE A SOURCE FOR IDEAS NOT YOUR OWN

The basic principle is simple: Cite a source for a borrowed idea whenever your readers might think you are claiming that you are its original source. But when you try to apply it, the rule becomes more complicated, because most of our own ideas come from some identifiable sources somewhere in history. Readers don't expect you to find and cite every distant source for every familiar idea. But they do expect you to cite the source for an idea when (1) the idea is associated with a specific person *and* (2) it's new enough not to be part of a field's common knowledge.

For example, psychologists claim that we think and feel in different parts of our brains. But no one would expect you to cite the source of that idea, because it's so familiar to psychologists that no reader would think you were taking credit for originating that idea. On the other hand, some psychologists argue that emotions are crucial to rational decision making. You would have to cite the source of that idea because it is so new and so closely tied to particular researchers.

> QUICK TIP
>
> **When to Cite Ideas**
>
> If you are a new researcher, you have a problem: You can't cite every borrowed idea, but how are you supposed to know which ideas are too familiar to cite? Here are some signs to look for:
>
> - If an idea is a main claim in the source, you should cite it.
> - If the source spends time showing how the idea differs from the ideas of others, you should cite it.
> - If the source cites an idea, you should too.
> - If more than one source uses the idea without citing it, then you don't have to cite it either.

6 DON'T PLEAD IGNORANCE, MISUNDERSTANDING, OR INNOCENT INTENTIONS

To be sure, what looks like plagiarism is often just honest ignorance of how to use and cite sources. In those cases, students defend themselves by claiming they didn't *intend* to mislead. The problem is, we read words, not minds. So think of plagiarism not as an act you intend but as one that others *perceive*. Avoid any sign that might give your readers a reason to suspect you of it. Whenever you put your name on a paper, you implicitly promise that you wrote every word that you don't clearly and specifically attribute to someone else.

Here is how to think about this: If someone read your paper immediately after reading your source written by Johnson. Would she think, *This sounds just like Johnson* or

I remember these words or *This idea must have come from Johnson.* If so, you must cite Johnson and set off any sequence of his exact words in quotation marks or a block quotation.

7 GUARD AGAINST INAPPROPRIATE ASSISTANCE

Before experienced writers turn in their work, they often show drafts to others for criticism and suggestions, and you should too. But teachers differ on how much help is appropriate and what help you should acknowledge. Most instructors encourage students to get general criticism and minor editing, but not detailed rewriting or substantive suggestions. You usually aren't required to acknowledge general criticism, minor editing, or help from a school writing tutor, but you must acknowledge help that's special or extensive. Your instructor, however, sets the rules, so ask.

PART III

UNDERSTANDING CROSS-CULTURAL INTERACTIONS

CHAPTER 9

LANGUAGE AND CULTURE

LANGUAGE AND COMMUNICATION

BY PAYAL MEHRA

> "You should say what you mean," the March Hare told Alice in Alice in Wonderland. "I do," Alice replied, "at least I mean what I say—that's the same thing, you know." "Not the same thing a bit!" said the Hatter, "You might as well say that 'I see what I eat' is the same thing as 'I eat what I see'"
>
> —Lewis Carol, Alice's Adventures in Wonderland, 1865

INTRODUCTION

Communication is the creative force that drives processes in organizations. Manifesting in dialogue, rhetoric, speech acts, and nonverbal expressions, communication processes drive, evolve, change, and unify organizations. Far from being merely a functional division in organizations, communication has now become a powerful enabler for the growth, development, and consolidation of organizations.

Payal Mehra, "Language and Communication," *Communication Beyond Boundaries*, pp. 49-65, 149-153. Copyright © 2014 by Business Expert Press. Reprinted with permission.

COMMUNICATIVE COMPETENCE

The essence of communicative competence is that language and culture are inseparable in expressing one's point of view. Linguistic knowledge includes grammar and the rules that govern discourse. Sociocultural knowledge involves the choices people make on the basis of their contextual background. Communication is integral to an organization, with various situations demanding different forms of communication that are culturally defined (Figure 9.1).

Figure 9.1 Antecedents of communication competence

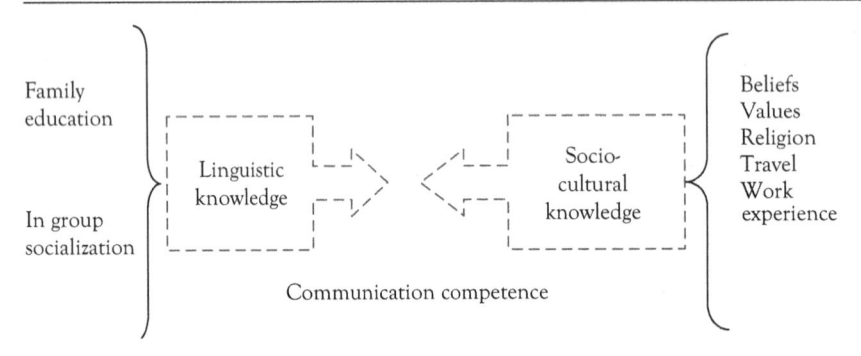

```
Family                                                        Beliefs
education  ⎫                                              ⎫  Values
           ⎬  ┌──────────┐        ┌──────────┐            ⎬  Religion
           ⎪  │Linguistic│  ──>   │  Socio-  │            ⎪  Travel
In group   ⎪  │knowledge │  <──   │ cultural │            ⎪  Work
socialization ⎭ └──────────┘      │knowledge │            ⎭  experience
                                   └──────────┘
                        Communication competence
```

LANGUAGE AND COMMUNICATION

Though technology has fueled globalization, technology alone cannot achieve globalization. The important role played by language as a sharing facility and an enabler of communication between individuals and companies (and countries) to communicate cannot be understated. Language itself is an evolved cultural pattern.

More international business is done between nonnative English speakers than between native English speakers. In 2005, *Newsweek International* published an article on the rise of English around the world. Quoting English language expert David Crystal (1997), the article reports that nonnative speakers of English now outnumber native speakers 3 to 1. There are more Chinese children studying English—about 100 million—than there are Britons. It concluded then that within a decade (by 2015), 2 billion people would be studying English and about half the world—some 3 billion people—would be speaking it.

As cross-cultural exchanges happen in a connected world, language remains in focus. It is important to take into account, however, that the pragmatic purposes of English in international business do not typically call for the same breadth of lexicon and grammar as some of the other activities. In fact, native speakers often need as much help as nonnatives when using English to interact internationally.

Research suggests that the English Lingua Franca (ELF) communication seems "too partial a view for globalized business." Failure to communicate in the language of the new country may result in pragmatic failure—the inability to understand what is meant by what is said. Pragmatic failure results in the misinterpretation of the utterances, the way the speaker intends them. This leads to frustration and cross-cultural communication breakdowns. The rise of Hinglish, Chinglish, and Spanglish is a positive step to reduce the linguistic ethnocentricity that had engulfed the world till sometime back.

> Media attention has now focused on a new phonetic writing system developed by an investment banker George Jabbour to assist new language learners read, understand, and speak their target language. A Syrian visiting England for higher studies, Jabbour had trouble pronouncing English words, which created stark barriers between the locals and foreigners. The new system, called *SaypU*, an acronym for *Spell As You Pronounce Universally*, can be applied to all languages; visitors to foreign countries would be able to read signs, maps, labels, and menus without learning a new writing system.
>
> *Source*: Meritt (2013).

According to Charles (2007), in the environment of global diversity, it is Business English Lingua Franca (BELF), and not ELF, that is going to pave the way for effective conduct of international business. The BELF approach differs from ELF in that the domain of the former is only business and its frame of reference is the globalized business community. "Whatever language becomes the lingua franca of global business, faster and more accurate translation services and products are needed" (Zipperer 2001).

> *Katakana eigo*
>
> In the Japanese language, consonants such as *v* are nonexistent. Consonants are always attached to the vowels and never used distinctly. This results in *katakana eigo* or English interpretation produced by joining the building blocks of the Japanese alphabet. Thus, first and fast may sound the same (fa-su-to) when spoken by the Japanese.
>
> *Source*: c JETRO (1999).

Studies indicate that the Internet use of Mandarin, Hindi, and Spanish is rising. Graddol (1997) cautions that if regional trading blocs increase in number and in influence, English could become irrelevant within some of the blocs. Similarly, if translation software improves, businesspeople might stop needing a common language altogether.

> When speaking English, the Japanese tend to confuse by and until. If the speaker says, "I will be in India until August 15" and actually meant that he would be reaching India by August 15, then serious communication errors may arise.

Charles (2007) described three responses companies can take to address language issues:

- Techno-oriented companies address the language issue by installing sophisticated language software or hiring translators.
- Rule-bound companies address the issue by standardizing the spoken and written communication language.
- Forward-looking companies address the language issue by enabling and facilitating the understanding of different cultures and the way of speaking. They do this by heightening the awareness of communicative and cultural diversity and increasing the English used globally.

THE RISE OF INDIAN ENGLISH: THE INTERNATIONAL LANGUAGE OF GLOBALIZATION

"Prepaid mobile phones have become so ubiquitous in India that English words to do with their use—recharge, top-up and missed call—have become common, too. Now, it seems, those words are transforming to take on broader meanings in Indian languages as well as in Hinglish" (Lahiri 2012).

In 2005, a new edition of the *Collins English Dictionary* included 26 neologisms of Indian origin. In a statement, the dictionary has officially acknowledged the role of Hinglish in the evolution of English. The *Concise Oxford Dictionary* the world's most credible collection of words has turned eclectic, incorporating several Indianisms. Many words of daily use in English are of Indian origin, including words such as shampoo, bangle, bungalow, jungle, mantra, pundit, and cot. Even though purists are agitated about it, the *Oxford Dictionary* has acknowledged "a public demonstration" as the meaning of "agitation," which is more in use in India and is vastly different from the traditional English usage as "irregular motion or disturbance."

According to a statement by Collins, "the inclusion of Hinglish words in the Dictionary marks an exciting development and a new phase of borrowing by English." Hinglish, it appears, is playing a greater role in the business world. According to the article, advertising has "started shifting from pure Hindi or English advertisements to Hindi with a few words of English thrown in." Multinational companies such as Domino's Pizza, Pepsi, and Coca Cola are using Hinglish to appeal to local sensitivities. Thus the Pepsi slogans include "Yeh dil maange more" ("Ask for more") and 'Bas abhi ke abhi' ("Want things right now"), while Coke relies on "Life ho to aisi" ("Life should be like this") and Dominos Pizza on 'Hungry Kya?' ("Are you hungry?").

LANGUAGE AND SPEECH ACTS

People belonging to different groups, subgroups, and communities have different ways of using language to communicate, and their ways of using speech define them as a group, subgroup, culture, and community. Thus, no two groups or communities have the same communicative competencies. The situation is compounded in a cross-cultural context because groups are defined or limited by their respective communicative competencies. For example, in comparison to the Danes, the French use verbs in an abstract manner; their nouns are also changed to verbs, imparting a rather abstract character to the French language. The French language uses a hierarchical structure in text and communication such that the information in sentences is often organized in subordinate structures (for example, by nonfinite verb forms). The Danish language uses a linear structure for presenting and organizing information in coordinate sentences, which have as their center, verbs in the finite form of past, present, or future (Lundquist 2009).

Deborah Tannen (1984) describes three broad levels of differences, which can create misunderstanding in a cross-cultural interaction:

- When to say
- What to say
- How to say, which includes pacing and pausing, listening, intonation and prosody, formulaicity, indirectness, and cohesion and coherence

The potential areas for misunderstanding are elaborated upon in the sections that follow (level 3 has been dealt with more elaborately in the next chapter).

WHEN TO SAY

When to say represents the most general level of communication that is relative to the culture. For instance, most East Asian cultures such as Japan, China, Taiwan, Thailand, Singapore, Korea, and a few African cultures such as Swaziland, Ethiopia, and Kenya value silence. In these cultures, when *not* to talk is a more appropriate question than when to talk. Silence in these cultures is also a form of communication. The Japanese word *haragei*, the Korean term *noon-chi*, and the Chinese term *mo-chi* indicate the value attributed to silence by the East Asian societies. Among Westerners, the Swedes and the Finns are more reticent than the French and Germans. Americans, the British, and Australians are referred to as the *talkative* cultures.

For many Easterners, silence does not indicate disinterest, inaction, or a failure to communicate as is commonly perceived in some Western societies (see Table 9.1 in the following text). Silence can communicate the following:

- The person is contemplating a response to a question
- The person is agreeing to what the other person is saying
- The person is expressing dissent
- The person is angry
- The person is anxious and suffers from communication apprehension
- The person is waiting for the seniors to speak up first

Table 9.1 Silence and its Interpretation in Diverse Cultures

S. NO.	SILENCE AS PERCEIVED BY EAST ASIAN CULTURES	SILENCE AS PERCEIVED BY EUROPEAN, AMERICAN, AND AUSTRALIAN CULTURES
1	Speech regarded as distraction to the thinking process; silence allows contemplation	Speech associated with expression and clarity of thought; silence regarded as uncomfortable break in conversation
2	Silence associated with wisdom; allows people to plan	Silence leads to awkwardness between the parties, especially when it is too long
3	Silence gives people time to collect thoughts before responding	Silence leads to view such people as unsocial and uncooperative
4	Silence helps people to interpret the speaker correctly	Silence creates ambiguity
5	Silence allows the speaker opportunity to rephrase the question	Silence results in waste of time and resources
6	Silence saves the face of the speaker especially when the receiver disagrees	Silence delays action; depicts apathy of the listeners
7	Silence saves the face of self, especially observed in persons with low level of English language fluency	Silence creates unwarranted judgments about competency and confidence
8	Silence is associated with power	Silence is deemed manipulative

Source: Nakane (2007).

Silence and its occurrence cannot be examined in isolation. Its basis lies in physical, psychological, linguistic, stylistic, and interactive factors. Experts also suggest that cultures can be mapped on a continuum from the most verbal to the most silent.

WHAT TO SAY

Once a decision has been made to talk, the next logical question is what to say. This includes the following speech acts: questions, agreement and disagreement, asking for information, humor and irony, opinions, compliments, apologies, and advice.

QUESTIONS

Socrates defined teaching as the *art of asking questions*. Asking questions is considered important to aid in the construction of meaning and to make sense of the information presented. It facilitates knowledge creation and dissemination. Questioning serves many useful purposes. It allows for reflection and internalization of the concepts, it is a form of feedback to the speaker, and it paves the way for greater interactivity and participation in the classroom. In most classrooms, questioning takes up almost a third of the teaching time.

Questioning is widely used in many corporate boardrooms. Google, a well-known tech company, prides itself on the culture of questioning that it has created in the organization.

Questioning is also deeply rooted in the psyche of the culture to which the person belongs. In societies that have a large power distance, there is great distance between the parents and the children, the teacher and the taught, the boss and the subordinate, and the government officials and the common person. Respect and obedience to the elders and those in power is expected, and any deviation from the same can be perceived as threatening (Hofstede et al. 2010). With respect to the education sector, teachers inspire awe and fear. Usually teaching is teacher centered with emphasis on rote rather than learning. Japan, China, South Korea, Singapore, India, and Mexico are examples of cultures that have a high power distance.

> In my class on intercultural communication, I observed that among the Europeans, the French asked the most questions, while the Swiss asked the least questions. Not surprisingly, the native Indian students asked the least number of questions in accordance with their cultural norms of deference.

In Korea, the teacher is revered like a king. Taiwanese students do not question the content or the teaching process at all out of respect for the teacher. In fact, many students in Taiwan prefer teacher-centered authority despite educational reviews calling for more student-centered learning. In Japan, students would rather ask other students than the teacher for clarifications, if any. Similarly, in Mexico and India, questions from students are highly improbable (even in higher education); the instruction style is lecture driven and teacher centered. In China, two broad strategies are common for eliciting responses—the hint strategy and the query strategy. Examples could be, "I feel that we should not go ahead with the project" (the aim was to know what the recipient felt). The query strategy is more direct, such as, "Do you have any suggestions?" or "What do you think of the proposal?"

EXPRESSING DISAGREEMENT

The *Oxford Dictionary* defines disagree as *to have or express a different opinion*. It may also imply attacking the position held by another person or silently conveying displeasure. In an American culture, it is considered a virtue to be assertive and expressive about one's views and opinions (Samovar and Porter 2001). In contrast, in the Japanese culture, it is important to avoid conflicts and maintain harmony; voicing one's opinion is a measured strategy rather than an impulsive one. Though Hofstede (1997) claimed that collectivist cultures were more indirect in saying no or refusing requests, studies report that cultures such as Korea and China are more direct than even the most individualistic cultures (Australia, for example, or even Great Britain). In a study of rhetoric in an actual business meeting, Yeung reported that the Chinese delegates asked more questions and made more requests than Australians, that Australians hedged more (using words like perhaps; I think that; Yes, but...), and that most Chinese delegates used more negative words to start their sentences (but, no) than the Australians.

> Chinese rule for disagreement: It's more important to give constructive suggestions than to show respect for the higher status of others. Australians preface their disagreements with "Yes, but..."
>
> *Source:* Spencer-Oatey (2000).

Some cultures tend to use mitigation devices to avoid direct confrontation. Fiona Johnson (2006) lists a following few:

Hedging   This is a strategy used to understate the illocutionary point of the utterance. The speaker avoids making a firm commitment. The words used are kind of, maybe, and I think so are used frequently by the Japanese to avoid a direct clash of ideas (Kobayashi and Viswat 2010). In India, if one has to disagree or decline an invitation, it is normal to use the euphemism: I'll think about it.

Downtoners   In this strategy, the tone or the vocal impact is sought to be reduced by modulating the impact of the utterance. Words used are probably, may, and perhaps.

Hesitators   In this strategy, the speaker deliberately hesitates to reveal qualms about the veracity of the idea proposed by another. Words used are err or umm.

Appealers   This strategy aims to appease the hearer directly so that a positive response is elicited from the hearer. Phrases include I agree with you, but…You may be right, but…You see….

Another category, the **reasoners** can be added. They try to reason out their viewpoint without appearing to be offensive. Phrases include the following: The way I see it… I'm against it because… Instead, I think that… I'm afraid I don't agree with you, because… The British often use this technique to disagree politely.

Yet another way to disagree in some culture is to offer solutions. These are the **solvers** and they use phrases such as I think we should… We could… One solution may be….

> Telling people how you feel about something requires a bit of finesse in some cultures. You have to be able to say what you want to say without offending the other person. For the British, this often means finding roundabout ways of saying what you want to say and using a lot of polite expressions in your speech. Frankness is something that English speakers do not necessarily appreciate.
>
> *Source*: Norman (n.d.).

EXPRESSING AGREEMENT

The simplest way to acknowledge an agreement is to nod one's head. Phrases include "Hmmm," "That's a good idea," "I think you are right," and "I completely agree with you." In Japan however, head nods are not to be interpreted literally (more on head nods in the next chapter). Their ways of expressing agreement are also rather ambivalent; agreement is more about the person, not the premise. Due to the collectivist orientation, Japanese differentiate between *honne* (their true feelings or opinions) and *tatamae* (the appropriate thing to say in a situation). This is a cause of deep-rooted frustration for non-Japanese business people as they are not able to make a distinction between what constitutes *honne* and what constitutes *tatamae*. The Japanese yes can mean anything from "I am understanding you," "I am listening to you," and "I am listening to you even if I do not agree with what you say," to "Please continue with what you are saying."

> In India, when a host inquires, "Would you like to have a cold drink?" it is almost customary to refuse the first time. The conversation would continue something like this: "No, I am quite full." This will prompt the host to say, "Oh! You hardly ate anything! A cold drink would do no harm." The guest would reply: "Well...alright. Just give me in a small glass." Indeed the guest would be quite taken aback if the host did not ask him or her again!

REQUESTS FOR INFORMATION

People belonging to high-context collectivist cultures typically require a lot of information to assist them in decision making. This is distinct from the low-context countries, which focus on the information that they need to know to complete the task assigned to them. For most Americans time is money, and they would rather not spend time on unnecessary information that does not add value. However, if a Japanese requires X information, it will be implicit that he or she would also like to have information Y and Z to successfully complete a task. Requests therefore in the Japanese culture are not explicit and clear; they merely indicate the starting point from which more such requests could follow. The requests are therefore characterized as vague, in piecemeal format, and requiring frequent follow-up by foreigners dealing with the Japanese.

In China, the situation is vastly different even if the country possesses somewhat similar cultural traits as the Japanese. The Chinese (as well as those from Taiwan and Korea) prefer to be direct in expressing requests for information and abstain from beating around the bush. Like the Japanese, a vast majority of Indians are indirect communicators and come to the point later on in the conversation especially when a relationship has not been established with the information seeker.

HUMOR AND IRONY

What results in laughter is not universal; it is dependent on many sociocultural variables. Humor may not always result in laughter and is not always regarded as amusing. Cultures have different interpretations of what constitutes humor. For the French, humor is more a play on words. Irony is characteristic of Danish humor. Indians cannot appreciate laughing at themselves, while they openly laugh at others' misfortunes.

Cultures also vary in their preference for topics of humor. Blonde jokes are common in the United States. Similarly, other cultures have a preference for jokes on mothers-in-law, wives, politics, and religion. In Japan, humor is governed by conventions such as those relating to harmony, cooperation, formality, and membership of an in-group. Humor in Japan is rarely spontaneous and impulsive. American humor tends to be rather over the top and exaggerated and ignores conventions of formality and hierarchy. A typical American sarcasm would be followed by "Just kiddin'." British humor tends to be dry and witty (often the Oscar Wilde variety), whereas Canadian humor is satirical in nature. Canadians tend to provoke people by making fun of them, and there have been instances in which Canada has been rebuked for political incorrectness. A well-known instance is that of the Canadian Prime Minister Pierre Trudeau (known for his unconventional ways) who was caught by photographer Doug Ball spinning a pirouette behind an oblivious Queen Elizabeth during a G7 Summit conference in the Buckingham Palace, London, England, on May 7, 1977. "The picture expresses his maverick anti-conformism, his democratic disdain for aristocratic pomp," noted Ball.

Irreverent body language?: Trudeau in focus
Source: Trudeau (1977).

In some countries such as Denmark and Belgium, people deliberately make light of topics that make people anxious, such as those related to death, old age, loneliness, and illness.

COMPLIMENTING

The convention of paying and receiving compliments differs across cultural boundaries. Praise and compliments play an important role in communication. Compliments fall into two major categories: those having to do with appearance (for a person as well as objects) and those having to do with ability (of the person or the specific act of ability). Wolfson (1983) regards rapport building as the primary function of compliments. She also indicates that expressions of gratitude, greeting, conversation starters, or leave taking are also different functions of compliments.

The functions of praise could be any one of the following:

- To encourage others: Teachers in any society would like to encourage young children with phrases such as "You can really draw well" or "That's a great piece of writing; well done and keep it up!"
- To build relationships: Praise is meant to make receivers feel good about themselves and is also about the person who is complimenting. Phrases include "That was a sumptuous feast!," or "You are so efficient!"
- To create an atmosphere of goodwill: This type of praise is given initially at the start of an important conversation so that the receiver(s) are appeased before any bad news or negative feedback is given. Thus instead of a greeting, the conversation would start with a praise or a compliment. Phrases include "Wow! Looking good!"; "Nice tie."

> Research by Li Feilin and Yu Gaofeng (2005) reveals interesting differences between the complimenting styles of the British, the Americans, and the Chinese. They observe that in the English language, people prefix the personal pronoun "I" before complimenting someone, such as "I love your dress!" The Chinese however use the second person to prefix the compliment in English language, for example, "You do this work really nicely!" Americans regard praise or compliments with respect to a person's ability a serious matter; hence only a qualified person can compliment somebody's achievement. This is not so with Chinese where usually a junior compliments the senior (rather than vice versa) so as to make an impression on him.

In some cultures, it is almost customary to disagree with a compliment. In India for example, if someone says, "This dress looks good on you," it is expected that the receiver would respond with something like this: "Oh, this? This is quite old! I purchased this in Delhi five years ago!" Even the Chinese respond with a disagreement to a compliment. They add a question and also a fault to the object of the compliment. "You like this watch? (question) Why, it's quite old and has at least two scratches!" (fault). On the contrary, Japanese do not feel the need to pay a personal compliment to their wives or children. Their compliments, when paid to others, are tempered with humility. For example, they may say, "Your country is so green and beautiful. In comparison my country looks like a marooned, dry island!" This kind of humility makes the recipient feel that the Japanese compliment is insincere and that the speaker is hoping that the recipient will use a disclaimer to counter the assertion, such as "No, no, even your country is very beautiful!"

Some cultures exaggerate when they compliment. For example, the British use hyperbole extensively to praise others. Arabs have a unique way of complimenting. Known for reciting couplets, proverbs, and poetry, they compliment using eloquent words and use metaphors, analogies, and imagery. Compliments are woven into the fabric of the Arab way of life. Complimenting is a way to appease, to flatter, and to indulge another mainly to serve self-interest. Arabs focus more on the eloquent delivery of the compliment than the compliment itself.

> When they enter a shop, Arabs might say something to this effect: "We have visited your shop because we understand that you are the best … give us a hefty discount and we will bring more customers to your shop."

GIVING AND RECEIVING ADVICE

Cultural nuances are also observed in the speech act of giving and receiving advice. When people make decisions, they usually seek advice from others. However, some advice is unsolicited and has the adverse effect of threatening the autonomy of the recipient. Unsolicited advice from relatives, friends, and strangers may appear inappropriate in cultural contexts when it is viewed as potentially intrusive and condescending to the recipient, as if to convey that the recipient lacks knowledge or the competency to make choices independently.

Collectivist cultures are known to be more tolerant of advice than individualistic cultures. In the United States and Western Europe, advice from relatives, friends, and strangers is seen as highly intrusive and that which fosters unnecessary relational interdependence. This is in contrast to Russia where almost anybody and everybody can give advice (Chentsova-Dutton and Vaughn 2011). In India, one is supposed to seek advice (even one is not in need of it) so as to give importance to a close relative, patriarchs in the family, bosses, and superiors. The central idea in this culture is to ensure that the decision has been made with the consent of all.

> I am a Dutch living in the UK and I totally agree that they (the British) are very closed on this subject (of giving and receiving advice). Whenever I am back in the Netherlands people in the shop talk to me or warn me when my kids are in trouble. In the UK it is just a big silence. (This) does not make me feel welcome. Even at work people don't really tell the way they see it. Which makes me feel lonely sometime. However this is how it is in the South of England. I also come in the North of England and people are their more curious and ask more. Which is nice (*sic*).
>
> *Source*: Meghan Fenn (2012).

Languages are used in two contexts—the language of ordinary, everyday conversation and the language of business. The language of business is the language of trade. The trade language can be the English language or its hybrid versions, or, a regional trade language such as Persian or Chinese. Either way, language should serve as the common ground that facilitates rather than hinders business. Translation services, interlocutors, and interpreters can be utilized to improve the quality and clarity of business conversations.

SUMMARY

1. Communication has now become a powerful enabler for the growth, development, and consolidation of organizations.

2. The essence of communicative competence is that language and culture are inseparable. Both linguistic as well as sociocultural knowledge is important for effectively expressing putting one's point of view.

3. Language itself is an evolved cultural pattern. Currently, the debate is that ELF communication seems too partial a view for globalized business and that it must be substituted by BELF.

4. Failure to communicate in the language of the new country may result in pragmatic failure—the inability to understand what is meant by what is said. If regional trading blocs increase in number and in influence, English could become irrelevant within some of the blocs.

5. Three broad levels of differences, which can create misunderstandings in a cross-cultural interaction are (1) when to say, (2) what to say, and (3) how to say (dealt with more elaborately in the next chapter).

KEY TERMS

- Communicative competence
- ELF and BELF
- Pragmatic failure
- Silence
- Speech acts

REFERENCES

c JETRO. *Communicating with Japanese in Business*, 1999, http://www.jetro.go.jp/costarica/mercadeo/communicationwith.pdf

Carol, L. "A Mad Tea Party." In *Alice's Adventures in Wonderland*. London, UK: Macmillan, 1865.

Charles, M. "Language Matters In Global Communication." *Journal of Business Communication* 44, no. 3 (July 2007), pp. 260–82.

Chentsova-Dutton, Y.E.; and A. Vaughn. "Let Me Tell You What to Do: Cultural Differences in Advice-Giving." *Journal of Cross-Cultural Psychology* 20, no. 10 (June 2011), pp. 1–17.

Crystal, D. *English as a Global Language*. Cambridge, MA: Cambridge University Press, 1997.

Feilin, L.; and Gaofeng, Y. "Cultural Differences in Compliments." *Canadian Social Science* 1, no. 1 (May 2005), pp. 68–72.

Graddol, D. *The Future of English*. London, UK: The British Council, 1997.

Hofstede, G. *Cultures and Organizations Software of the Mind. Intercultural Cooperation and its Importance for Survival*. New York, NY: McGraw-Hill, 1997.

Hofstede, G.; Hofstede, G.J.; and Minkov, M. *Cultures and Organizations: Software of the Mind*. 3rd ed. New York, NY: McGrawHill, 2010.

Johnson, F. "Agreement and Disagreement: A Cross-Cultural Comparison." *BISAL* 1 (2006), pp. 41–67, http://www.bisal.bbk.ac.uk/publications/volume1/pdf/Fiona_Johnson_pdf

Kobayashi, J.; and L. Viswat. "Intercultural Communication Competence in Business: Communication Between Japanese and Americans." *Journal of Intercultural Communication* no. 26 (July 2011), p. 1.

Lahiri, T. "How Tech, Individuality Shape Hinglish." *The Wall Street Journal*, January 21, 2012.

Lundquist, L. *Humour as a Mediator in Cross-Cultural Professional Settings. Examples from Danish and French.* Working paper no. 66. International Center for Business and Politics Copenhagen Business School, 2009.

Meghan Peterson Fenn. *Is giving parenting advice in Britain taboo*, 2012, http://www.bringingupbrits.co.uk/blog/is-giving-parenting-advice-in-britain-taboo

Meritt, A. *News Report in the Telegraph.* (March 20, 2013).

Nakane, I. *Silence in the Multicultural Classroom: Perceptions and Performance.* Amsterdam: John Benjamins, 2007.

Norman, L. *How to Express Agreement and Disagreement in English*, n.d., http://www.ehow.com/how_6785120_express-agreement-disagreement-english.html#ixzz2NyWf9YIB

Samovar, L.A.; and R.E. Porter. *Communication Between Cultures.* 4th ed., Belmont, CA: Wadsworth, 2001.

Spencer-Oatey, H. *Culturally Speaking: Managing Rapport Through Talk Across Cultures.* 2000. New York, NY: Cassel Academic

Tannen, D. "The Pragmatics of Cross-Cultural Communication." *Applied Linguistics* 5, no. 3 (1984), pp. 189–95, http://xa.yimg.com/kq/groups/23344266/839912215/name/the_pragmatics_of_cross-cultural_communication.pdf

Trudeau, P. "Trudeau's Pirouette." *Iconic Photos*, May 7, 1977, http://iconicphotos.wordpress.com/2009/06/19/trudeaus-pirouette/

Wolfson, N. "An empirically Based Analysis of Complimenting in American English." In *Sociolinguistics and Language Acquisition*, eds. N. Wolfson; and E. Judd, 82–95. Rowley: Newbury House, 1983.

Zipperer, J. "Global Languages Aren't Universal." *Internet World* 7, no. 12 (June 2001), pp. 14–5.

CHAPTER 10

NONVERBAL CODES AND CULTURE

NONVERBAL MESSAGES

BY PAYAL MEHRA

Fie, fie upon her! There's language in her eye, her cheek, her lip, Nay, her foot speaks; her wanton spirits look out at every joint and motive of her body.

—Ulysses in William Shakespeare's Troilus and Cressida, IV.5.54-57

INTRODUCTION

From the time Charles Darwin published his epoch study—*Expressions of the Emotions in Man and Animals* in 1872, researchers from diverse disciplines such as anthropology, sociology, and, now, management, have been interested in exploring body language and its interpretation in various cultures. Nonverbal communication is an outward reflection of a person's emotional condition. More than verbal communication, it is the nonverbal communication that reveals the true attitudes and emotions of people, often without their conscious awareness. People both consciously and subconsciously tend to reveal their likes and dislikes through their body language.

Nonverbal communication is a product of culture and tends to be interpreted in a culture-specific way. People from native cultures speak their own language and follow particular cultural norms. In a multicultural

Payal Mehra, Selection from "Nonverbal Messages," *Communication Beyond Boundaries*, pp. 67-76, 149-153. Copyright © 2014 by Business Expert Press. Reprinted with permission.

workplace, negative micromessages may be sent to members of minority or ethnic groups (people who are perceived to be different from the majority), even if their verbal messages are polite and courteous. Negative micromessages can include a sneer, a cynical smile, raised eyebrows, a casual shrug, a smug facial expression, and the like. This subtle form of communication complicates relationships and provides a subconscious source of misunderstandings across cultures. It also has the potential to affect performance and output.

> Randhir Garg, an Indian, working as a guest worker in Great Britain, is regarded by fellow British employees as nonassertive and lazy. Though they do not say anything to him verbally, they send him micromessages conveying a negative stereotype. Garg feels like an outsider, thus affecting his performance in the team.

Nonverbal communication includes all forms of communication excluding the language used to speak or write. Three types of nonverbal communication will be discussed in this text: body language (facial expressions, gestures, posture, and body movements); physical environment (using physical space, distance and proximity norms, and territorial control); and personal attributes (such as appearance, voice, and touch). Technically, the study of body language is termed as kinesics, oculesics, proxemics, haptics, vocalics, chronemics, and environment.

Nonverbal communication is very important in international business, partly because verbal communication can be (more often than not) misleading or unreliable. This is especially true in international business negotiations, cross-country presentations, international product launches, as well as all communication related to mergers and acquisitions. International marketing often relies on the nonverbal communication of target population participants in focus group discussions for brand decisions.

TYPES OF NONVERBAL COMMUNICATION

Nonverbal communication can be classified into two categories: conscious messages and subliminal messages. Senders of conscious messages are aware that they are sending out a particular message and that the message has a definite implication.

For example, a thumbs-up signal by an American is positive, denoting good job or go ahead. Receivers of the conscious nonverbal message know that the message is a positive one and a sign of motivation. In contrast, subliminal messages appeal to the subconscious mind of the receiver. A receiver is not consciously aware of the nonverbal message. Organizations that require its employees to wear uniforms subliminally communicate position, authority, and a desire for belongingness among those wearing them. The advertising media also uses subliminal messages. For example, in a movie, an actor is seen drinking cola of a reputed company. The use of these products in the movie would not be classified strictly as advertisements. However, the mere association of the movie with the brand and the product transmits subliminal messages that influence the viewers.

Nonverbal messages can be involuntary as well as voluntary. People unintentionally convey many messages through their facial expressions, hand movements, and eye contact. It is often said that liars can be caught merely by telltale signals: shifty eyes, gestures of touching nose and ear, and even by the way they smile. Because involuntary communication is unplanned, it represents a better assessment of people's true intentions than verbal messages. Nonverbal communication can also be voluntary. People knowledgeable about body language can control their nonverbal responses. They take special care to avoid the telltale signs that may reveal their true intent.

FUNCTIONS OF NONVERBAL COMMUNICATION

Mindful nonverbal communication has the following distinct functions:

ENHANCING, ASSERTING, AND REFLECTING IDENTITIES

Nonverbal cues serve as identity badges. We tend to respond to others on the basis of stereotypes rather than personal content characteristics. The face, hair, eyes, clothes, and accessories are interpreted by others through the medium of stereotypes. Accent, posture, and gesture also reveal group membership (Asian? American? Japanese?). Categorical slotting takes place as a result of speech patterns, physical cues (such as hair and skin color), and clothing. Vocalics such as speech, accent, pitch intensity, volume, and articulation also characterize cultural origins. We tend to like people who sound like us in contrast to those who sound very different.

EXPRESSING EMOTIONS

Feelings and attitudes are inferred from kinesics and vocalics. The human face is said to be capable of producing 2,50,000 facial expressions. Culture shapes emotional expressions. Subconsciously, through the cultural reinforcement process, people internalize the nonverbal rules of their culture. They react spontaneously to situations through learned behavior. It is thus that human beings acquire nonverbal display rules. They learn when to suppress emotions and how and when to convey emotions. Thus, collectivists will learn to suppress display (to maintain relationships and preserve harmony), while the individualists will learn to express display of emotions, feelings, and behavior.

Though members of various cultures universally acknowledge happiness and surprise, feelings of disgust, anger, unhappiness, or hurt are more obviously demonstrated by the expressive cultures better than the reserved cultures. Additionally, the smile can be interpreted in different ways. While in the United States the smile is an expression of joy, in Japan, it may imply a myriad of emotions (including embarrassment, displeasure, or anger). Russians, for example, rarely smile at the beginning of a negotiation, but as it progresses in a favorable manner, they start to smile. In terms of vocalics, the Arabs, Italians, and Greeks tend to raise their voices and argue passionately; while they are not angry, to an American they might appear to be so. From an Arab's point of view, the American tone may sound cold, distant, and aloof, but to an Asian it may sound too aggressive and harsh. Thus, cultural relativism can impact how people perceive each other.

Meaning of a smile in various cultures

United States:	Friendliness
Asia:	Friendliness, covering for emotional pain, embarrassment, anger
Russia:	Agreement, satisfaction

MANAGING CONVERSATIONS

People use kinesics and oculesics (eye contact) to manage their conversations with each other. Kinesics includes emblems, illustrators, regulators, and adaptors, and each of these has a specific communication objective. They are not, however, mutually exclusive. An emblem is an intentional hand gestures that has a specific meaning attributed to it. Consider the *ok* sign, for example. The use of this signal means good in the United States, money in Japan, a sexual insult in Greece, zero in French, and vulgar in Russia. The thumbs-up gesture means good or great in the United States and Great Britain, but is offensive to Arabs. The use of gestures may lead to misunderstandings, as a polite greeting in one culture may be considered rude in another culture.

Meaning of hand gestures in various cultures

Italy	In counting, thumb means one and index finger means two
Australia	Index finger is one and middle finger is two
United States	*V* is for victory with outward palm
Great Britain	*V* is for victory when the palm faces the receiver; it is an insult when palm faces the speaker (same for Australia, New Zealand)
Japan, Korea, Taiwan	*V* with outward palm (facing the receiver), especially when photographed
Philippines	*V* is for peace
Vietnam	*V* is for hello
Indonesia	Index finger is used to stop public transport
United States	People are beckoned with palm up
Korea	People are beckoned by snapping fingers
Europe	Thumbs-up gesture means one
Greece	Thumbs-up means "one up to you"
United States	Handshake to greet
Japan	Bow to greet (depth of the bow indicates respect for seniority and position)

Illustrators are hand gestures that complement the spoken words. These gestures help to visualize the imagery and are the most pictorial of the nonverbal gestures. These are mostly used to illustrate directions. The Italians, Greeks, and Spaniards use more illustrators than the Americans. Arabs, South Americans, and Egyptians use animated illustrators. Belgians, Finns, and those from Asian cultures use fewer illustrators. The Arabs do not gesture or eat with the left hand as it is perceived as unclean. Members of some Asian countries refrain from patting the head, as the head is considered sacred.

Regulators are vocalics, kinesics, and oculesics to regulate the flow of conversation. As with emblems, they are also culture specific. Interruptions, for example, are regulators as is the use of silence. Brazilians interrupt twice as much as the British or Americans. In Bulgaria, when people nod their heads, it means no, but in other parts of the world, nodding means yes. The French also like to interrupt with interjections such as an exclamation, a remark, a protest, or even laughter. Pauses and filler cues such as "uh huh" (British) or "hai hai" (Japanese) are also regulators as is eye contact. Regulators, like other nonverbal gestures, have the potential to create misunderstandings when used across cultures.

Adaptors are essential postural changes at a low level of awareness. Seldom intentional, adaptors are often true indicators of what a person is thinking because people perform these movements at a subconscious level. For example, a slumped posture conveys boredom and disinterest, while an erect posture suggests enthusiasm and vitality. Similarly, leaning forward suggests keen listening and active involvement while leaning away indicates disinterest and boredom. Other examples of adaptors include fiddling with one's hair (low involvement), chewing fingernails (anxiety), tapping one's foot and leg (impatience), playing with jewelry (nervousness), and cracking knuckles (awkwardness).

Extent of eye contact and its implication in various cultures

Minimal or very less eye contact:	Far East Asian countries
Moderate eye contact:	Thailand, India, Pakistan, Korea, Africa
Firm eye contact:	United States, most parts of northern Europe, Turkey
Intense eye contact:	Saudi Arabia, Italy, Spain, Greece, parts of South America

Meaning of raised eyebrows in various cultures

Germans	Brilliant!
Arabs and Chinese	Disagreement

IMPRESSION FORMATION

Impression formation occurs throughout the process of communication. An individual's personality, physical attributes, profession, and behavior create an impression on the receiver. Positive impression formation is often related to the person's posture, style of walking, voice modulation, eye contact, dress, and accessories. However, norms regarding what constitutes professionalism vary across cultures. While some types of business attire are universally acceptable in all cultures, the same may not hold true for eye contact, voice modulation, and posture. In the United States, for example, assertiveness is a valued trait but this may not hold true for many South Asian countries. A positive impression in these countries is associated with passive behavior (especially when lower in hierarchy), a reserved communication style, and minimal display of gestures.

INTERPRETING NONVERBAL MESSAGES

Nonverbal messages must be interpreted in totality and not in isolation because most messages have more than one possible interpretation. Nonverbal messages are often rooted in cultural contexts. For example, it may appear perfectly normal in many cultures to lightly pat a child's head, but the gesture has a negative connotation in Thailand. Similarly, in some cultures, direct eye contact is preferred, while in others, a direct gaze is considered offensive. South European countries are more physically demonstrative than the north European countries.

> In a negotiation process, the Americans erroneously concluded that the Chinese were in agreement with their proposal. Every time the Americans expressed a viewpoint, they were met with silence and an impassive gaze. Because there was no overt resistance, the Americans felt confident about their proposal. The confidence was misplaced, however.

HANDSHAKES

It is important to consider the effects of cultural differences when interpreting handshake cues. For example, in the Middle East, the grip is more gentle than executive in nature. In most Asian countries, direct eye contact is avoided when shaking hands. It is considered suspicious in the United States and in Latin American countries when people avoid eye contact while shaking hands. In Islamic countries, it is taboo to shake hands with women. Women also avoid touching gestures such as the shoulder pat. In the United States, women are accustomed to using the executive grip when shaking hands with both men and women. In India, businessmen also prefer the executive grip; however, only a few women use it; most women prefer the gentle touching of the fingers or the *limp fish* handshake, which can be misinterpreted in other cultures as a sign of weakness. In many countries including India, shoulder pats, kissing on the cheek, embraces, or other types of touching are considered a violation of one's personal space, especially between strangers. In Japan, the custom is to bow, although visiting dignitaries need not do so. U.S. President Obama was criticized by the U.S. media for bowing too low to the point of depicting extreme servility to his Japanese counterpart (see picture in the following text):

President Obama: Bowing too low?
Source: *The Telegraph* (2009).

> U.S. President George Bush in 1992 toured Australia and gave a peace sign in the form of a V gesture to a group of farmers in Canberra. He apparently wanted to appease the farmers who were protesting U.S. farm subsidies. The signal backfired; the outward facing V sign in Australia is an insulting and hostile gesture.
>
> *Source*: Tarpley and Chaitkin (2004).

North Americans, for example, value privacy; therefore they have fairly wide proxemic requirements in contrast to Latin Americans who have little concept of privacy. The British maintain greater distance than the French, who are a more high-contact culture than the former. Similarly, an Arab's concept of personal space is very different from that of an American (see the following illustration). As with other types of nonverbal communication, space and distance are open to misinterpretation and misunderstandings. A too-close proximity is often viewed as invading the privacy and space of another person. People tend to react, become defensive in their behavior, and actually move away from the person who they perceive as invading their space.

An Arab greeting an American

Preferred distances between people belonging to different cultures:

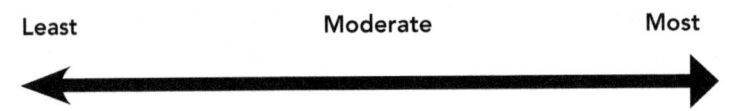

Least   Moderate   Most

⟵——————————————————⟶

Arabs, Latin Americans, Greeks, Turks, French, Italians, Indians, Japanese, Chinese, Thai, British, Germans, Dutch, Americans

Hall distinguishes two types of spatial arrangements that can convey different types of meaning and hinder effective communication: the sociofugal space (greater distance between the manager and the subordinates expressed by placement of furniture and room arrangement), and the sociopetal arrangement (minimal distance between the manager and subordinates resulting from room and furniture arrangement).

> Japanese office seating arrangements are designed to facilitate control and quick interpersonal communication. The manager sits in a far corner to supervise ably the subordinates who sit facing each other, each with a small desk. The manager's desk is slightly bigger than that of the subordinates. In the conference room, the seating is strictly hierarchical, with the manager sitting at the head of the table and the subordinates sitting in decreasing order of hierarchy.
>
> *Source:* Nishiyama (2000).

REFERENCES

Nishiyama, K. "Barriers to International Business Communication." In *Doing Business with Japan: Successful Strategies for Intercultural Communication.* Honolulu, HI: University of Hawaii press, 2000.

Tarpley, W. G.; and A. Chaitkin. *George Bush: The Unauthorized Biography,* 651. San Diego, CA: Progressive Press paperback edition, 2004. Web link to Chapter -XXV- Thyroid Storm, January 3, 1992.

The Telegraph. *Barack Obama Criticised for 'treasonous' Bow to Japanese Emperor,* November 16, 2009, http://www.telegraph.co.uk/news/worldnews/barackobama/6580190/Barack-Obama-criticised-for-treasonous-bow-to-Japanese-emperor.html

CPSIA information can be obtained
at www.ICGtesting.com
Printed in the USA
FSHW012038310819
61593FS

REDEFINING GOVERNMENT'S ROLE IN THE MARKET SYSTEM

*A Statement on National Policy
by the Research and Policy Committee
of the Committee for Economic Development*

CED

July 1979

Library of Congress Cataloging in Publication Data

Committee for Economic Development. Research and Policy Committee.
 Redefining government's role in the market system.

 Includes bibliographical references.
 1. Economic policy.   2. United States—Economic policy.   3. Industry and state—United States.
I. Title.
HD82.C573 1979   338.973   79-15717
ISBN 0-87186-068-6

First printing: July 1979
Second printing: April 1981
Paperbound: $5.00
Library binding: $6.50
Printed in the United States of America by Kearny Press, Inc.
Design: Harry Carter

COMMITTEE FOR ECONOMIC DEVELOPMENT
477 Madison Avenue, New York, N.Y. 10022
1700 K Street, N.W., Washington, D.C. 20006

Contents

RESPONSIBILITY FOR CED STATEMENTS ON NATIONAL POLICY 6

PURPOSE OF THIS STATEMENT 9

1. INTRODUCTION AND SUMMARY OF RECOMMENDATIONS 13

   Changing Role of Government 15
   Assessing the Costs, Benefits, and Side Effects 16
   Making Use of the Market System 18
   New Political Restraint 19
   The Problem of Government Involvement 20
   Summary of Recommendations 21

   New Criteria to Screen Requests for Government Intervention 22
   Improving Procedures for Screening Policy Proposals 23
   Evaluating the Effectiveness of Policy 25
   Special Presidential Action 26
   Publicizing Ineffective Government Involvement 26

   Implications of Improving the Policy-Making Process 26

2. THE MARKET SYSTEM AND GOVERNMENT'S ROLE IN THE ECONOMY: STRENGTHS AND LIMITATIONS 29

   The Market System's Strengths 29
   The Market System 32
   The Market System's Limitations 34
   The Government's Strengths 34
   What the Market System Does 35
   The Government's Limitations 37

3. THE GROWING ROLE OF GOVERNMENT IN THE ECONOMY: EXPENDITURES AND INDIRECT INCENTIVES 40

   Growth of Public Expenditures and Employment 41
   Growth of Government Indirect Incentive Policies 44
   Special Tax Arrangements 46
   Subsidies 47
   Loans and Loan Guarantees 50
   How to Control the Growth of Government Expenditures and Indirect Incentive Programs 53

4. **THE GROWING ROLE OF GOVERNMENT IN THE ECONOMY: REGULATION**   56

   Growth and Scope of Government Regulation   57

   Regulatory Techniques   59

   Costs of Regulation   60
      Direct Costs: Government Expenditures   62
      Indirect Costs: Changes in Production   62
      Indirect Costs: Restrictions on Operation   65

   Indirect Costs: Inefficiencies in Production   66

   Benefits of Regulation   67
      Regulatory Constraints on Drug Innovation   68

   Net Benefits of Regulation   73

   Conclusions about the Growth of Government Involvement   75
      Problems in Achieving New Regulatory Goals:
         The Consumer Product Safety Commission   76

5. **WEAKNESSES IN THE CURRENT POLICY-MAKING PROCESS**   79

   Pressures of the Political Environment   80

   Processes that Determine Policy: Budget and Appropriations, Legislative and Authorization, and Management Accountability   82

   Policy Review and Program Evaluation   84

   Improving Control over Policy: Congressional and Executive Recognition of the Problem   86

6. **RECOMMENDATIONS FOR SCREENING, ADOPTING, AND DESIGNING GOVERNMENT ACTION**   91

   Recommendations for Screening   92

   Recommendations for Selecting and Designing a Specific Kind of Government Involvement in the Market System   97

   Methods of Involvement that Should Be Reassessed: Four Case Studies   99
      Utilizing the Price Mechanism: Environmental Policy   100
      Implications of the Zero-Risk Principle   100
      Avoiding Undesirable Side Effects of a Subsidy: Housing   103
      Internalizing the Costs of Accidents and Illness: OSHA   104
      Coordinating Involvement Techniques: Transportation   106

   Conclusions   107
      Summary of Criteria for Screening, Adopting, and
         Designing Government Actions   108

7. A COMPREHENSIVE APPROACH FOR DISCIPLINING
   POLICY DECISIONS   110

   Phase 1: Screening the Objective, Method, and Impact
      of Proposed Policies   113
   Phase 2: Evaluating the Effectiveness of Policies   115
      *Implementing Phase 1: Recommendations for Screening
         the Objective, Method, and Impact of Proposed Policies   116*
      *Implementing Phase 2: Recommendations for Evaluating the
         Effectiveness of Policies   120*
   Additional Procedures for Screening and Evaluating
      Public Policies   123
      Direct Expenditure Programs   123
      Indirect Incentive Policies   128
      Regulations   129
   Phase 3: Ensuring that Program Evaluation Leads
      to Policy Changes   130
   Phase 4: Recommendations for Reviewing
      the Policy-Making Process   132
   Conclusions   132
      *Implementing Phase 3: Recommendations for Ensuring
         that Program Evaluation Leads to Policy Changes   133*
      *Implementing Phase 4: Recommendations for Reviewing
         the Policy-Making Process   135*

MEMORANDA OF COMMENT, RESERVATION, OR DISSENT   136

OBJECTIVES OF THE COMMITTEE FOR ECONOMIC DEVELOPMENT   144

FIGURES

   Chapter 3
      1. *Growth in Public Employment*   43
      2. *Growth in Public Expenditure*   43
      3. *Changing Distribution of Federal Expenditure*   45
      4. *Differentially Lower Tax Treatment*   47
      5. *Summary of Federal Subsidy and Related Program Costs*   49
      6. *New Federal Credit Extended, Fiscal Years 1977 to 1979*   51

   Chapter 4
      7. *Estimates of Increased Production Costs from OSHA Standards*   63

Redefining Government's Role in the Market System

Responsibility for CED Statements on National Policy

The Committee for Economic Development is an independent research and educational organization of two hundred business executives and educators. CED is nonprofit, nonpartisan, and nonpolitical.

Its purpose is to propose policies that will help to bring about steady economic growth at high employment and reasonably stable prices, increase productivity and living standards, provide greater and more equal opportunity for every citizen, and improve the quality of life for all. A more complete description of CED is to be found on page 144.

All CED policy recommendations must have the approval of the Research and Policy Committee, trustees whose names are listed on page 7. This Committee is directed under the bylaws to "initiate studies into the principles of business policy and of public policy which will foster the full contribution by industry and commerce to the attainment and maintenance" of the objectives stated above. The bylaws emphasize that "all research is to be thoroughly objective in character, and the approach in each instance is to be from the standpoint of the general welfare and not from that of any special political or economic group." The Committee is aided by a Research Advisory Board of leading social scientists and by a small permanent professional staff.

The Research and Policy Committee is not attempting to pass judgment on any pending specific legislative proposals; its purpose is to urge careful consideration of the objectives set forth in this statement and of the best means of accomplishing those objectives.

Each statement is preceded by extensive discussions, meetings, and exchanges of memoranda. The research is undertaken by a subcommittee, assisted by advisors chosen for their competence in the field under study. The members and advisors of the subcommittee that prepared this statement are listed on page 8.

The full Research and Policy Committee participates in the drafting of findings and recommendations. Likewise, the trustees on the drafting subcommittee vote to approve or disapprove a policy statement, and they share with the Research and Policy Committee the privilege of submitting individual comments for publication, as noted on pages 7 and 8 and on the appropriate page of the text of the statement.

Except for the members of the Research and Policy Committee and the responsible subcommittee, the recommendations presented herein are not necessarily endorsed by other trustees or by the advisors, contributors, staff members, or others associated with CED.

Research and Policy Committee

Chairman: FRANKLIN A. LINDSAY
Vice Chairmen: JOHN L. BURNS / *Education and Social and Urban Development*
E. B. FITZGERALD / *International Economy*
HOWARD C. PETERSEN / *National Economy*
WAYNE E. THOMPSON / *Improvement of Management in Government*

A. ROBERT ABBOUD, Chairman
The First National Bank of Chicago

[1] ROY L. ASH, Chairman
AM International, Inc.

JOSEPH W. BARR
Washington, D.C.

HARRY HOOD BASSETT, Chairman
Southeast Banking Corporation

JACK F. BENNETT, Senior Vice President
Exxon Corporation

[1] CHARLES P. BOWEN, JR.
Honorary Chairman
Booz, Allen & Hamilton Inc.

JOHN L. BURNS, President
John L. Burns and Company

[1] FLETCHER L. BYROM, Chairman
Koppers Company, Inc.

ROBERT J. CARLSON
Senior Vice President
Deere & Company

RAFAEL CARRION, JR.
Chairman and President
Banco Popular de Puerto Rico

WILLIAM S. CASHEL, JR., Vice Chairman
American Telephone & Telegraph Company

JOHN B. CAVE, Senior Vice President
Finance and Administration
Schering-Plough Corporation

EMILIO G. COLLADO, President
Adela Investment Co., S.A.

ROBERT C. COSGROVE, Chairman
Green Giant Company

W. D. DANCE, Vice Chairman
General Electric Company

JOHN H. DANIELS, Chairman
National City Bancorporation

W. D. EBERLE, Special Partner
Robert A. Weaver, Jr. and Associates

WILLIAM S. EDGERLY
Chairman and President
State Street Bank and Trust Company

FRANCIS E. FERGUSON, President
Northwestern Mutual Life
  Insurance Company

JOHN H. FILER, Chairman
Aetna Life and Casualty Company

E. B. FITZGERALD, Chairman
Cutler-Hammer, Inc.

JOHN M. FOX, Retired Chairman
H. P. Hood Inc.

[1] DAVID L. FRANCIS
Chairman
Princess Coals, Inc.

WILLIAM H. FRANKLIN
Chairman of the Board (Retired)
Caterpillar Tractor Co.

JOHN D. GRAY, Chairman
Omark Industries, Inc.

H. J. HEINZ II, Chairman
H. J. Heinz Company

ROBERT C. HOLLAND, President
Committee for Economic Development

EDWARD R. KANE, President
E. I. du Pont de Nemours & Company

[2] CHARLES KELLER, JR.
New Orleans, Louisiana

[1] PHILIP M. KLUTZNICK
Klutznick Investments

RALPH LAZARUS, Chairman
Federated Department Stores, Inc.

FRANKLIN A. LINDSAY, Chairman
Itek Corporation

J. PAUL LYET, Chairman
Sperry Rand Corporation

G. BARRON MALLORY
Jacobs Persinger & Parker

[1] WILLIAM F. MAY, Chairman
American Can Company

THOMAS B. McCABE
Chairman, Finance Committee
Scott Paper Company

GEORGE C. McGHEE, Corporate Director
  and former U.S. Ambassador
Washington, D.C.

E. L. McNEELY, Chairman
The Wickes Corporation

[1] J. W. McSWINEY, Chairman
The Mead Corporation

RUBEN F. METTLER, Chairman
TRW, Inc.

[1] ROBERT R. NATHAN, Chairman
Robert R. Nathan Associates, Inc.

VICTOR H. PALMIERI, Chairman
Victor Palmieri and Company Incorporated

HOWARD C. PETERSEN
Philadelphia, Pennsylvania

C. WREDE PETERSMEYER,
Bronxville, New York

R. STEWART RAUCH, JR., Chairman
The Philadelphia Saving Fund Society

JAMES Q. RIORDAN, Executive Vice President
Mobil Oil Corporation

WILLIAM M. ROTH
San Francisco, California

HENRY B. SCHACHT, Chairman
Cummins Engine Company, Inc.

ROBERT B. SEMPLE, Chairman
BASF Wyandotte Corporation

ROCCO C. SICILIANO, Chairman
Ticor

ROGER B. SMITH, Executive Vice President
General Motors Corporation

CHARLES B. STAUFFACHER, President
Field Enterprises, Inc.

WILLIAM C. STOLK
Weston, Connecticut

WILLIS A. STRAUSS, Chairman
Northern Natural Gas Company

WALTER N. THAYER, President
Whitney Communications Corporation

WAYNE E. THOMPSON, Senior Vice President
Dayton Hudson Corporation

SIDNEY J. WEINBERG, JR., Partner
Goldman, Sachs & Co.

GEORGE L. WILCOX, Director-Officer
Westinghouse Electric Corporation

[1] FRAZAR B. WILDE, Chairman Emeritus
Connecticut General Life Insurance Company

RICHARD D. WOOD, Chairman and President
Eli Lilly and Company

[1] Voted to approve the policy statement but submitted memoranda of comment, reservation, or dissent or wished to be associated with memoranda of others. See pages 136-143.
[2] Voted to disapprove this policy statement.

NOTE / A complete list of CED trustees and honorary trustees appears at the back of the book. *Company or institutional associations are included for identification only; the organizations do not share in the responsibility borne by the individuals.*

Subcommittee on Regulation and the Role of Government in the Economy

Chairman
W. D. EBERLE, Special Partner
Robert A Weaver, Jr. and Associates

[1] E. SHERMAN ADAMS
New Preston, Connecticut

[1] ROY L. ASH, Chairman
AM International, Inc.

JOSEPH W. BARR
Washington, D.C.

JACK F. BENNETT
Senior Vice President
Exxon Corporation

THEODORE F. BROPHY, Chairman
General Telephone & Electronics Corporation

ALEXANDER CALDER, JR.
Chairman
Union Camp Corporation

THOMAS S. CARROLL, President
Lever Brothers Company

SAMUEL B. CASEY, JR., Chairman
Pullman Incorporated

ROBERT C. COSGROVE, Chairman
Green Giant Company

JOHN DIEBOLD, Chairman
The Diebold Group, Inc.

FRANCIS E. FERGUSON, President
Northwestern Mutual Life Insurance Company

WILLIAM S. FISHMAN, Chairman
ARA Services, Inc.

[1] TERRANCE HANOLD
Minneapolis, Minnesota

RODERICK M. HILLS
Latham, Watkins and Hills

TOM KILLEFER
Chairman and President
United States Trust Company of New York

FLOYD W. LEWIS, President
Middle South Utilities, Inc.

[1] WILLIAM F. MAY, Chairman
American Can Company

CHARLES A. McLENDON
Executive Vice President
Burlington Industries, Inc.

RENE C. McPHERSON, Chairman
Dana Corporation

RUSSELL E. PALMER
Managing Partner
Touche Ross & Co.

[1] D. C. SEARLE
Chairman, Executive Committee
G. D. Searle & Co.

WILLIAM P. SIMMONS, President
First National Bank & Trust Company

L. EDWIN SMART, Chairman
Trans World Airlines

RICHARD M. SMITH, Vice Chairman
Bethlehem Steel Corporation

ROGER B. SMITH, Executive Vice President
General Motors Corporation

J. PAUL STICHT, President
R. J. Reynolds Industries, Inc.

JOHN H. WILLIAMS, Chairman
The Williams Companies

RICHARD D. WOOD
Chairman and President
Eli Lilly and Company

Ex Officio

JOHN L. BURNS

FLETCHER L. BYROM

ROBERT C. HOLLAND

FRANKLIN A. LINDSAY

WAYNE E. THOMPSON

*Nontrustee Member

HARRY C. McPHERSON, JR.
Verner, Lipfert, Bernhard, McPherson and Alexander

[1]Voted to approve the policy statement but submitted memoranda of comment, reservation, or dissent or wished to be associated with memoranda of others.

*Nontrustee members take part in all discussions on the statements but do not vote on it.

Advisors to the Subcommittee

SAMUEL B. CHASE, JR.
Golembe Associates

LYLE C. FITCH, President
Institute of Public Administration

MARVIN H. KOSTERS
Director, Center for the Study of Government Regulation
American Enterprise Institute for Public Policy Research

WILLIAM A. MORRILL
Senior Fellow
Mathematica Policy Research, Inc.

MICHAEL H. MOSKOW
Vice President of Corporate Development and Planning
Esmark, Inc.

WALLACE E. OATES
Department of Economics
Princeton University

ANTHONY G. OETTINGER, Director
Program on Information Resources Policy
Harvard University

WILLIAM POOLE
Professor of Economics
Brown University

EZRA SOLOMON
Dean Witter Professor of Finance
Graduate School of Business
Stanford University

PETER O. STEINER
Professor of Economics and Law
The University of Michigan

Project Director

KENNETH McLENNAN
Director of Industrial Studies
Committee for Economic Development

CED Staff Advisors

FRANK W. SCHIFF
Vice President and Chief Economist

KENNETH M. DUBERSTEIN
Director of Business-Government Relations and Secretary, Research and Policy Committee

SEONG H. PARK
Economist

Consulting Editor

BARBARA WHITESIDES
Newton, Massachusetts

CED Project Staff

JACK B. LIPTON
Policy Analyst

LORRAINE MACKEY
Administrative Assistant

Purpose of This Statement

FOR MORE THAN THIRTY-FIVE YEARS, the Committee for Economic Development has been concerned with strengthening and improving this country's economic system, with bringing about steady economic growth without inflation, and with achieving high levels of employment and productivity. However, it is becoming increasingly clear that forces of a longer-term and chronic nature are having a critical impact on the increasingly unsatisfactory performance of some areas of this nation's economy. We are concerned that the largely unguided growth of government involvement in the economic system is threatening the achievement of this nation's economic *and* social goals.

It is ironic that government, to which the nation has often turned for assistance in meeting these goals, has now become a major contributor to inadequate national economic performance. We found that, increasingly, the public is becoming aware that much government involvement has slowed the growth of the economy, has decreased services delivered per tax dollar, and has contributed to inflation. There are more and more signals—both from the public and from government itself—that the country is now seeking more effective control over government involvement in the economy. President Carter recently underscored this when he said that "for too long we have acted as if we could throw another law or another rule at every problem in our society without thinking seriously about the consequences."

Focus on the Long Term

This policy statement is the result of two years of research, study, and deliberation by the CED Subcommittee on Improving the Long-Term Performance of the U.S. Economy and the Subcommittee on Regulation and the Role of Government in the Economy.

CED launched this project with a 1977 seminar, "Major Changes Likely to Face Our Economy in the Future." The business, government, and academic experts who participated in that inaugural session concluded that the relationship between the economy and government is changing and that the system through which that relationship is expressed is not adapting fast enough. The participants concluded that government is placing increasingly excessive demands on the private sector and that the results are decreased productivity and increased inflation.

Under the chairmanship of William D. Eberle, the Subcommittee on Regulation and the Role of Government in the Economy was established to analyze these issues. It was the consensus of the trustees and advisors who participated in this project that the process of public policy making should be reformed if the nation is to achieve its longer-term objectives.

In this statement, we stress primary reliance on the market system. However, we recognize that the market system is not an end in itself but the most efficient and effective means of achieving greater productivity, economic growth, and social diversity.

In preparing this statement, the subcommittee commissioned a number of research studies, one of which, *Strategic Planning in Business and Government,* by Michael Moskow, was published in December 1978 as a CED supplementary paper.

In addition, this report drew extensively from the experience of a number of other CED subcommittees examining other key economic and social problems such as jobs for the hard-to-employ, long-range energy policy, and technology policy.

Redefining Government's Role

This statement focuses on the growth and nature of direct expenditure programs; indirect incentive policies such as tax incentives, loans, and loan guarantees; and regulations and their effects on markets. It concludes that the current federal policy-making process makes it difficult to strike a reasonable balance between strengthening the market and furthering social goals.

The report offers what we believe to be a coherent approach to determining the nature and degree of government involvement in the private economy required to achieve legitimate social and economic objectives. It emphasizes the importance of establishing criteria for government involvement, of testing the effectiveness of new and ongoing programs, and of assessing the overall economic and social impact of new programs.

It also stresses that to avoid distortions, the problems of overall economic efficiency and the problems of social equity must be handled separately. It warns against using broad economic policies rather than specific income supplements to achieve specific social goals, such as maintaining artificially low energy prices to cushion the burden on a small segment of the population.

One of the most important recommendations in this statement is that the overall impact of any regulation on the economy as a whole must be considered *when the regulation is being formulated.* Further, both legislators and regulators must consider the enormous costs of trying to achieve a completely risk-free environment. Attempts to achieve zero risk as opposed to acceptable, realistic standards have severely strained large segments of the economy and contributed little additional environmental protection.

We hope this policy statement can help bring about a broader understanding of the impact that government actions have on the economy as a whole. It is essential to redefine the government's role in the economy, but it will not be an easy task, and there is no one, simple solution. Reversal of the tendency toward ad hoc expansion of government will require commitment, patience, and courage from business leaders, government officials, labor leaders, and most important, the public.

Special Contributions

The subcommittee that prepared this statement included a number of trustees and advisors with extensive experience in both business and government. A list of all subcommittee members and advisors appears on page 8.

We are especially indebted to the chairman of the subcommittee, William D. Eberle, of Robert A. Weaver, Jr. and Associates and former

United States special representative for trade negotiations, for his skillful and persuasive leadership. Special recognition is also due to project director Kenneth McLennan, CED's director of industrial studies, for his clear and incisive approach to this critical and complex set of problems.

We are also grateful to the Andrew W. Mellon Foundation for its generous support of the CED project on Improving the Long-Term Performance of the U.S. Economy. The process of study and exploration that led to the preparation of this statement would not have been possible without the foundation's encouragement and assistance.

Franklin A. Lindsay, *Chairman*
Research and Policy Committee

1.

Introduction and Summary of Recommendations

A STRONG COMPETITIVE MARKET SYSTEM is necessary to this country's social and economic welfare. When it functions effectively, it serves the nation by stimulating the efficient provision of goods and services. Moreover, it promotes business investments in research, new equipment, and other capital goods necessary for improvements in productivity and economic growth. The market system benefits a broad spectrum of the society—workers, consumers, and businesses. It also provides resources to support social programs and improve the quality of life.

In response to the demands of voters and organized interest groups, the political system, whether intentionally or unintentionally, has often reduced the effectiveness of markets. Excessive, ill-planned regulation and excessive, poorly designed government expenditure and subsidy programs have interfered with the market system to the detriment of society.

The expansion of some direct expenditure programs and indirect subsidies has burdened the taxpayer and contributed to large budget deficits and inflation. Overregulation has seriously eroded the effectiveness of some markets and created enormous costs in terms of higher prices and premature changes in capital equipment that have not usually led to technological progress. These actions have contributed to inflation by raising costs of production, reducing productivity, and retarding economic growth.

This Committee believes that the country would be well served by freeing markets from ill-designed government constraints. This statement presents a comprehensive framework for redefining government's role in the market system. We believe that if the criteria we set forth and the procedures we recommend are implemented, they can contribute to curtailing government expenditure programs and regulations that are not justified and to reshaping those that are. Government programs and regulatory policies need to be justified on the basis of both their specific goals and their potential effects on the overall economic system. When new initiatives are implemented, the effectiveness of government policies should be periodically evaluated to determine whether existing programs should be modified or eliminated.

Our analysis is concerned with federal activities, with what Congress, the executive branch, and the independent regulatory agencies should consider doing to improve the public policy process. We recognize that state and local governments also have an enormous impact on every area of the private sector. And although this statement does not deal directly with state and local government activities, many of the principles we recommend can and should be applied to them.

This statement focuses on federal policies that directly affect the operation of markets, including regulatory policies, some expenditure programs, and a wide range of indirect policies such as subsidies, loans, and loan guarantees. It does not discuss such macroeconomic policies as monetary and fiscal, wage and price, and international trade policies, which also have a pervasive influence on markets. Prior CED policy statements have dealt at length with these subjects.[1] We recognize that our recommendations may require modification when applied to such

---

1. In many of its previous policy statements, CED has presented recommendations for achieving economic stabilization and growth. See *High Employment Without Inflation* (1972), *Fighting Inflation and Promoting Growth* (1976), *The Economy in 1977–78: Strategy for an Enduring Expansion* (1976), and *Jobs for the Hard-to-Employ: New Directions for a Public-Private Partnership* (1978).

issues as national security, foreign policy, and some defense policies, all of which have an impact on the market system. Nevertheless, we believe the concept of periodic evaluation should be applied to all types of government policy.*

CHANGING ROLE OF GOVERNMENT

The public sector of the economy has grown rapidly. There has been a proliferation of new social responsibilities that various groups have asked government to assume. As a result, the federal government has multiplied its area of involvement in the market system. More and more government effort is being directed toward cushioning individual risks and regulating personal and institutional conduct with which government was not previously concerned. The *cumulative* impact of these actions now impinges on all participants in the economy—employers, investors, workers, and consumers—whether in the public, nonprofit, or private sectors.

The combined total of federal, state, and local government expenditures, subsidies, credit guarantees, and other indirect programs has also increased sharply, and government expenditures are now equivalent to almost one-third of the gross national product, compared with one-quarter twenty years ago. Most of this increase in government expenditures is attributable to the rapid expansion of federal transfer payments to individuals and grants-in-aid to states. Over the past two decades, the combined value of these federal expenditures has expanded more than tenfold.

In some cases, government is stepping in because business did not respond to public demand for such measures as safer working conditions, an improved environment, and safer products. Business also contributes to government's expansion into the market system when it seeks controls on costs and prices or restrictions limiting the entry of new competitors into some industries.

The political system, with its goals of improving public well-being and achieving greater equality, is exerting more and more pressure on the economic process, which emphasizes efficiency. Even with the growing recognition that government action needs to be more cost-effective, there will undoubtedly be some conflict between the perceived goals of greater social responsibility and greater efficiency. Yet, in order to achieve a particular social goal, it can be self-defeating to reduce the efficiency of the market system. Although such action may benefit a few groups, the

*See memorandum by E. SHERMAN ADAMS, page 136.

interference with the market can be detrimental to the majority. Instead, this country must learn better ways of *using* markets to help achieve social goals.

Because both future improvements of society and its present condition depend on the health of the economy, the proposed solution to a given problem must take into account its impact on the effectiveness of markets. Government policies must be designed and implemented through programs that take full advantage of market forces and minimize discouragement of productive investments.

ASSESSING THE COSTS, BENEFITS, AND SIDE EFFECTS

Government involvement in markets costs this country billions of dollars.[2] These costs produce certain benefits to *some* groups, but it is often arguable whether such benefits are worth the cost. More important, the high cost of such government involvement causes a misallocation of resources that reduces the overall productivity of the economy. In some cases, benefits outweigh the cost of lower productivity improvement and economic growth; but in many cases, they do not. It is estimated that in 1974-75, indirect costs of environmental and worker safety and health regulations reduced the annual change in output per unit of input by 0.5 percentage points. This is equivalent to about one-fifth of the nation's average annual rate of growth since the end of World War II.[3]

This impact on economic growth would be less serious if the cost of meeting regulations, such as environmental standards, was imposed through one-time capital expenditures. However, regulatory policies that

---

2. A recent study of forty-eight large corporations, all members of the Business Roundtable, estimated the extra cost of regulations by six regulatory agencies at $2.6 billion in 1977. The study did not include indirect costs such as higher costs of innovation and construction of new plants and equipment. A variety of these indirect costs discourage capital investment and distort existing resources, which reduces the overall productivity of the economy. Arthur Andersen and Company, *Cost of Government Regulation Study*, Executive Summary, March 1979.

3. See Edward F. Denison, "Effects of Selected Changes in the Institutional and Human Environment upon Output per Unit of Input," *Survey of Current Business* 58, no. 1 (January 1978): 21–44.

require the adoption of the best available technology and the pursuit of zero-risk goals imply continual changes in standards. For example, there have been many changes in environmental and health and safety regulations since 1975, and the annual reduction in productivity because of these indirect costs has undoubtedly risen since then. Many forms of regulation stimulate a trend toward rising costs of production that, unless offset by rapid technological change, make it difficult to avoid chronic inflationary pressure in the economy. The cost of regulation as a result of inflationary impact is difficult to measure, but it is real and affects all groups in society.

Regulations are often contradictory and confusing. For example, Environmental Protection Agency and Interior Department regulations concerning the mining and burning of coal seriously constrain Department of Energy programs encouraging the use of coal. On a smaller scale, Health, Education, and Welfare Department regulations require that plastic liners be used in hospital wastebaskets for hygienic reasons, but the Occupational Safety and Health Administration (OSHA) prohibits their use, calling them a fire hazard. There is currently no effective procedure for minimizing inconsistencies among regulations. Both the Office of Management and Budget and the new Regulatory Council have recently compiled a useful inventory of forthcoming regulations. This is a good beginning, but it does not go far enough.

The cost of government involvement has taken many forms. Ill-considered government policies have led to artificial price restraints on scarce commodities, contradictory and ineffective expenditure programs, price-fixing, and limiting free entry into markets.

Both Congress and the executive branch have proposed reforms to check government expansion, and more and more states are putting the question of substantial tax relief on the ballot. However, even when taxpayers rebel, they do not often agree on what constitutes excessive government involvement. Virtually every economic, social, political, business, and ideological group wants something supported, regulated, or banned by government. And although there is evidence of a general public demand for cuts in government spending, there is also continued public support for improvements in some government programs.

Government can find it difficult to resist the temptation to do something for the benefit of some groups, even when this is accomplished at a large cost to the rest of society. Government frequently fails to consider whether a given problem really does need and justify public intervention.

Even when action appears justified, legislators and administrators have no effective way of determining the best manner in which government help should be given.

There are services, such as national defense, a system of law and order, and basic public education, that only government can and should guarantee. But there are other services that government cannot and should not provide. In order to redefine government's role in the market system, politicians, administrators, and the public can and should learn to ask the following critical questions about proposed policies: What evidence shows that a problem actually *requires* government involvement? What *form* should that action take? Can government action be *effective?* What are the *costs, benefits,* and *side effects?*

MAKING USE OF THE MARKET SYSTEM

The existence of competitive markets has been extremely important to this country's economic and political development. Historically, the function of business has been to supply the public with goods and services and to provide jobs and income, thereby increasing the nation's wealth. The economic growth and high standard of living this nation has achieved are largely measures of business's success in carrying out its economic responsibilities.

The competitive market is usually the most effective vehicle for allocating resources to produce most of the goods and services this country needs. It is generally efficient and flexible, and it can respond more quickly than government to the changing needs and preferences of individuals. Therefore, when government acts to correct or aid the market, that action should be conceived and executed insofar as possible in a way that works with the market, not against it. Where competition is absent, government has a responsibility to restore it. Where the market fails to take into account the costs of pollution or to supply adequate product information, government has a responsibility to provide the needed incentive.*

We believe that there are broad economic and social problems whose solutions depend on making greater use of the market system, rather than on relying on government. Once the political decision has been made that some type of government action is needed, legislators and those responsible for implementing policy should proceed to choose carefully *how* and *when* it should become involved. Rather than considering all choices available, policy makers far too often automatically increase specific public

*See memorandum by ROBERT R. NATHAN, page 136.

expenditures in the belief that spending alone can solve the problem. When regulation appears necessary, policy makers usually choose a command-and-control system, specifying not only the required results but also the method by which those results must be achieved. In this way, antipollution and safety specifications, for example, tend to become ends in themselves and even fail to achieve the goal of cleaner air or safer workplaces.

Detailed rules governing specific kinds of behavior are the most common form of government regulation. However, in many industries, cleaner air or safer workplaces could be achieved at less cost if government set the goals, timetables, and penalties and left it to industry to find the most efficient means of achieving the required results. For example, OSHA has usually preferred to demand changes in plant design rather than to permit the adoption of effective alternatives such as personal protection devices (safety goggles, ear plugs, and so on), even when such devices could secure a safe and healthy working environment at a small fraction of the cost of changing production methods or machinery.

NEW POLITICAL RESTRAINT

When, where, and how government becomes involved in markets or reduces its influence in markets are always political decisions. Legislators and other elected officials at all levels of government make these decisions based on their sense of the will of their various constituents. *Reform of the government decision-making process therefore must emerge from the political process.*

Political leaders need to recognize that the efficient operation of the market system and government's reduced role in it are crucial to solving the country's problems. In particular, they should, wherever possible, provide the participants in markets with an incentive and/or penalty to correct their own limitations and should convince voters that they will benefit from government involvement that is cost-effective and complements the performance of markets.

Voters have already clearly begun to realize that some government involvement has contributed to slower economic growth and raised prices and that in many areas services are inefficiently provided. Voters want government to be responsive *and* responsible. The powerful constituency for cost-effective government is ready to respond to political leadership. Referenda, elections, and polls have impressed many elected representatives with the fact that the public is demanding greater government efficiency and less government involvement.

We believe that the pursuit of responsible government policies is now also good politics. Politicians and concerned citizens currently recognize that it is in their interest to reappraise the impact of government actions on the long-term, overall health of the economy.

THE PROBLEM OF GOVERNMENT INVOLVEMENT*

On the basis of the analysis contained in subsequent chapters, this policy statement draws the following conclusions:**

- The expansion of government's role in markets has in many cases impaired the performance of the U.S. economy.

- The trend toward accelerating inflation, lower productivity, and sluggish economic growth has been exacerbated by the expansion of government expenditure programs and by regulatory policies that reduce the productivity of the economy.

- The growth of some public expenditure programs and some indirect incentive programs has made it difficult to reduce large federal budget deficits. Regulations have increased the costs of production, reduced productivity, discouraged capital investment, and raised prices, often without providing adequate compensating benefits.

- Government policy makers have often failed to recognize that the market system is an effective way of achieving policy goals and that the output of the market system must be permitted to expand in order to provide benefits to the public—consumers, workers, and shareholders.

- Improved economic performance and the achievement of social goals require that government involvement be reduced and that ineffective and inconsistent government programs be eliminated.

- When government involvement is justified, markets should be used wherever possible to implement policies. Restricting the operation of the market system or failing to encourage competitive markets is often the most inefficient way of achieving desirable economic and social goals simultaneously.

*See memorandum by PHILIP M. KLUTZNICK, page 137.
**See memorandum by FRAZAR B. WILDE, page 138.

● Weaknesses in the current policy-making process within the political system have initiated and continued to support the trend toward ineffective government interference with markets.

● The goal of slowing the growth of aggregate government expenditure should be supported. This type of constraint on the political decision-making process will not by itself solve the problem, but it will help.

● The decision-making process for public policy must provide policy makers with the information to redefine government's role and to modify counterproductive expenditure programs and regulations systematically.

SUMMARY OF RECOMMENDATIONS

We believe that the recommendations presented in this statement offer one approach toward a systematic and practical way of acting on these conclusions. Our recommendations suggest that proponents of major new policies state the objectives of proposed government action clearly enough to permit future evaluation of whether the objective is being met, state the potential impact on overall economic objectives, and present evidence to justify government's involvement and choice of technique. They also require that the results be independently evaluated relative to the goals and projections.

If these recommendations are put into practice, proponents of any major policies will learn to weigh what they promise more carefully and policy makers will have to take responsibility for the ineffectiveness as well as the effectiveness of any new actions.[4]

The recommendations summarized here are discussed in greater detail in subsequent chapters.

---

4. The terms *policy* and *program* are frequently used interchangeably in discussions of the role of government in the market system. In this statement, *government policy* is used to describe the general approach to carrying out a responsibility or dealing with a problem. A particular policy is likely to include a number of programs to implement the policy. For example, the government's welfare policy consists of a number of programs. We recommend requiring proponents of new *policies* to state their objectives in specific terms that will permit evaluation of whether these objectives have been achieved. Such evaluation requires scrutinizing *programs* or *groups*

New Criteria to Screen Requests for Government Intervention

We have developed a series of questions for screening government actions that could affect the market system. These questions are grouped under three criteria that should be satisfied with evidence before government action is taken. These criteria require defining the necessity for government action in terms of a market limitation, a social or political objective, and the feasibility and cost-effectiveness of the action. If these criteria are applied by policy makers, it will be easier to respond effectively to public pressure *and* to consider the overall impact of political decisions on the performance of the economy.

We recommend that the following three criteria and related questions (discussed in detail in Chapter 6) become the standard process for screening requests for government involvement.

1. Which type of market limitation (if any) is the government action attempting to correct? Absence of competition is one example of a market limitation. *Is government action necessary to correct this limitation?*

> What is the policy's objective?
>
> Will the policy increase competition by reducing restrictions on entry, by improving information, or by eliminating restraints on the price mechanism?
>
> Is government action required because the market is producing some undesirable side effect such as pollution?
>
> What impact will this have on other overall economic objectives, such as improved technological innovation, satisfactory economic growth, reduction of inflationary pressures, and a high level of employment?

---

of programs, rather than *policies*. In the case of government regulations, the term *policy* is used not only to describe the general approach to the problem but also to identify the techniques used to carry out the general policy. These implementation techniques are described as *policies* or, simply, *regulations*. The recommendations apply only to major policies. It is recommended that the Administration and Congress define the term *major* on the basis of the Council on Wage and Price Stability's recent experience in reviewing major regulations.

2. What social and/or political goal is the government seeking? A minimum standard of living for some citizens and equal opportunity for all citizens are examples of social objectives. *Is government action necessary to achieve these objectives?*

>What is the policy's objective?

>In what manner will the beneficiaries gain?

>Which citizens will bear the cost?

>What impact will this have on other overall economic objectives?

3. Is the proposed government solution to the problem feasible and cost-effective? There is a great distinction between the *desirability* of achieving certain objectives and the *feasibility* of achieving them. If it is decided that government action to correct a market limitation or achieve a social objective is justified, policy makers (in the Administration, in Congress, and in the independent regulatory agencies) should specify exactly how its action will achieve the stated objective and should demonstrate that it is cost-effective.

>Could the stated goal of the proposed government involvement be achieved more efficiently by eliminating an existing government involvement?

>Can the stated goal be achieved by *any* conceivable government action?

>What will the stated goal cost?

>What are the proposal's probable side effects, and what will they cost?

Policy makers should not automatically assume that government action is the best way to deal with an economic problem or achieve a social goal. Government involvement should be considered only if the market system is clearly incapable of dealing with the problem.*

Improving Procedures for Screening Policy Proposals

It is the President's responsibility to see that our recommended (or similar) criteria are utilized in decision making in the executive branch,

---

*See memorandum by ROBERT R. NATHAN, page 138.

and it is Congress's responsibility to see that the criteria are applied in legislative branch decisions.

There is no one simple way to bring about a more effective and systematic approach to government involvement in the market system. However, we believe that the following recommended actions will improve the effectiveness of public policies.*

Setting Criteria. The President should propose to Congress and should establish within the executive branch a list of criteria (such as those we have suggested) for determining the purpose, feasibility, and probable consequences of all major administrative and legislative proposals. Each bill or administrative proposal should clearly identify whether the proposed action meets the three criteria for screening a *new* government action or the criterion for eliminating an *existing* government involvement. The criteria listed on pages 92 to 97 have been proposed for this purpose.

Establishing Goals. The President should propose to Congress and should direct the executive branch to include a clear statement of objectives and anticipated results in each major bill or proposed administrative action. All statements of administrative agencies' objectives and expected results should be reviewed within the Administration.

Congress should also consider passing general legislation requiring every federal agency issuing regulations or conducting public programs to take into account various broader economic objectives that will be specified by Congress. Congress should take action to ensure that similar requirements are applied to the independent regulatory agencies.

If Congress requires broader economic objectives to be taken into account, it will in some instances mean amending the enabling legislation covering regulatory agencies. Congress itself may have originally designed the enabling legislation so that it actually prevented the President and the independent regulatory agencies from taking broader economic objectives into account when initiating regulatory policies.

Congress should be sure that its own legislation passes similar tests and that, in the case of complex laws, the legislative history accompanying new legislation provides additional needed clarification.

Choosing Methods. The President should propose to Congress and should establish within the executive branch a preferred order for the

---

*See memorandum by ROY L. ASH, page 139.

choice of methods of involvement. This preferred order should encourage the greatest reliance on markets. All major decisions to implement a new policy should be accompanied by an explanation of why a particular method was chosen over all other available methods.

Evaluating the Effectiveness of Policy

The Administration should develop a system for testing the effectiveness of major new policy proposals and selectively reviewing major ongoing federal programs. Under this system, a report comparing the results with the original goals should be made to the President on the second and fifth or sixth anniversaries of any new legislation.

Congress should consider requiring that each bill with a significant economic impact should include a funding provision for program evaluation. The primary oversight responsibility for each program should be assigned to a specific committee, which should hold oversight hearings at least once every five or six years. The oversight committee should request the appropriate agency, an outside independent group, and/or the General Accounting Office to prepare an evaluation report that would be part of the oversight hearings. The hearings should assess whether the programs have measured up to their original objectives. We also recommend that the budget and appropriations processes be strengthened to complement the screening and evaluation proposals.

Every four years, the Speaker of the House, the House minority leader, and the Senate majority and minority leaders should appoint a bipartisan commission of experts to appraise the effectiveness of the congressional oversight process.

The General Accounting Office should provide expert advice on evaluation procedures, assist in oversight proceedings, and provide staff to evaluate the oversight process.

A program should be instituted for coordinating the expiration and evaluation dates of interrelated programs, for shifting all permanently authorized programs to a periodic reauthorization schedule if they could be more effectively handled this way, for scheduling periodic evaluations of all permanently authorized programs, and for providing for evaluations by more than one committee when jurisdictions overlap.

The applications of these evaluation recommendations to major existing policies will make it easier to reduce existing government involvement by eliminating ineffective programs and policies.

Special Presidential Action

Once every eight years, the President should appoint a special commission of outstanding public and private leaders to consider the current relationship between government and the market system, to review government's methods of involvement in the market system, and to make recommendations to the President and Congress for improvements.

Publicizing Ineffective Government Involvement

Reforming the process that results in government involvement in the markets requires highlighting important issues in the arena of public debate. Requiring executive agencies to describe their least effective programs is a possible way of accomplishing this. Another way is to require that the Government Operations Committee in the House and the Governmental Affairs Committee in the Senate prepare annual oversight reports that indicate what changes actually occurred as a result of both favorable and unfavorable oversight reviews. These committees should call on the General Accounting Office, the Congressional Budget Office, and the Congressional Research Service for staff support in preparing the annual oversight reports. These reports should clearly identify if and how each part of the legislative process and the bureaucratic structure responds to the policy changes proposed in the reformed oversight process.

IMPLICATIONS OF IMPROVING THE POLICY-MAKING PROCESS

Implementation of the recommendations offered in this policy statement requires no new agency. However, our proposals for screening, adopting, and finally designing public policies and for periodically evaluating them do imply that congressional committee staff should be strengthened so that they can interpret evaluation studies. This does not mean that there should be an increase in the overall number of staff assigned to congressional committees. Our proposals do mean that modest additional staff resources with the necessary analytic skills will be required to strengthen some of the congressional-support organizations, such as the Congressional Budget Office and the General Accounting Office, for conducting evaluations.

In the executive branch of government, our proposals can be implemented by reallocating existing resources. Most agencies already have substantial budgets for research and evaluation. We believe these funds can be reallocated to provide the professional staff and technical support for screening, adopting, and designing new proposals and for evaluating existing programs.

The success of our proposals for redefining government's role in the market system will depend on whether policy makers follow the reformed process for screening and reviewing major policies. Our proposals contain several concepts which attempt to ensure that policy makers justify their actions and *provide support to those policy officials in the Administration and Congress who want to curtail or modify ineffective policies.*

For each branch of government, there is provision for certifying that proponents of new policies are in compliance with the requirements for the screening, adopting, and designing of proposals. In the executive branch, certification is provided by the Office of Management and Budget or some other unit within the Executive Office of the President. In Congress, the Rules Committees would perform this task based on the advice of either the Congressional Budget Office or the General Accounting Office.

Compliance with the screening process on the part of the independent regulatory agencies is encouraged through requiring the Congressional Budget Office or the General Accounting Office to review proposed major regulations for compliance with the recommended procedures. At the public hearing, the congressional-support organization (CBO or GAO) should present its assessment of whether the agency has considered the potential impact of the proposed rule on overall economic objectives as well as the impact on the stated purposes of the regulation. This requirement does not restrict the statutory authority of the independent regulatory agencies to issue new rules, but it does provide the public with information on the potential effect of proposed rules before they are implemented.

Our recommendations also propose evaluation procedures that will identify the successes and failures of major existing programs and regulatory policies. Our suggested procedures ensure that the results of these evaluations become part of the public debate. Ineffective programs and regulations may, of course, survive this debate, but the failure of policy makers to correct failures will become more obvious.

If an approach similar to the one we are recommending is adopted, we are confident that public policies will be improved. There is reason for our optimism. Considerable bipartisan support now exists for a number of legislative proposals that are similar in intent to our recommendations. Over thirty regulatory reform bills (including an Administration bill) and many bills designed to reform ineffective direct expenditure programs have recently been introduced in Congress. During the Ninety-sixth Congress, several of these bills will be seriously considered for enactment. Regulatory reform and the control of direct expenditure programs are now clearly legislative priorities of the Administration and Congress. This demonstrates the strong desire of some public officials to improve the policy-making process.

2.

The Market System and Government's Role in the Economy: Strengths and Limitations

THE UNITED STATES RELIES MORE HEAVILY than most nations (even industrialized ones) on its market system in the belief that the economy is best served by a large private sector with only limited government influence on resource allocation and pricing decisions. In contrast, the majority of the world's population lives in countries in which the central government plays a much stronger role in directing the economic system and in which the market system is used less frequently to decide what, how, and for whom goods and services are produced.

Countries that possess healthy market systems produce a very large share of the world's output. This is not entirely an accident of history.

THE MARKET SYSTEM'S STRENGTHS

The greatest strengths of the market system lie in its efficiency and flexibility.

The system responds to the preferences of individual buyers so that what is produced is decided automatically, without any centralized government planning.

It is responsive to wants and scarcities, and through the profit mechanism's automatic system of rewards and penalties, it encourages an efficient allocation of resources.

It is flexible and corrects errors before there is a major imbalance between what individual products are produced and what is demanded.

It provides both short-run and long-run incentives that encourage growth and innovation.

Efficient production in the competitive marketplace is fostered when business attempts to optimize its long-run profits. That attempt requires firms to use resources efficiently and to use the most effective production methods, thus minimizing private and social costs. Only if business is successful, earns profits, and makes investments will the economy be able to increase future job opportunities, curb inflation, raise the real income of workers, and provide the tax base necessary for financing other social objectives.

The market mechanism permits economic decisions by individual and institutional buyers and sellers on a decentralized basis and yet interrelates their myriad decisions. Individuals and businesses can determine for themselves how to use their economic resources: to consume, to invest, or to save. By establishing the prices that are paid for products and for the resources used to produce them, the market mechanism rewards production of goods and services that buyers judge worth their cost and penalizes those that buyers judge not worth their cost. In doing so, it promotes the efficient use of the nation's productive resources because it encourages the shift of resources toward increased production of what buyers want most. According to Swedish economist Assar Lindbeck:

> It is exactly the market system, with competition and free entry, that allows a rather far-reaching decentralization of economic decisions and initiatives in a world with strong interdependence between the decisions and activities of various economic agents. Without a reasonably well-functioning market system, a far-reaching centralization of economic decision-making and responsibilities would be necessary; such a situation would largely destroy pluralism.

This is perhaps easiest to see if we try to visualize what the economic system would look like without markets for goods, labor, and capital. For then it would be necessary to have some central agency that determined what the preferences of individual consumers were, or should be; that told firms how and what to produce, qualitatively and quantitatively; that decided to whom different goods and services should be delivered and what new products should be introduced.

A heavy reliance on markets has saved us from: a strongly centralized command economy, where pluralism could hardly exist because pluralism presupposes decentralized decision-making and a considerable autonomy of households, firms, and other organizations that are engaged in economic activities, including the production and distribution of information and of what we call culture.[1]

The system of rewards and penalties that lies at the heart of a competitive market endows it with vital self-correcting forces. Buyers who are careless in their choice of purchases must live with, and learn from, their mistakes. Producers who fail to recognize changes in the wants of buyers as expressed in market demand also risk losses. So do those who fail to economize in the use of labor, capital, and natural resources. Wage and salary differentials, as well as employment opportunities, generally guide workers into the most productive pursuits, as measured by the value of their output.

Dynamic change is indispensable to long-run economic progress, and producers in a competitive market cannot long continue to employ obsolete methods of production or to produce goods that are outmoded. The pursuit of economic rewards (wages, profits, dividends, or rents) is crucial in motivating investment and reallocating resources efficiently. The rewards provided by the market system encourage improvements in technology and the development of new products. Once market pressures to correct errors and impel improvements are perceived, change is rapid. In most cases, the less the market system is controlled and the more competitive it is—both nationally and internationally—the speedier its self-correcting adjustments are. Flexibility in the pursuit of economic returns is the market's hallmark.

---

1. Assar Lindbeck, *Can Pluralism Survive?* Eleventh Annual William K. McInally Memorial Lecture, Graduate School of Business Administration, University of Michigan (Ann Arbor: University of Michigan, 1977), pp. 8–9.

THE MARKET SYSTEM

The *market system* is one way of organizing the economy to decide what, how, and for whom goods and services are produced. The *public sector,* overseen by the government, is another way and is characterized by some form of government planning. In the public sector, both the choice of the goods and services produced and the nature of decisions leading to their production are quite different from those in the market system.

In the market system, individual (and institutional) consumers and producers make decisions on the basis of prices and costs. In the public sector, voters and legislators or appointed officials make decisions on the basis of political criteria. National defense, education, and subsidies to cultural activities, to farmers, and to specific industries are financed out of taxes paid by all consumers, even though the average consumer may not consume some of these goods and services. The supply of goods and services responds to social pressure and political power. In the market system, economic purchasing power determines what is demanded and supplied. However, the legitimacy of both systems lies in what they can achieve for all citizens.

The boundary between the market system and the public sector is often unclear. There is interaction between producers in the market system and producers in the public sector. For example, there is a large segment of privately owned economic activity in which the government controls the operation of the price mechanism and entry of firms into the industry. The nature of an industry, such as the utilities and, in the past, railroads, may protect the producer from the entry of new firms and give him or her potential monopoly power over prices. Similarly, some goods and services are produced by nonprofit organizations in the private sector but with production subsidized by the government. Such organizations are not part of the public sector; neither are they always part of the market system. In some segments of the health care industry, for example, government involvement may be so extensive that it affects the supply and demand for the service and severely restricts the operation of the price mechanism.

Even though the market system relies on the price mechanism and places no explicit restrictions on entry, there is great variation among individual markets. The degree of competition within markets varies according to the number of buyers and sellers, the information available to consumers, the geographic area of the market, importance of transportation costs, and the availability of competing products. In the private sector, markets vary greatly in the degree of competitiveness, ranging from relatively competitive local or national markets to relatively noncompetitive local or national markets. In all cases, however, the consumer has a choice.

Even when a few large firms dominate an industry, the consumer is still likely to have a considerable number of options. Entry into less competitive markets is never entirely restricted. There is always some competition, and the price mechanism makes possible the efficient allocation of resources. Public policy should not strive to restrict the operation of the price mechanism; rather it should provide the environment that makes markets competitive both domestically and internationally. Public policy to ensure competition in markets should not be determined statistically by the number of firms in the industry; rather, it should be based on whether the consumer benefits from efficient production and has alternate sources of supply. In addition, antitrust policy should recognize that foreign competition is an important consideration in determining the degree of competition in markets.

THE MARKET SYSTEM'S LIMITATIONS

Both the existence and the efficiency of the market system depend on the broader sociopolitical environment. The market system cannot do all the work of the nation. For example, it does not guarantee a safe environment. But stepping in to correct or supplant the market has become a very complicated and difficult task. For example, in some cases, individual customers at a grocery store cannot reasonably be expected to protect themselves fully against harmful ingredients in the absence of minimum standards of labeling set by the government. Yet, it is sometimes difficult to define minimum standards of safety and to apply them without raising costs excessively.

The market system does not always *guarantee* competition. There can be too few active sellers or buyers in a particular marketplace to offer the alternatives needed to protect the interests of all participants.*

Finally, the market system provides little or no payment to individuals who cannot or do not produce what other people want and, in contrast, rewards providers of scarce goods or services that are in great demand. People can occupy strategic economic positions because of fortuitous circumstances as well as because of hard work and foresight. The resulting distribution of income and wealth is not always considered just. The market system on its own extends no direct helping hand to those who cannot participate in it.*

THE GOVERNMENT'S STRENGTHS

The government's strengths can correct the market's limitations. Business leaders and the public have long recognized that government has a responsibility to establish the rules of the game for participants in the economic system. These rules include protecting against collusive or uneconomic predatory actions to restrict competition, recognizing property rights, enforcing contract rights, establishing standards of societal performance, and maintaining adequate information for buyers. All these rules are essential if the market system is to live up to its potential. Accordingly, the system's advocates support antitrust policy. However, such policy must take into account the expansion of international markets and international competition and the magnitude of the financial investment necessary to achieve the benefits of new technology in some industries.**

*See memoranda by FLETCHER L. BYROM, page 139.
**See memorandum by ROBERT R. NATHAN, page 140.

WHAT THE MARKET SYSTEM DOES

Let us consider the city of New York. Without a constant flow of goods in and out of the city, it would be on the verge of starvation within a week. A variety of the right kinds and amounts of food is required. From the surrounding counties, from 50 states, and from the far corners of the world, goods have been traveling for days and months with New York as their destination.

How is it that 12 million people [in the New York City area] are able to sleep easily at night, without living in mortal terror of a breakdown in the elaborate economic processes upon which the city's existence depends? For all this is undertaken without coercion or centralized direction by any conscious body! . . . Hundreds of thousands of commodities are produced by millions of people more or less of their own volition and without central direction or master plan.

This functioning alone is convincing proof that a competitive system of markets and prices — whatever else it may be, however imperfectly it may function — is not a system of chaos and anarchy. There is in it a certain order and orderliness. It works.

A competitive system is an elaborate mechanism for unconscious coordination through a system of prices and markets, a communication device for pooling the knowledge and actions of millions of diverse individuals. Without a central intelligence, it solves one of the most complex problems imaginable, involving thousands of unknown variables and relations.

Source: Paul A. Samuelson, *Economics,* 10th ed. (New York: McGraw-Hill Book Company, 1976), pp. 41–42.

Increasingly, government has also attempted to define and enforce standards of fairness and ethical behavior in both labor and product markets. This is an exceedingly difficult and, in some cases, a questionable role of government. The government can act constructively when private-market participants fail to take into account important public consequences of their actions. Until recently, excessive environmental pollution occurred mainly because public and private polluters were not motivated to change and were able to ignore the costs their effluents imposed on others. In principle, the legal system now provides a check on polluters. But government action through economic incentives may be an appropriate alternative if it reduces burdensome litigation and permits the adoption of the least costly corrective measures in order to achieve relative environmental objectives.

The government can play an important role by fostering equal opportunity. Freedom of opportunity to enter and participate in the market system either as an employee or as an employer or entrepreneur is important to the effectiveness and legitimacy of the market system.

The government can and must directly pay for what are called *public goods*. Public goods are products or services that people need and use collectively and that only government should procure (even if decentralized private markets could provide them). National defense, foreign policy, the judicial system, and protection of human and property rights at home are all collective needs. Similarly, the government needs to guarantee the availability of certain goods and services, such as basic education, to all.

Government is responsible for much more than the efficient operation of the market system; it is also responsible for some degree of equity in society. However, the goals of equity and efficiency are sometimes in conflict with each other. Government programs to promote equity are likely to result in lower efficiency of the market system. Tax policies and income-maintenance programs can reduce productive effort, and interference with the price mechanism can distort the use of productive resources. Few would deny that there is a need to make a compromise between efficiency and equity.

> Correcting deprivation and preserving economic efficiency are both desirable goals, which unfortunately sometimes conflict with each other. Of necessity we must live with compromises between the two. We cannot aid low-income groups to the point of destroying the incentive system of the market that marshalls the effort and economic activity.... Nor can we

tolerate kids with empty stomachs, adults selling apples, and oldsters with begging cups in the name of a greater aggregate real GNP. There are serious, legitimate grounds for debate and controversy among informed citizens about how much assistance should be provided.[2]

Resolving any conflict between the goals of equity and efficiency will remain a crucial issue for all groups in society. We believe that in addition to making an important contribution to the societal wealth that is needed to sustain and improve the quality of life, business has a responsibility to foster social equity by responsible behavior in product and labor markets. However, if public policies are necessary to meet equity objectives, through either tax or expenditure programs, they should insofar as possible minimize market distortions through creating disincentives for the participants in the market system. Attempts to achieve equity objectives through interference with the price mechanism can be particularly harmful to efficiency. Consequently, equity objectives are often never achieved. Rent control is a classic illustration of failure to achieve greater equity through restricting the price mechanism. Rent control has not only reduced the supply of housing units in the market but has also failed to assist most of those in need of housing.

The solution to many problems of inequity depends on a strong, productive economy. The elderly, the disabled, and the unemployed are indirectly supported by a system that creates greater opportunities for their participation. A productive economy is also necessary to finance government assistance programs.

THE GOVERNMENT'S LIMITATIONS

If one of government's strengths lies in establishing the rules of the game for the market, one of government's limitations lies in its tendency to lose sight of the purpose of the game, which is to benefit all participants in the economic system—consumers, workers, and shareholders. These benefits will be achieved only if there are adequate incentives, including profits, to stimulate the saving and investment necessary for economic growth.

---

2. Arthur M. Okun, *Capitalism and Democracy: Some Unifying Principles,* The Columbia University, McGraw-Hill Lectures on Business and Society, October 31, 1978, p. 12.

Ineffective government intervention frequently results from the way policy decisions are reached. Public policies aimed at correcting the shortcomings of the private-market system often do not succeed. Government often attempts to do more than it can. Decisions in the political process frequently confuse means with ends. Political solutions to economic problems often tend to be shortsighted, choosing immediate benefits that result in even greater long-run costs. Examples of these confusions can be found in wasteful regulations aimed at protecting workers and consumers, in artificial restraints on price increases for scarce commodities, in a confusing and often inconsistent array of tax and welfare programs, and in statutes and regulations (often rationalized on other grounds) that fix prices or deny free entry into markets for the purpose of protecting established interests.

Government has inadequate mechanisms for self-correction compared with those provided by market forces. Civil servants face no equivalent of operating losses, disappearance of customers, creditors' suits, or threatened bankruptcy, all of which impel changes. Outmoded programs perpetuate themselves, often vigorously supported by a coalition of their beneficiaries, administrators, employees, and legislative creators or overseers. Adaptation of spending, taxing, loan-guarantee, and regulatory programs to changing needs and technology is slow, and too little attention is given to finding better ways of dealing with public needs. The tax burden of many programs is so widely distributed that these programs generate little political opposition. As a result, it is difficult to terminate small programs, and there is little opposition to new ones, which are frequently designed to have larger budgets in future years. However, if the direct and indirect costs of programs that seem individually insignificant are added up, it may become clear that their total cost may have a detrimental impact on the economic system.[3]

Legislators, administrators of expenditure programs, and regulators are slow to respond because the evidence that a change is needed must be obvious and persuasive not only to the regulator but also to a large sector of the regulated. Even after the need is obvious, information must be gathered, hearings held, orders issued, and appeals accommodated, resulting in further delay. Moreover, for the regulated, regulation may

---

3. For further discussion of this problem, see Michael H. Moskow, *Strategic Planning in Business and Government* (New York: Committee for Economic Development, December 1978), pp. 30–31.

ultimately become an end in itself because it provides security, regardless of the cost to society.

Legislation covering many expenditure programs and regulations tends to be out of date because it was framed according to an earlier situation in an industry, an old technology no longer widely used, previous standards of quality, and the earlier scope of the market. Regulation tends to insulate firms against pressures to reduce costs and prices and thereby reduces pressures to enlarge markets.

Government regulatory policy has resulted in excessively detailed and restrictive government actions. The reasons for this development include excessive reliance on legal processes of resolving complaints, regulation by forbidding a practice rather than by requiring a result, the complexities of many of the problems that government programs are intended to solve, and the difficulty of measuring success in solving them.

The result is a ponderous and conflicting array of government programs and regulations that often unintentionally or inappropriately benefit particular groups at the expense of others. Private economic stakes in political decisions are so large that government is under pressure to benefit special rather than national interests. Policy makers must improve their mechanism for screening the proposals of special-interest groups so that the nation and its people can receive more benefit from the market system than they do now.

3.

The Growing Role of Government in the Economy: Expenditures and Indirect Incentives

ONE OF THE MOST IMPORTANT RESPONSIBILITIES of government is providing the framework for economic stabilization and growth. The fiscal and monetary policies through which government fulfills this responsibility influence the climate in which the market system functions. This chapter focuses on the growth of the more specific forms of government involvement through expenditure and indirect incentive policies such as subsidies, special tax arrangements, loans, and loan guarantees. This type of involvement results in important economic interactions with a wide range of individual markets. (Chapter 4 describes government's administrative interaction with markets through regulation and appraises the growth of regulation. The discussion of these two types of policies has been separated because each is determined through different procedures and any improvements in policy making must recognize these differences.)

Any attempt to redefine government's role in the market system must recognize the significance for the operation of the market system of the expansion of expenditure programs. For example, the growth of a federal employment and training program to $12 billion in annual expenditures or the introduction of a major new defense program has considerable influence in a large number of individual markets.

Another reason for reviewing expenditure growth is that it is frequently difficult to distinguish the market implications of some expenditure programs from the market implications of regulations. Legislative proposals affecting the health care industry are introduced ostensibly as expenditure programs and included in the annual budget. Many of these legislative proposals, such as those concerned with containing the increase in hospital costs, do involve federal expenditures, but their regulatory impact is frequently as important as their expenditure impact. Such legislation, if enacted, will affect the market for health care services. Therefore, any attempt to discipline government's role in the market system must recognize the growth in both federal expenditures and federal regulations.

GROWTH OF PUBLIC EXPENDITURES AND EMPLOYMENT

Over the past two decades, government's involvement in the market system has burgeoned. Public employment now represents almost 17 percent of total civilian employment (see Figure 1), an increase of about 5 percentage points (or 40 percent) in twenty years. This increase has occurred entirely among state and local employees. Total government expenditures (federal, state, and local) are now equal to about 33 percent of GNP[1] (see Figure 2). Both federal and state-local expenditures have increased in importance to the rest of the economy. Federal expenditures

---

1. Each of these percentages is inexact. For example, the distinction between workers in a public transit system and those in a privately operated transit system or between teachers in public and private education systems is indeed a fine one, especially when the private systems receive substantial subsidies from government. Similarly, government expenditures are not a reliable measure of the role of government. A specific government policy may have far more economic influence than its budget indicates.

have now risen to 22.4 percent of GNP; state and local expenditures have also increased, but about half of this growth is due to the rise in federal grants to state and local governments.

The nature of government's new level of involvement can be illustrated by examining the changing distribution of expenditures. Figure 3 shows that the composition of federal purchases of goods and services has changed significantly. As is to be expected in peacetime, the relative importance of defense expenditures has diminished rather significantly over the past twenty years. This decline contrasts with the growing importance of nondefense expenditures. The most significant change in the pattern has been the rapid increase in domestic transfer payments and federal expenditures through grants-in-aid to state and local governments. Between 1957 and 1959, spending for domestic transfer payments and grants-in-aid was equivalent to 5.4 percent of GNP; but between 1977 and 1979, it is estimated to equal 12.7 percent of GNP. This reflects the expansion of social programs during the 1960s and 1970s as well as a substantial increase in grants-in-aid. This rise and shift in government expenditures has contributed to a larger public sector by increasing the number of employees at the state and local levels needed to deliver expanded social services. Such changes have also altered the nature of the private sector by affecting the mix of goods and services it produces.

What has stimulated the trend toward a larger public sector? Consumption of personal services has increased as real family income has risen. There has been an overall increase in demand for services traditionally supplied by government, such as education, outdoor recreation in parks, and highways. This increase appears to be associated with the growth in real family income. In addition, demographic changes in the population, as well as political pressure, have caused a rapid expansion in transfer payments to individuals.

A rapid rise in living standards has increased the public sector in other ways as well. Higher levels of real income have permitted the public to demand that the government deal with problems, such as greater pollution and congested highways, that are some of the unintended effects of economic growth.[2]

---

2. William J. Baumol and Wallace E. Oates, "The Cost Disease of the Personal Services and the Quality of Life," in *The Urban Economy*, ed. H. Hochman (New York: W. W. Norton, 1976), pp. 41–56.

Figure 1: Growth in Public Employment

Public Employment as Percent of Civilian Employment

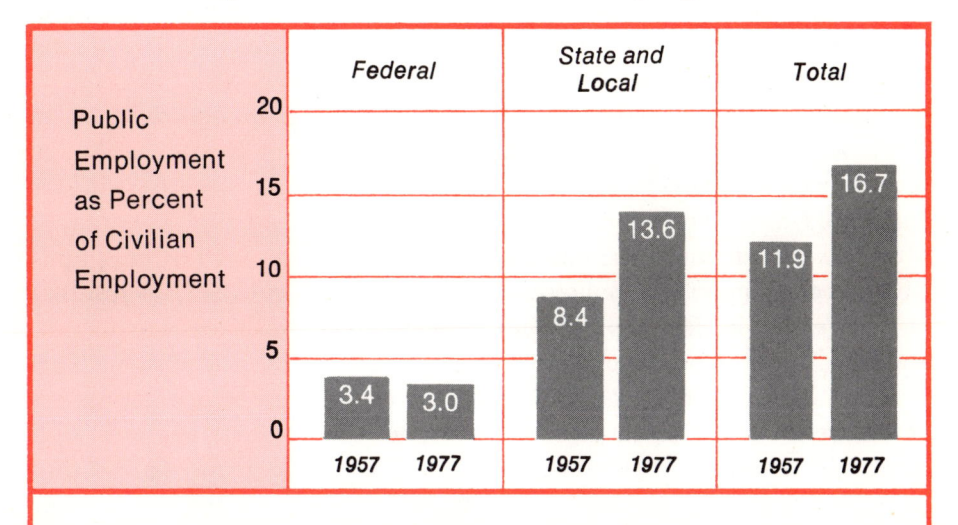

	Federal	State and Local	Total
1957	3.4	8.4	11.9
1977	3.0	13.6	16.7

Figure 2: Growth in Public Expenditures[a]

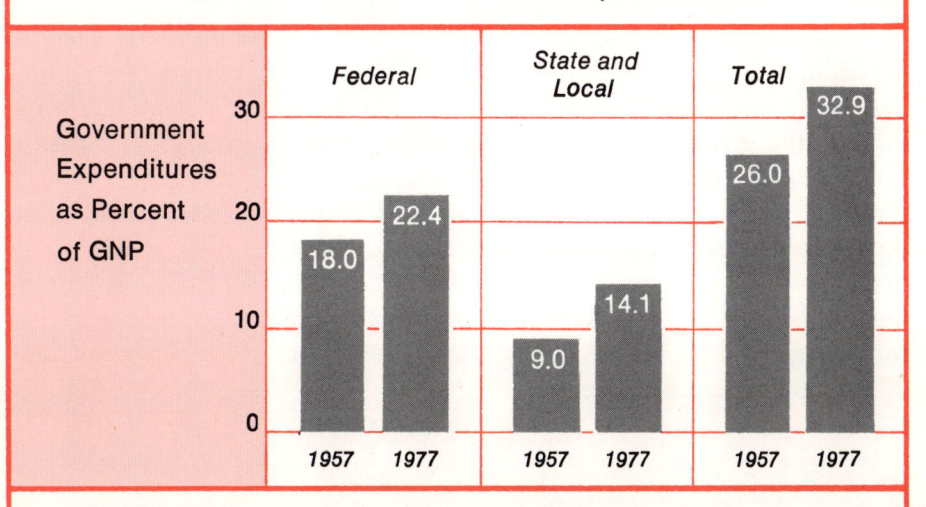

Government Expenditures as Percent of GNP

	Federal	State and Local	Total
1957	18.0	9.0	26.0
1977	22.4	14.1	32.9

[a] Federal grants to state and local governments are included in both federal and state and local expenditures, but the duplication is eliminated in the combined total.

Source: Office of Management and Budget, Executive Office of the President, *Special Analyses: Budget of the United States Government, Fiscal Year 1979* (Washington, D.C.: U.S. Government Printing Office, 1978), Special Analyses B and H.

In general, expanded population, increased urbanization, and the technologies of mass production, mass distribution, and mass communication have yielded, as by-products, a host of social and environmental problems that no advanced industrial society has been able to avoid or to remedy. In the United States, as in other nations, public response to these modern problems has impelled the government to try to assuage such difficulties as best it could. In the process, government expenditures and employment have mounted.

The growth and distribution of direct federal expenditure programs have become important policy issues. Expenditure growth has resulted in a larger public sector in which decisions about what services to produce and how to produce them are essentially political decisions. This general trend has produced a multitude of sometimes conflicting expenditure programs. Because of the nature of the public decision-making process, it has become increasingly difficult to modify many expenditure programs or even to eliminate them when the need for them no longer exists. This has produced a relative decline in the role of markets within the economy.

The changing distribution of government expenditures has affected individual markets in the private sector. Defense expenditures for capital equipment are mostly made up of purchases through contracts with firms in the private sector; nondefense expenditures are mostly for programs implemented through agencies in the public sector. Even though there has been an increase in nondefense purchases from the private sector, that increase has not been enough to offset the relative decline in private-market contracts that has occurred as a result of the decline in defense expenditures. This would not be an important problem except for the fact that in many cases markets are a more efficient way of producing goods and services.

GROWTH OF GOVERNMENT INDIRECT INCENTIVE POLICIES

In addition to direct expenditures, the federal government uses a broad array of indirect policies, including special tax arrangements, various forms of subsidies, direct loans, and loan guarantees, to achieve its diverse goals. These instruments are another avenue through which government has become more heavily involved in the economic system.

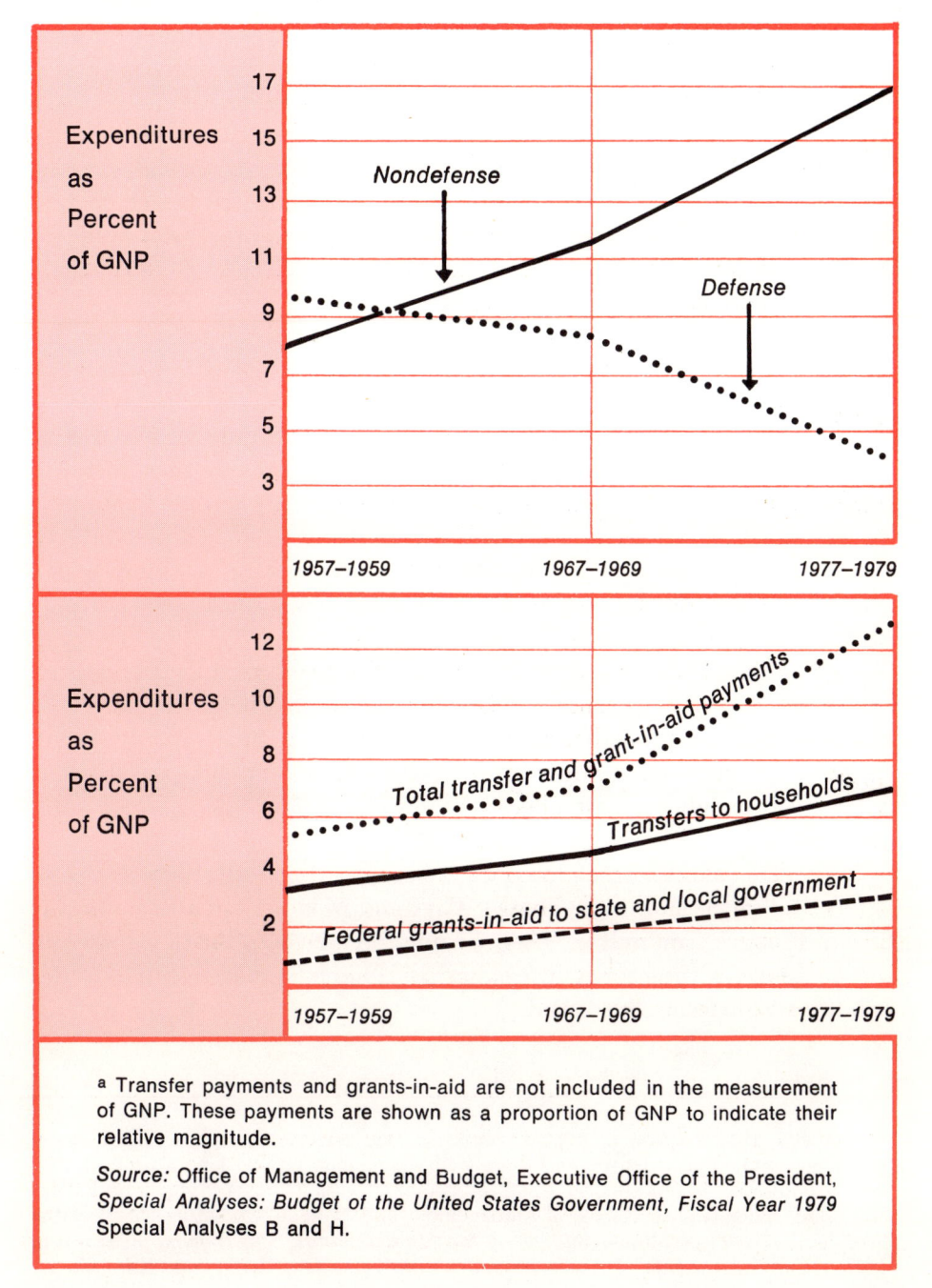

Figure 3: Changing Distribution of Federal Expenditures

Expenditures as Percent of GNP

Nondefense

Defense

1957–1959   *1967–1969*   *1977–1979*

Expenditures as Percent of GNP

Total transfer and grant-in-aid payments

Transfers to households

Federal grants-in-aid to state and local government

1957–1959   *1967–1969*   *1977–1979*

[a] Transfer payments and grants-in-aid are not included in the measurement of GNP. These payments are shown as a proportion of GNP to indicate their relative magnitude.

Source: Office of Management and Budget, Executive Office of the President, *Special Analyses: Budget of the United States Government, Fiscal Year 1979* Special Analyses B and H.

Special Tax Arrangements

Differential tax treatments are exceptions to the normal structure of the individual and corporate income tax.[3] The purpose of these special arrangements is either to encourage a particular economic activity (such as investment, home ownership, or state and local borrowing) or to assist individuals (such as the aged or the unemployed) in special circumstances. Figure 4 shows the magnitude of such tax treatment that is applied to individuals and organizations in various functional areas of government activity as reflected in the U.S. budget. That overall magnitude has more than doubled during the 1970s.

The 1978 estimate of the aggregate magnitude of differential tax arrangements is only approximate. In fact, it is impossible to sum up accurately all the individual special tax arrangements. The opportunity to benefit from such a tax arrangement may place the individual or corporate taxpayer in a different marginal tax bracket. Because the effect this opportunity has on the aggregate tax situation of all taxpayers can only be estimated, it is not accurate to aggregate numerous differential tax arrangements. Similarly, the definition of what constitutes a differential is arbitrary because the normal tax structure is based on subjective judgment.

Differential tax arrangements are likely to have considerable impact on economic behavior in many individual markets. There are, however, two important questions that should be asked about their growth: What type of economic behavior does the government wish to influence? Is this policy instrument the most effective way to achieve the government's objective?

Specific changes in the tax code are reviewed periodically within the executive branch and in the House Ways and Means Committee and the Senate Finance Committee. There is now greater coordination between the decisions of these committees and the budget process in which expenditure policies are reviewed.

---

3. Actually, the situation is not so simple as this statement implies. There is no historical normal tax structure, and there is no agreement on how long a new tax provision should be termed *abnormal* before becoming *normal*. For a discussion of these and other difficulties, see Office of Management and Budget, Executive Office of the President, *Special Analyses: Budget of the United States Government, Fiscal Year 1976* (Washington, D.C.: U.S. Government Printing Office, 1975), pp. 101–102.

Figure 4: Differentially Lower Tax Treatment (billions)

	1970	*1975*	*1978*
Agriculture	$0.9	$1.1	$1.1
Health	3.2	5.8	9.8
Manpower	0.6	0.7	4.3
Education	0.8	1.0	1.7
International	0.3	1.5	2.1
Housing	8.7	12.9	16.0
Natural resources and energy	2.0	4.1	3.1
Transportation	—	0.1	0.9
Commerce and industry	14.1	19.3	33.8
Other	9.4	13.1	22.6

Source: Joint Economic Committee, U.S. Congress, *Federal Subsidy Programs* (Washington, D.C.: U.S. Government Printing Office, October 1974), p. 5; and Office of Management and Budget, Executive Office of the President, *Special Analyses: Budget of the United States Government, Fiscal Year 1979,* pp. 148–174.

Subsidies

Subsidies are sometimes justified by their supporters as promoting economic growth, maintaining full employment, protecting defense production capability, fostering price stability, and influencing the balance of trade. Unlike government regulations and other policy instruments, subsidies do not *compel* businesses or individuals to behave in a particular way. What they do is *encourage or discourage* particular private-market behavior.

The magnitude of federal subsidies and related programs in terms of gross budgetary costs is presented in Figure 5. Although the 1978 figures are limited in their scope and do not include some of the newer programs, they clearly show the growing importance of subsidies and related programs in the economy. Figure 5 shows that from 1970 to 1975, there was a rapid increase in such programs. Over the last several years, growth slowed substantially; and in 1978, these forms of subsidy were equivalent to about $37 billion. In 1975, the most recent year for which data are complete, benefit-in-kind subsidies (consisting of the provision of goods and services, especially for food and health, at less than cost) were by far the most important. Direct cash subsidies are next in importance; their greatest expansion has been in the areas of manpower, education, and housing. Credit subsidies are much less significant, and their magnitude has fluctuated over the past decade.

A traditional rationalization for a subsidy is that it corrects market limitations. For example, an industry possessing a natural monopoly might be regulated through subsidies. In that case, prices are set at levels that cannot cover the firm's overhead. By subsidizing such an industry, the government permits prices to fall to a level that encourages enough demand to allow the industry to take advantage of the economies of scale inherent in its technology. In recent years, government has granted subsidies to semiprivate corporations operating postal services, passenger railroads, and satellite communications because these industries have characteristics of a natural monopoly.

A similar argument is used to justify subsidizing an industry that will have beneficial side effects. For example, renovation of slum housing benefits not only the houses improved but also the entire neighborhood. In such cases, there is usually not sufficient private incentive to encourage firms to take action. A subsidy may restore that incentive.

Broadly defined, subsidies include not only direct cash payments to private groups but also special tax preferences, low-interest loans, and purchase or sale of goods and services at other than market prices.* A subsidy involves a change in an existing price or cost relationship made by the government in expectation of, or in return for, certain behavior by the recipient. For example, the federal government has made considerable use of credit guarantees since the 1930s. These guarantees influence the allocation of resources and represent a cost when made, even though they appear as a government expenditure only if the government has to honor the repayment of the loan.

In recent years, indirect subsidies (farm price supports, public housing) have been used extensively to raise or stabilize the income of specific groups, even though it is often argued that direct cash transfers are a more efficient means of accomplishing this aim.

*See memorandum by E. SHERMAN ADAMS, page 140.

Figure 5: Summary of Federal Subsidy and Related Program Costs (billions)

	Direct cash subsidies 1970	Direct cash subsidies 1975	Direct cash subsidies 1978	Credit Subsidies 1970	Credit Subsidies 1975	Credit Subsidies 1978[a]	Benefit-in-kind subsidies 1970	Benefit-in-kind subsidies 1975	Benefit-in-kind subsidies 1978[a]	Total order of magnitude 1970	Total order of magnitude 1975	Total order of magnitude 1978[a]
Agriculture	$4.4	$0.6	N/A	$0.4	$0.7	$1.7	—	—	—	4.8	1.4	1.7
Food	—	—	—	—	—	—	1.5	5.9	8.8	1.5	5.9	8.8
Health	0.8	0.6	—	—	—	—	4.6	10.2	17.3	5.4	10.5	17.3
Manpower	2.0	3.3	—	—	—	—	0.1	0.1	—	2.0	3.4	0.0
Education	1.9	5.0	—	0.1	0.1	0.4	0.4	0.4	—	2.4	5.5	0.4
International	0.1	—	—	0.6	0.9	1.5	—	—	—	0.7	0.9	1.5
Housing	0.1	1.7	—	3.0	0.1	3.7	—	—	3.0	3.0	2.8	6.7
Natural resources and energy	0.1	0.1	—	—	—	—	0.1	0.1	—	0.1	0.3	0.0
Transportation	0.3	0.6	—	—	—	0.1	0.2	1.7	—	0.5	2.2	0.1
Commerce	2.0	0.3	—	0.1	—	0.6	1.8	1.9	—	3.9	2.2	0.6
Other	—	—	—	0.1	0.1	—	—	—	—	0.1	0.1	0.0
Total order of magnitude[b]	11.6	12.3	N/A	4.1	2.9	8.0	8.8	20.2	29.1	24.5	35.4	37.1

[a] Estimate based on incomplete data. [b] Individual items may not add to totals because of rounding error. The total order of magnitude for 1978 will be greater than $37.1 billion when direct cash subsidies are included.

Source: Joint Economic Committee, U.S. Congress, *Federal Subsidy Programs: A Staff Study* (Washington, D.C.: October 18, 1974) p. 5. The data for fiscal years 1970 and 1975 are taken directly from the 1974 JEC staff study. The data have been updated to 1978. The inclusion of benefit-in-kind subsidies is an arbitrary decision; these programs could also be categorized as transfer payments.

Like many other government policy instruments, subsidy programs exist primarily to alter the distribution of resources in the private sector. Within the private-market system, subsidies offer rewards, either in money or in kind, as inducements to change. However, subsidies sometimes support inefficient practices and consequently cost more than their own cash value.

Government use of subsidies as an instrument to influence the production of goods and services in the economy may indeed be justifiable. Unfortunately, subsidies can produce undesirable biases in production. For example, over half of all transportation subsidies are in the form of capital grants to urban mass transit systems, but only small (though gradually increasing) amounts are available for operating such systems. In addition, the availability of government credit guarantees encouraged rapid rail construction, despite considerable evidence that such systems do little to relieve automobile congestion and are much more expensive than express bus systems on freeways.[4] Furthermore, that portion of the capital grants going to the purchase of buses appears to have resulted in premature replacement of buses.[5]

Similar unintended results are common in federal grants to public education. There has been a strong bias toward using such funds for capital plant, equipment, and buildings despite the fact that such expenditures do not have a significant effect in producing better education.

Policy makers need a rational basis for choosing the most effective way of achieving a stated economic goal. At the very least, the costs and benefits both of proposed subsidy programs and of alternative economic instruments should be analyzed.

Loans and Loan Guarantees

Government loans and loan guarantees play an important role in stimulating economic activity and allocating economic resources. Over

---

4. George W. Hilton, "The Urban Mass Transportation Program," in *Perspectives on Federal Transportation Policy*, ed. James C. Miller III (Washington, D.C.: American Enterprise Institute, 1975), pp. 139–141.

5. William B. Lilley III, "Transit Lobby Sights Victory in Fight for Massive Subsidy Program," *National Journal* 4, no. 10 (March 4, 1972): 393–403; and "Mayors and White House Prepare for Battle over $40-billion Subway Programs for 1970s," *National Journal* 4, no. 12 (March 18, 1972): 484–492.

Figure 6: New Federal Credit Extended,
Fiscal Years 1977 to 1979 (millions)

Type of Credit Assistance	1977	1978[a]	1979[a]
Direct loans, on budget	$21,854	$29,361	$26,575
Direct loans, off budget	13,558	16,871	17,575
Guaranteed loans[b]	40,794	44,669	53,354
Total	76,206	90,901	97,504

[a] Estimates. [b] Primary guarantees, adjusted.
Source: Office of Management and Budget, Executive Office of the President, Special Analyses: Budget of the United States Government, Fiscal Year 1979, Special Analysis F, pp. 127, 128, 140.

the past decade, the federal government has in a variety of ways supplied 10 to 15 percent of the total funds in U.S. credit markets.

Many federal agencies have authority to make direct loans. In 1977, the outstanding loans from these agencies amounted to $100.9 billion; the amount will rise to about $137 billion in 1979 as a result of the expansion of existing loan programs and the initiation of new programs. New transactions have grown rapidly for some programs in the Department of Housing and Urban Development, the Department of Health, Education, and Welfare, and the Department of Transportation and for international defense agreements.

The federal government also guarantees loans by insuring the principal and/or interest on loans supplied by private lenders. Federal participation in loan guarantees has been rising and currently covers over $200 billion in outstanding loans.

The growth and relative importance of these forms of government involvement are summarized in Figure 6. *Various forms of new federal* *credit are currently being extended at the rate of a little less than $100 billion per year.* The amount of credit generated through loan guarantees is slightly greater than the amount generated through direct loans, and the use of guarantees is expanding at a much more rapid rate.

The growth of loan guarantees has been dramatic. There are now over sixty loan-guarantee programs, compared with only twenty-four in 1960. Housing programs still account for about 80 percent of these guarantees. In recent years, new programs have been established for education, railroad assistance, emergency farm credit, and various energy programs.[6] In addition, the overall nature of the loan guarantee is changing. Until 1960, almost all loan-guarantee programs covered their cost, including allowance for repayment. They were provided for farm operations, Federal Housing Administration property improvement, mortgage insurance, and veterans programs guaranteeing mortgages. However, over the past twenty years, the proportion of loans that are likely to cover their cost has declined. The government has increasingly guaranteed loans involving higher risk. For example, loan guarantees have been extended to students, small businesses, and tenants displaced by urban renewal. Although the government may feel these groups are worthy of receiving credit on preferential terms, the risk of default is obviously greater. The government has also guaranteed loans for a limited number of very large projects, such as Amtrak and Conrail. The degree of risk involved in such guarantees is difficult to estimate, but it is certainly greater than that involved in the traditional guarantee programs prior to 1960.

Over the years, government loans and loan guarantees have proved to be a relatively successful tool for stimulating economic activity. However, the rapid growth and change in the nature of loans and loan guarantees have raised some concern about their cost. The objective of guarantees is generally to attract private capital *to* investments that are judged to be socially worthy. However, because the magnitude of loan guarantees has become very large, it is inevitable that this process is attracting private capital *away from* other investments. Yet, the question of what activities are deprived of capital is never asked. The government needs to develop a method of deciding which programs are worth their cost.

---

6. See Allen Schick, *Congressional Control of Expenditures* (Washington, D.C.: U.S. Government Printing Office, 1977), p. 88.

HOW TO CONTROL THE GROWTH OF GOVERNMENT EXPENDITURES AND INDIRECT INCENTIVE PROGRAMS

Government expenditure and incentive programs are powerful tools of public policy. Their growth has affected the distribution of the nation's resources. They have influenced technological change, capital investment, economic growth, and the aggregate level of employment. *It is essential that the direct and indirect costs of these powerful policy instruments be clearly identified and that their effectiveness be assessed.*

The budget and appropriation processes identify the cost of most federal expenditures, although these processes exercise less control over indirect incentive programs. Rising budget costs of separate expenditure programs are visible, but these are only the direct costs. The indirect costs that many expenditure programs impose on workers, employers, and consumers are not visible in the budget. Even though the federal budget identifies the direct costs, the policy makers' ability to control the expenditure level for a large proportion of programs in the budget is severely limited. Some 75 percent of the federal budget is said to be relatively uncontrollable. For example, federal entitlement programs such as revenue sharing, housing payments, social security and railroad retirement, Medicare, and Medicaid are, in effect, permanent appropriations and under current law are not subject to annual action by Congress.[7]

Control can be exercised only by amending the law covering a program. Changing politically popular entitlement programs is especially difficult if it requires a change in law, but that is no reason to regard expenditures for these programs as uncontrollable. The term *uncontrollable* is quite misleading because it is obvious that many programs described as *controllable* are also difficult to modify substantially or eliminate. Most of the defense budget is controllable, but it is unrealistic to assume that policy makers are free to eliminate most of the defense budget, though the nature of defense programs can be changed. Systematic evaluation of all programs should provide the evidence for modification no matter how these programs are described in the budget.

---

7. A detailed discussion of this issue is beyond the scope of this policy statement. For a further discussion, see Schick, *Congressional Control of Expenditures*, pp. 1–15.

The fact that spending levels are so difficult to adjust for many politically popular entitlement programs, such as social security, is all the more reason for periodically reviewing their purpose and effectiveness.

An additional limit on the overall ability of Congress to appraise individual expenditure programs is its source of information. Today, the main source of information about these programs remains the Administration, and Administration reports are frequently supportive of existing programs. No currently established committee (such as the Appropriations Committees or congressional staff units) is equal in resources to bureaucratic agencies. Nevertheless, this Committee believes that the House Ways and Means Committee and the Senate Finance Committee should continue to review proposed special tax arrangements and examine the effectiveness of existing arrangements. In addition, the Budget Committees should continue to exercise their existing authority over special tax arrangements. That authority includes estimating the projected magnitude of the arrangements over a five-year period and comparing them with other instruments of aggregate economic policy.

Identifying the effect of indirect policies is more difficult than identifying the cost of expenditure programs. The cost of subsidies is also estimated and presented as part of the budget, but it is much more difficult to estimate the cost of loans and loan guarantees. These costs can take several forms. If marginal borrowers default, government must obviously bear the cost. In addition, government interest rates are usually only slightly above the rate that the U.S. Treasury pays for money and substantially below the rate in the private market. Borrowers are therefore receiving a substantial interest subsidy that currently amounts to over $2 billion annually.

This policy instrument may therefore involve a cost through driving up interest rates in sectors that receive less capital. Consequently, if federal loan guarantees continue to expand, some worthwhile projects in the private sector will have more difficulty receiving financing.

Loans and loan guarantees enable the government to support potentially worthwhile economic activity. However, as in the case of other incentive mechanisms, there is no effective congressional procedure for deciding which loan program should be eliminated, expanded, or modified.

The Federal Financing Bank's activities, which currently finance over $15 billion in new guaranteed loans per year, are not considered along with the budget and therefore do not compete with other priorities within the overall budget. In addition, several other agencies have lending authority and are also outside the budget review. Loan guarantees as well as direct loans to off-budget agencies[8] are not reviewed as part of the budget process. Federal funds for these agencies and all loan guarantees are, of course, subject to the rather loose control of the authorizing limit set by Congress. Assessment of most loan programs is made by the agencies that are responsible for administering them. However, because new loans and loan guarantees function as revolving funds, federal agencies do not have to go to Congress for additional authority. Consequently, there is little opportunity outside the executive branch to review the effectiveness of these policy instruments.

The rapid growth of federal expenditures and indirect incentive programs has important implications for the economy. The major issue raised by the increasing use of these policy instruments is inadequate public and congressional control over them. Congress exercised only limited control over their expansion and has no effective process for reviewing their worth. Many of these programs may stimulate economic activity in specific markets and benefit the overall performance of the economy. However, others may bias the types of goods and services produced in ways that could have a negative impact on the economy. In addition, the growth of both expenditures and indirect policies has made it more difficult to avoid large budget deficits.

---

8. Several agencies, including the FFB, are not part of the budget process. Among these off-budget agencies are the U.S. Postal Service, the Rural Telephone Bank, and the U.S. Railroad Association.

4.

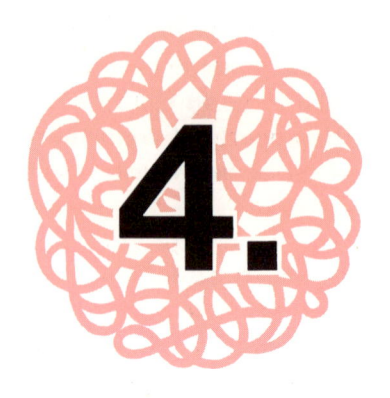

The Growing Role of Government in the Economy: Regulation

GOVERNMENT'S REGULATION OF THE MARKET SYSTEM has been the most rapidly growing form of government expansion in the last twenty years. In addition, regulation is as poorly controlled as expenditures and indirect incentive policies are. This chapter examines the growth of regulation, the techniques used to pursue regulatory goals, and the costs and benefits of regulation.

Some degree of government regulation of private business is a necessity in a highly developed nation. The Constitution provided Congress authority for regulating interstate commerce. However, government regulation on a national scale did not actually commence until the passage of the Interstate Commerce Act in 1887. Since then, the regulatory function of government has expanded to the point where virtually every industry and every household are affected in some visible way.

Regulation to achieve social goals is not a new phenomenon. Regulation of the sale of food and drugs was initiated at the beginning of the century, and regulation affecting employment conditions was well established before 1940. However, in the past decade, there has been a much greater emphasis on the achievement of social goals through regulation. Since 1970, Congress has created several regulatory agencies with very broad responsibilities (e.g., the Environmental Protection Agency, the Occupational Safety and Health Administration, the Consumer Product Safety Commission). These new agencies deal mostly with the health and safety of individuals. They have wrestled with difficult fundamental issues such as: What is an adequately safe environment? In its attempt to change the behavior of individuals and businesses, what degree of safety should the government prescribe when some degree of risk is inevitable?

These problems of health and environment are among the most important issues facing those who make public policy. Everyone aspires to live and work in a safe environment. However, few agree on the lengths to which government should go to promote that goal. Moreover, if that goal includes unreasonable standards or if it is pursued too rapidly, the costs of meeting it are extremely high.

The economic impact of regulation is substantially larger than is currently measured in government statistics. Within the federal budget, the relatively small budget for a particular small agency may place enormous power in the hands of a few civil servants. A regulatory agency is likely to influence the economy to an extent far beyond its budget or the number of its employees. The resources needed to achieve regulatory goals are not expended directly by government. Instead, businesses pass some of the cost on to buyers in the form of higher prices and to suppliers, employees, and investors in the form of slower price increases, smaller wage increases, and reduced dividends and retained earnings. The result is higher costs of production and reduced output in the industries affected. Achieving a social goal through regulation may result in a slower growth in business output and consequently in the creation of fewer private-sector jobs.

GROWTH AND SCOPE OF GOVERNMENT REGULATION

When the rules and procedures associated with government programs and contracts are added to direct and prescriptive methods of involvement, it becomes clear that the scope of government influence on the market is much greater than could possibly be indicated by government revenues or expenditures alone. A recent Congressional Budget Office review of the magnitude of government regulations[1] identified thirty-three federal departments and agencies engaged in activities that affect

> the operating business environment of broad sectors of private enterprise, including market entry and exit; rate, price, and profit structures; and competition
>
> specific commodities, products, or services through permit, certification, or licensing requirements
>
> the development, administration, and enforcement of national standards, violations of which could result in civil or criminal penalties or which result in significant costs

Requirements imposed on business through government regulations are especially stringent in the domains of medical care, urban transit, occupational safety and health, and environmental protection. Elaborate policies attempt to reduce labor market discrimination and encourage government contractors to increase the participation of minorities and women in the economic system. This type of government involvement, termed *social regulation*,[2] contrasts with the economic objectives of other regulations. Conflicts arise when social regulation hurts the market's efficiency because this creates a trade-off between social and economic goals.

Major sectors of the economy are subject to industry-specific regulations by federal, state, and local authorities. The communications industry (radio, television, telephone, and telegraph) is subject to the regulations of the Federal Communications Commission. The transportation industry is subject to many regulatory authorities, including the Interstate Commerce Commission, the Civil Aeronautics Board, and the

---

1. U.S. Congressional Budget Office, "The Number of Federal Employees Engaged in Regulatory Activities," Staff Paper presented for the Subcommittee on Oversight and Investigation, Committee on Interstate and Foreign Commerce, U.S. House of Representatives, August 1976, pp. 1–2.
2. See, for example, the discussion of regulatory reform in Council of Economic Advisors, *Economic Report of the President* (Washington, D.C.: U.S. Government Printing Office, 1978), pp. 206–216.

Federal Maritime Commission. The auto industry is subject to regulations established by the National Highway Traffic Safety Administration, which reviews the safety performance of automobiles, and by the Environmental Protection Agency. Similarly, the drug industry is heavily regulated by the Food and Drug Administration. The construction industry, another important part in the economy, is one of the most extensively regulated. It faces a complex array of sets of regulations promulgated mainly by individual state and local authorities.

Government has regulated financial institutions for decades. At least eight federal agencies are now involved: the Department of the Treasury, the Federal Reserve Board, the Federal Deposit Insurance Corporation (FDIC), the Federal Home Loan Bank Board, the Federal National Credit Union Administration, the Securities and Exchange Commission (SEC), the Commodity Futures Trading Commission, and the Department of Labor (which oversees employee pension funds). In addition, insurance and banking are regulated by many state agencies.

REGULATORY TECHNIQUES

The most widely used regulatory techniques are detailed rules governing specific kinds of behavior. For example, licenses are required in order for individuals or businesses to sell services in such industries as communications and transportation and in many professional occupations. Safety standards and pollution controls are typically required in terms of detailed equipment specifications, rather than in terms of results. Affirmative action guidelines include procedural rules that influence hiring practices. Farmers are given quotas and acreage allotments. Local zoning ordinances specify where various types of buildings can be built. Real estate transactions must meet a variety of standards if a home is to be financed under the Veterans Administration home loan program.

Many regulatory techniques apply to the public sector as well as to the private sector. For example, the principles underlying federal contract compliance to ensure equal employment opportunity apply to public employers who receive government contracts. Similarly, specifications for urban transit buses are now being mandated for public as well as private systems receiving subsidies from the Urban Mass Transportation Administration.

Historically, regulation has tended to focus more on the means of achieving a policy objective than on the objective itself. Consequently, each new problem government tries to solve hatches a new set of detailed rules. In some cases, it can be legitimately argued that specific standards are easier to observe (and therefore easier to enforce) than performance goals. For example, it is cheaper to inspect a plant to see if it has a specific smokestack than to monitor the plant's air emissions continuously. However, economists have argued that the same results could often be achieved at less cost through greater reliance on economic incentives, by minimum performance standards, and by relying on self-certification of compliance, with appropriate penalties for inaccurate certification.

Another prominent regulatory technique is the establishment of an independent commission or other power to approve maximum and/or minimum prices. Such bodies currently regulate telephone communications, air and surface transportation, banking (in the form of interest ceilings), electric power, and oil.

In principle, control over prices is usually intended to achieve what a well-functioning competitive market would achieve if such a market existed. There is a limit to the regulator's ability to determine what a competitive price would be. In practice, regulators permit regulated industries considerable latitude in price setting, even though in these industries the criterion for price setting is usually the achievement of a fair rate of return on assets and/or the establishment of fair ceilings on prices, as in the case of energy.

Although this rate-of-return regulation is necessary in some industries, it has disadvantages. In the field of transportation, for example, it may also lead to cross-subsidization of markets, a situation in which service is provided to some markets at even less than actual cost, with the deficit made up from profits. Another possibility is that regulated firms will compete away the extra profit through various types of nonprice rivalry. The airline industry is an example. Until recently, the Civil Aeronautics Board mandated the rate of return for the airline companies, which resulted in a spiral of rising prices followed by competitive increases in flight frequency. The results were sparsely filled flights and unimpressive profits.

COSTS OF REGULATION

Regulation is presumably instituted to provide certain public benefits. The question is: Are there always benefits worth the inevitable costs? Although it is impossible to measure all the benefits of regulation, it is possible to measure some of the costs. Both the decision to regulate and the selection of a particular type of regulation should be based on whether the benefits to society exceed the costs. However, the exact value of the benefits of regulation is frequently difficult to estimate. Even if the economic, political, and social benefits seem obvious, it is important to know at the very least which types of regulation are the most economical.

Costs of regulation include expenditures by agencies enforcing regulation, increases in production costs resulting from regulatory standards, secondary increases in production costs resulting from inefficient uses of resources in producing a given quantity of goods and services, and economy-wide inefficiencies brought about by producing too much or too little of a given product or, in some cases, by not producing a product at all.

A recent study by Arthur Andersen and Company for the Business Roundtable estimated the annual cost of complying with the regulations of six federal agencies; the cost for 1977 is limited to incremental costs, that is, the additional costs over and above the costs that would have been incurred in the absence of any new federal regulations. For example, on their own initiative, large corporations have established extensive worker health and safety programs. The study measures the costs in excess of what the forty-eight participating companies would have spent for existing health and safety programs.

The study estimated that the forty-eight corporations spent $2.6 billion in incremental costs. The Environmental Protection Agency regulations accounted for $2 billion, or 77 percent of the $2.6 billion total for all six agencies combined. The remaining 23 percent was distributed among the other agencies as follows: Equal Employment Opportunity, 8 percent; Occupational Safety and Health, 7 percent; Department of Energy, 5 percent; Employee Retirement Income Security Act, 2 percent; and Federal Trade Commission, 1 percent.[3]

This study estimated only the direct costs to industry; it did not include indirect costs of unintended consequences, which are difficult to measure but real and very high nonetheless.

---

3. Arthur Andersen and Company, *Cost of Government Regulation Study for the Business Roundtable,* Executive Summary, Chicago: March 1979.

Direct Costs: Government Expenditures

At the federal level, the direct costs of operating regulatory agencies are easy to measure. The Congressional Budget Office compiled a list of the federal agencies engaged in regulatory activity in 1976; it determined the number of employees primarily engaged in regulatory activities and the costs of that work.

In 1976, 92,172 man-years were spent in regulatory activities, at a cost of $2.854 billion; this included some 7,300 man-years in positions such as public information, consumer education, legislative liaison, and research. Most of these direct expenditures resulted from a few activities requiring field inspections. Over 16,000 man-years in the Department of Agriculture were devoted to meat and poultry inspection and agricultural disease and pest control. Most of the 8,000 positions in the Department of Health, Education, and Welfare were in the Food and Drug Administration. The Departments of the Interior and Transportation also devoted many man-years to inspection for safety: mining safety (Department of Labor), aviation safety (Federal Aviation Administration), and water safety (Coast Guard).

Enforcing regulations that affect the entire economy requires an enormous number of inspections. Agency heads often argue that they are operating with a skeleton staff, to the detriment of all concerned. In addition, many critics charge that regulation is ineffectual because the agencies cannot come close to matching their industries in technical expertise and information. Acceptance of either of these two arguments leads inevitably to an increased government sector.

The administrative costs of staffing and budgetary outlays by state and local governments would add substantially to the federal figure. Unfortunately, data about these expenses are lacking. Similarly, no comprehensive information is available on the high legal costs incurred by large and small firms engaged in formal proceedings before regulatory agencies.

Indirect Costs: Changes in Production

Changes in production mandated by regulatory standards are often very costly. For example, direct specifications of health, safety, or environmental standards increase production costs for most firms. Although it is not possible to identify all the costs of providing healthy conditions and safe products, it is possible to look at the additional costs

Figure 7: Estimates of Increased Production Costs from OSHA Standards

Standard	Five-Year Capital Expenditures (millions)	Annual Operating Expenditures (millions)
Noise (90 decibels)	$10,500	NA
Coke-oven emissions	$450–$860	$170–$1,150
Inorganic arsenic	NA	$110
Benzene	$267	$74

Source: OSHA-commissioned studies reported in Albert Nichols and Richard Zeckhauser, "Government Comes to the Workplace: An Assessment of OSHA," *The Public Interest,* 49 (Fall 1977): 39–69.

incurred as a result of a specific set of regulatory requirements, even though some of those expenditures might have been made in response to market forces.*

Estimates of increased production costs have been made for three important sets of regulations. The Occupational Safety and Health Administration (OSHA) commissioned a series of studies of the five-year capital and operating costs incurred by various actual and proposed regulations.[4] Changes in standards for noise have been the most costly; it is estimated that even the ninety-decibel standard for noise levels in a workplace (which is not the most stringent) will cost $10.5 billion in capital expenditures over the next five years. Other estimates are listed in Figure 7. Although estimates of *total* costs incurred because of present OSHA regulations are crude, they may exceed $3 billion per year in capital investment alone.

---

4. The numbers cited are reported in Albert Nichols and Richard Zeckhauser, "Government Comes to the Workplace: An Assessment of OSHA," *The Public Interest* 49 (Fall 1977): 36–69.

*See memoranda by E. SHERMAN ADAMS and by DAVID L. FRANCIS, page 141.

These OSHA standards have been criticized by business executives as both costly and misguided. For example, many industry spokesmen have argued that use of protective headgear is a far less expensive way to prevent hearing loss. (Such gear is commonly worn by airport employees.) There is also evidence that given more pay, workers are willing to accept a limited level of occupational risk.[5] Consequently, it may be inappropriate to set most standards in an attempt to achieve a risk-free environment. Workers themselves are prepared to accept *some* degree of risk, although some specified minimum acceptable level of risk may be quite appropriate.

The high cost of complying with OSHA standards described in Figure 7 reduces investment in new capital plants and equipment. This results in an inadequate supply of raw materials and equipment required by U.S. industry. For example, the United States used to be self-sufficient in the production of coke for industry but now imports over 10 percent of its requirements from abroad. Inadequate capital investment in coke production facilities, partially because of OSHA standards, has affected the U.S. balance of payment and reduced employment opportunities in this country.

The regulatory cost increases in the automobile industry have been thoroughly studied. In 1972, a committee of the U.S. Office of Science and Technology estimated that the safety standards and emission controls then scheduled for implementation in the 1976 model year (but subsequently delayed into the 1980s) would add $873 to the retail price of an average car.[6] At a 1976 rate of domestic production for U.S. sales of 7,838,000 cars,[7] this would have amounted to $6.8 billion a year in increased costs to consumers.

Another example of increased production costs is in residential construction, where local building codes may continue to specify certain standards long after technological progress has made them obsolete. In

---

5. Richard Thaler and Sherwin Rosen, "The Value of Saving a Life: Evidence from the Labor Market," in *Household Production and Consumption*, ed. T. Terleckyj (New York: Columbia University Press, 1976), pp. 265–298.

6. *Cumulative Regulatory Effects on the Cost of Automotive Transportation (RECAT)*, Final Report of the Ad Hoc Committee to the Office of Science and Technology (Washington, D.C.: U.S. Government Printing Office, February 1972), p. 74.

7. U.S. Department of Commerce, "Current Business Statistics," *Survey of Current Business* 57, no. 7 (July 1977): 5–40.

1968, the National Commission on Urban Problems (the Douglas Commission) studied the additional construction costs incurred because of outmoded building code requirements. They concluded that if regulations were changed to permit the substitution of new construction materials, the result would be a savings of 5.2 to 8.3 percent of the construction cost of a typical house.[8] The commission concluded that the savings would be increased to 15.3 percent if there was increased uniformity among local jurisdictions.[9] With residential construction contributing $60.5 billion to GNP in 1976, the costs of meeting building code regulations over and above those regulations necessary for building safety could be as high as $9.3 billion per year.

Indirect Costs: Restrictions on Operation

The third broad category of regulatory costs stems from restrictions on the amount of economic activity performed by the firm resulting in inefficient production. For example, the method of distributing acreage allotments among farmers is certain to result in some good land remaining idle while poor land is farmed, thereby increasing the cost of production. Railroads have too much track capacity because of Interstate Commerce Commission refusals to permit abandonments and too few cars because of low per diem rates set for intercompany car rentals. Before 1971, regulated inland water carriers were prohibited from combining regulated and unregulated barges in a single tow.

The trucking industry is also subject to considerable regulation; its effect on the cost of transportation to consumers of the service is currently the subject of considerable controversy. A Brookings Institution study based on the regulations affecting surface transportation in the early 1970s estimated that these restrictions, all told, raise the cost of carrying freight by $3.4 to $5.6 billion annually.[10] (Although some of the

---

8. National Commission on Urban Problems, *Building the American City* (Washington, D.C.: U.S. Government Printing Office, 1968), as reported in Sharon Oster and John Quigley, "Regulatory Barriers to the Diffusion of Innovation: Some Evidence from Building Codes," *Bell Journal of Economics* 8 (Autumn 1977): 368.

9. Oster and Quigley, "Regulatory Barriers to the Diffusion of Innovation: Some Evidence from Building Codes," p. 365.

10. Thomas G. Moore, "Deregulating Surface Freight Transportation," in *Promoting Competition in Regulated Markets*, ed. Almarin Phillips (Washington, D.C.: Brookings Institution, 1975), pp. 57–69.

views expressed in this study have been challenged, recent changes in regulations have been made to eliminate some of the practices criticized in the study.) In addition, many investigators have argued that because regulated rail and truck rates are identical, much traffic is shipped at a higher actual cost than would occur if prices were set by the market. The study estimates the cost of this misallocation at $0.2 to $2.9 billion per year.[11] These costs would be higher when stated in 1979 dollars.

INDIRECT COSTS: INEFFICIENCIES IN PRODUCTION

When government regulates prices in an industry, the risk of unnecessary inflation is sometimes present. (Regulation's contribution to inflation has recently become an important concern within the executive branch.) Most economists believe that prices in at least some regulated industries are maintained excessively above costs. At its extreme, this is the regulated-cartel argument: that regulation permits firms which would otherwise compete to act like a cartel and reap profits as a pure monopoly. In a more moderate form, the argument is simply that prices are kept somewhat above their competitive level, with the extra revenues going to subsidize other parts of the regulated firm's business, for example, to maintain product quality and image, to pay for advertising, to provide higher than necessary payments to management or union labor. All these decisions will actually reduce profits for the industry and may simply encourage inefficient operators. In any case, if demand is even somewhat responsive to price, setting too high a price will result in too little production, which will harm those consumers who cannot pay the high price. In fact, one of the main problems in regulated industries may be that there is insufficient incentive to keep costs as low as possible.[12]

---

11. Moore, "Deregulating Surface Freight Transportation," pp. 69–72.
12. Richard Posner has reviewed the results of studies of several industries, including physicians services, milk production, and airlines, that, at least for the late 1960s, claim regulation has raised prices in these industries well above what they would have been if regulations had not existed. Richard A. Posner, "The Social Costs of Monopoly and Regulation," *Journal of Political Economy* 83 (August 1975): 818.

Innovation is the sign of a healthy market system, but regulation often inhibits it. An institutionalized regulatory environment is likely to lead to bureaucratic inertia, which may limit the ability of firms to respond positively to changes in market conditions (a phenomenon well illustrated by the railroad industry). Furthermore, uncertainty on the part of regulated businesses about what will be allowed may inhibit investment in new facilities and decrease the rate of economic growth. Both inertia and uncertainty are likely to affect the rate of innovation in regulated industries, though there is little agreement yet on the extent of that effect.[13]

Perhaps most important of all, regulation tends to induce undesirable innovations by encouraging high capital intensity and, in some cases, poorly directed product improvements. For example, there is some evidence that the introduction of the DC-7 propeller aircraft in the 1950s was an unwarranted innovation in view of the imminent introduction of jets. This DC-7 might not have been built without the excessive rivalry in service quality encouraged by CAB price regulation.[14]

BENEFITS OF REGULATION

The cost of regulation retards the rate of economic growth.[15] However, this fact alone does not argue against regulations. Part of their benefit may be improved *quality* of growth. In general, the social benefits of government regulations are difficult to quantify. At the very least, regulations benefit the economic system and society generally when they are used to eliminate imperfections in the market system.

Almost everyone supports the intent of many government regulations: safer working conditions, better products for the consumer, elimina-

---

13. For the proceedings of a conference on this issue, see William Capron, ed., *Technological Change in Regulated Industries* (Washington, D.C.: Brookings Institution, 1971).

14. Aaron J. Gellman, "The Effect of Regulation on Aircraft Choice" (Ph.D. diss., Massachusetts Institute of Technology, 1968).

15. See Edward F. Denison, "Effects of Selected Changes in the Institutional and Human Environment upon Output per Unit of Input," *Survey of Current Business* 58, no. 1 (January 1978): 21–44.

REGULATORY CONSTRAINTS ON DRUG INNOVATION

Drugs have become medicine's most important and most cost-effective technology. The prospects for discovering and developing effective new medications have never looked better. Yet, over the past fifteen years, the rate at which new drugs have been developed and approved in this country has declined significantly. A decade and a half ago, new chemical entities were introduced at a rate of forty-two a year; in recent years, the rate has fallen to sixteen, a decrease of 62 percent. Furthermore, the United States is lagging significantly behind the United Kingdom and other advanced nations in the introduction of new drugs.*

In 1962, the average research and development cost per new chemical entity approved was about $4 million. Today, that cost averages $50 million. Moreover, it now takes seven to ten years to bring a new drug to market. It took about two years only fifteen years ago.

Government has a responsibility to maintain safeguards to protect patients. However, there is a broad consensus in the United States today that regulatory impediments and restrictions have seriously hampered progress in drug innovation. For example, HEW Secretary Joseph Califano has spoken of the need for "cutting out the incredible underbrush of regulation and the hesitation and difficulty in getting a safe drug out to the American people more promptly."**

Unrestrained growth in the number and complexity of U.S. drug regulatory requirements has substantially increased the costs associated with

---

*William M. Wardell, "A Close Inspection of the 'Calm Look' Rhetorical Amblyopia and Selective Amnesia at the Food and Drug Administration," *Journal of the American Medical Association* (May 12, 1978): 2004.

**Joseph Califano, Statement at the press conference making public the proposed Drug Regulation Reform Act of 1978, March 16, 1978.

research while providing little or perhaps no additional protection to patients. In addition to the delays caused and the costs imposed by the quantitative expansion of regulatory requirements, the increasingly broad regulatory overview of research adopted by the FDA, which now extends even to the earliest stages of the research process, has created difficult problems because at this critical early stage information is limited, judgments are difficult to make, and delay and wasted effort are extremely disruptive to the momentum of the research process.

As regulatory controls and research costs have escalated, it is not surprising that there has been a substantial shift of expenditures by U.S. companies from drug discovery to drug development.† The probable consequence of this shift in resources will be a reduction in the likelihood of breakthrough drug discoveries in American pharmaceutical laboratories. In fact, five of the seven economically most important drugs introduced for general use in the United States between 1970 and 1977 were of European origin.

In a recent issue of a leading medical magazine, a prominent cardiologist discussed seven cardiac drugs not available to American physicians, even though some are widely used abroad.†† Aside from the humane costs of this "drug lag" in terms of therapy delayed or denied, excessive regulation also has had substantial economic costs for patients. Consider, for example, the recent controversy about the alleged overuse of coronary bypass surgery for angina pectoris at an average cost of more than $12,000 per procedure. Some of the surgery could surely have been avoided had modern antianginal drugs available abroad also been available for use in the United States as an alternative treatment.

---

†Lewis Sarett, "FDA Regulations and Their Influence on the Future of R&D," *Research Management* (March 1974): 18–20.

††Michael J. Halberstam, "Who's Lagging Now?" *Modern Medicine* (September 15–30, 1978): 10.

In short, the effects of overregulation of pharmaceutical research and innovation are numerous and profound. Escalating regulatory constraints have meant delays for patients and doctors in availability of new drug products (which has tended to force the utilization of more expensive forms of patient care), a profound stifling of the research necessary for new drug discovery, a shift in allocation of resources from research to development, diminished returns for industry on research and development investment, and movement of American research and development to other countries.

A number of positive steps could be taken to facilitate pharmaceutical innovation: *The President could require* the Food and Drug Administration to make encouragement of therapeutic research and innovation a coequal responsibility with that of ensuring the safety and effectiveness of new drugs. *The Department of Health, Education, and Welfare could prepare an annual drug innovation report* that would analyze and evaluate the effects of FDA regulatory policies and actions on drug innovation and safety in terms of the overall social and economic objectives of U.S. health care. Also, whenever new regulations are proposed, HEW could be required to issue research-impact statements assessing their impact on drug innovation. *A Presidential commission comprised of patient and medical practitioner representatives could be formed* to review the HEW annual drug innovation report and research-impact statements and to report to the President annually on their findings. *The responsibility for monitoring early-stage clinical research could be placed in the hands of existing research review committees* at medical institutions where clinical pharmacology is practiced. Such use of these committees would eliminate unnecessary regulatory delays in the critical early stages of the research process while ensuring the scientific merit of the studies and protection

tion of discrimination in employment, and reduction of environmental pollution. Each of the programs devoted to these goals has yielded some benefits to groups in society and, at times, to business in particular.

of research subjects. *A new approval standard on which the safety and efficacy of a drug is assessed* ought to be established. There is general agreement that decisions regarding the safety and efficacy of a new drug are ultimately benefit-risk judgments and that the law and regulations should explicitly accept this. What is needed is a practical, commonsense standard which recognizes that the objective is therapeutic progress, not the ultimate in experimental elegance. *In order to expedite the regulatory process, a certified summary could be adopted as the primary document for regulatory review,* rather than the present requirement to submit voluminous and often duplicative raw data. A properly prepared summary, endorsed by a panel of experts, could provide all essential information in systematic form and reduce the need to review *all* scientific data, thus expediting the decision-making process. *To broaden its regulatory perspective, the FDA could make greater use of advisory committees* in helping resolve complex and difficult scientific questions. *Consideration should be given to changing the law regulating the issuance of patents* so that the effective date of U.S. patent issuance coincides with the FDA's approval to market a new drug. (As a result of lengthy regulatory procedures, the effective patent life for a new drug has shrunk to about nine years, in contrast with the seventeen years typical for most other products.) *A program of postmarketing surveillance and continuing investigation of new drugs* could be used to expedite the approval of the drug while at the same time permitting the early detection of adverse reactions.

The Administration and Congress should examine these and other proposals as part of their effort to achieve regulatory reform. The process recommended in Chapters 6 and 7 of this policy statement for screening and reviewing regulations provides policy makers with a framework for considering these proposals affecting the pharmaceutical industry.

There has been a vast increase in the amount of information manufacturers are required to provide consumers about their products. Sometimes that information is very detailed and not readily comprehended by consumers. However, surveys indicate that many consumers make use of product information in purchase decisions.[16]

Air and water quality in the United States has been significantly improved by environmental regulations. Levels of carbon monoxide and sulfur dioxide (both proven causes of respiratory illness) have declined in urban areas across the country. Many rivers once badly polluted with industrial and organic wastes are now open (at least in parts) for fishing and swimming. Thus, although the environmental controls imposed on industry have added to inflation and caused financial burdens on many companies and unemployment in some, a strong conceptual case can be made for the *purpose* of some such regulation.[17]

Fuel economy standards mandated by the government also show positive results when viewed in terms of the nation's economy. These measures help the nation decrease its reliance on foreign sources of oil, which strengthens the country's economy, and a "stronger economy will produce a better atmosphere for the automobile industry." In addition, it is claimed that consumers will save hundreds of dollars in fuel costs over the life of their vehicles subject to these standards.[18] However, this saving must be balanced against the increased cost of meeting current and projected fuel economy standards.

In regard to automobile safety regulations, the General Accounting Office has estimated that occupants of model year 1973 automobiles were about 30 percent safer than occupants of pre-1966 vehicles, which did not have to meet federal safety standards. Furthermore, a National Highway Traffic Safety Administration report states that "the fatality rate has been reduced (since 1966) 40 percent, from 5.7 to 3.3 deaths per 100 million miles of travel. Had the fatality rate remained at the 1966 level, nearly 200,000 more persons would have been killed since that year, and

---

16. Murray L. Weidenbaum, *Business, Government and the Public* (Englewood Cliffs, N.J.: Prentice-Hall, 1977), pp. 13–14.

17. It has, however, sometimes proved difficult to develop empirical evidence to support the benefits of specific environmental regulations. For example, a careful study of automobile pollution was unable to demonstrate a significant relationship between mortality and the controlled auto pollutants. See Lester Lave and Eugene Seskin, *Air Pollution and Human Health* (Baltimore: Johns Hopkins University Press, 1977).

18. National Highway Traffic Safety Administration, "The Benefits of Automobile Regulations" (June 1978), p. iii.

an additional 35,000 would have died in 1977 alone."[19] However, the contribution of safety regulations to the reduction of deaths per 100 million miles of travel since 1966 has been challenged.[20]

NET BENEFITS OF REGULATION

Regulation undoubtedly provides noticeable benefits to many groups, and many proponents of regulation claim that the prohibition of some economic activity does result in positive progress. Despite the benefits provided by regulation, the issue for public policy is whether the costs imposed by particular regulations in fact offset the benefits achieved.

No balanced evaluation of the broad impact of government regulation can conclude that government always makes decisions in the country's best interests. Numerous adverse side effects and costs often overshadow benefits. Therefore, there is a need to demonstrate the existence of real net benefits and the feasibility of the government's plan to achieve them.

Although there is currently no accurate estimate of the overall cost of regulation, evidence about the costs of specific regulations shows that they are substantial.[21] In some cases, these costs are unnecessary because some regulatory policies are achieved through several overlapping layers of laws. For example, laws fostering equal employment opportunity, environmental protection, product labeling, and health and safety make business subject to federal, state, and sometimes local regulations. This redundancy of regulatory administration may produce unnecessary costs and lengthy delays. Because such duplication increases the cost to the participants in the market system, it should be avoided wherever possible. The appropriate level of government to implement these policies will

---

19. National Highway Traffic Safety Administration, "The Benefits of Automobile Regulation," p. iii.

20. See Sam Peltzman, *Regulation of Automobile Safety* (Washington, D.C.: American Enterprise Institute, 1975).

21. There have been several estimates that the aggregate cost of regulation ranges from about $60 billion to over $100 billion per year. The validity of these estimates has been widely criticized by reliable researchers. See U.S. General Accounting Office, *An Economic Evaluation of the OMB Paper on "The Costs of Regulation and Restrictive Practices"* (Washington, D.C.: U.S. Government Printing Office, 1975).

vary according to the goal of the policy. It is recognized, of course, that justifiable arguments can be made for regulatory systems that contain competitive alternatives, such as the dual banking system, and that a monolithic regulatory administration is not necessarily the best solution.

There does not appear to be an effective control mechanism for assessing regulatory programs either within the executive or within the legislative branch of government. The federal government's normal review process does not cover the regulations emanating from the independent regulatory agencies. When the law asks the head of an agency to promulgate new regulations, the executive branch cannot *effectively* review those regulations.

Within Congress and the independent regulatory agencies, there has been a failure to ask systematically what problems regulations were attempting to remedy, whether they were important enough to require action, whether regulations were the best way of remedying that problem, and if so, whether the cost of regulations could be reduced.

Government has accordingly found itself trying to regulate areas in which the extent and nature of the problems are not clearly delineated and in which the results of specific regulation policies are uncertain. For example, the public has asked the government to protect young children from unsafe and hazardous toys. The benefits of this regulation may be substantial, and the goal is certainly desirable. But government has not yet found a way to determine quickly whether these consumer products are safe. Some public groups have advocated protecting young children from more than physical hazards; they have proposed that certain types of advertising be banned on children's television programs. These groups claim that young children are in no position to judge the desirability of the products advertised. The protection of children from unsafe toys has drawn the government into an important but difficult area of public policy; if government tries to protect children from commercial television as well, it will have entered a completely uncharted area of public policy. The protection will be based on standards determined by a government official without any evidence that the government knows what is right for young children or that they will benefit from the regulation.

Expansion of administrative constraints is not confined to the social policies enacted in the 1970s. Earlier industry-specific regulations included such areas as banking, railroads, and trucking. With rare exceptions, regulation of these industries has not decreased. Although it has pushed the government farther into controversial areas, the political process has rarely withdrawn government from regulating specific industries when the need for controlling them is no longer appropriate.

Many policy makers in the executive branch and Congress now want to reform the design of regulations to ensure that they result in *net* benefits. Policy makers are hampered by lack of coordination and lack of authority. There is currently no coherent framework for analysis or evaluation, nor are there any commonly accepted criteria for judging when and to what extent regulation is worthwhile.

CONCLUSIONS ABOUT THE GROWTH OF GOVERNMENT INVOLVEMENT

Although expanding expenditure programs and the spread of regulations may have benefited particular groups, they have sometimes not been beneficial to those they were intended to help. More important, the expansion of government's role in the market system has had serious consequences for the performance of the economy.

The growth of government expenditure programs has made it difficult to reduce large federal budget deficits and has thereby contributed to inflation. Regulations affecting specific industries have sometimes protected firms by restricting the entry of new firms, thus reducing competition and encouraging inefficient production. Regulations designed to improve the physical environment and to protect workers' and consumers' health and safety have frequently established zero-risk goals. The higher price of achieving zero risk compared with the price of achieving some acceptable minimum standard of risk has imposed enormous costs on the market system. Some of these costs have been borne by consumers and workers. The pursuit of unrealistic mandatory standards has therefore raised costs of production, reduced productivity, and contributed to inflation. Regulations have also told business how to produce goods and services and when to change the technology used in production. Potential capital investment in the market system has been diverted away from the goal of economic growth and toward achieving zero-risk standards of environmental quality, health and safety, and product safety.

Government policy makers have consistently failed to recognize that the market system is the most effective way of implementing policy goals and providing benefits to the public—consumers, workers, and shareholders. The achievement of both improved economic performance and social goals requires that the extent of government involvement be reduced and that ineffective and inconsistent government programs be eliminated.

When government has a legitimate role to play in securing the well-being of society, it frequently does so by failing to use the market system constructively or by failing to improve competition in markets. This approach to policy is often the most inefficient way of achieving desirable economic *and* social goals.

PROBLEMS IN ACHIEVING NEW REGULATORY GOALS: THE CONSUMER PRODUCT SAFETY COMMISSION

The Consumer Product Safety Commission (CPSC) began operation in 1973 amid expectations that it would soon develop into an aggressive, cost-effective regulatory agency. However, by 1978, CPSC's disappointing performance provoked serious congressional discussion about abolishing the agency. The commission has been awarded provisional funding through 1981. Future appropriations are contingent upon positive progress in regulating safety in the marketplace.

The problems confronting CPSC were not anticipated when the agency was created. The agency's enabling legislation, the Consumer Product Safety Act, now appears gravely flawed. This legislation grafted together several safety statutes and mandated that the existing branches of the authorizing agencies (e.g., sectors of the Food and Drug Administration, the Department of Health, Education, and Welfare, and the National Bureau of Standards) be housed under CPSC. Coordinating these existing government safety bureaus to function as one cohesive safety agency proved to be one of CPSC's most formidable obstacles. The legislation also called for mandatory product standards, but for a number of reasons, including inadequate resources, CPSC promulgated only three mandatory standards in five years.*

The current policy-making process within the political system has initiated and continued to support increasing interference with the market system. Policy makers need to find an approach that eliminates unnecessary government interaction with the market system and controls government actions, whether regulations or expenditures, that *are* necessary.

Within the executive branch, Congress, and the independent regulatory agencies, there is currently no effective system for determining

---

Yet, for all CPSC's problems, it is clear that the climate for product safety has changed for the better. Industry's strongest incentive to manufacture safe consumer products has been the spiraling cost of product liability court cases. Although this development is not directly related to CPSC, the agency has helped reduce the number of hazardous consumer products. Aided by amendments to the Consumer Product Safety Act and a better comprehension of its mission and its failings, the agency has begun to cope with the task of regulating the safety of over 10,000 consumer products. Mandatory standards are now being augmented by voluntary standards. The agency also emphasizes product information and education programs and a cooperative effort with other safety agencies in the area of chronic hazards (e.g., carcinogens).

The commission's experience to date has demonstrated that the best intentions of government can run afoul. Under the congressional threat of termination, the agency may yet prove efficient and effective. CPSC's first frustrating years have shown how difficult it can be in government to move from promise to performance.

---

* The CPSC inherited four laws from other agencies and has experienced modest success under these. Standards for childproof bottle tops, cribs, lead in paint, vinyl chloride sprays, and several other products have been promulgated.

whether regulations or government expenditure programs are successful or not. One approach is to reduce the aggregate growth of government expenditures. That will provide policy makers with an additional incentive to reconsider the worth of existing programs, but it will not ensure that the most ineffective policies will be changed. In addition, policy makers in the political system require a mechanism for measuring the *performance* of programs against their objectives.

5.

Weaknesses in the Current Policy-Making Process

POLICY MAKERS IN THE ADMINISTRATION and Congress currently exercise inadequate control over the expanding role of government in the economy. This weakness in the policy-making processes has resulted in excessive government involvement in markets to the detriment of both economic and social objectives.

The relationship between government and the market system has been an issue since the founding of the Republic. Alexander Hamilton and Thomas Jefferson took opposing positions on the same issue two hundred years ago. Hamilton favored a strong role for the national government: "I acknowledge . . . on my part towards a liberal construction for the powers of the national government" (letter, 1792). And while he was secretary of the treasury, the federal government funded foreign and domestic debt, assumed state debts, provided adequate federal revenue, and established a national bank. Hamilton advocated the use of taxation "to equalize the condition of the citizens" (letter, 1792). On the other hand, Jefferson stated in his 1801 Inaugural Address that government "shall restrain men from injuring one another, shall leave them otherwise free to regulate their own pursuit of industry and improvement."[1]

This chapter examines current policy making in the context of the political system: Why do administrators, politicians, and judges alike pay too little attention to the long-term welfare of the nation's economy? What allows them to overlook the effect of their decisions on the contribution of the market system to employment, relative price stability, and improvement in economic growth?

PRESSURES OF THE POLITICAL ENVIRONMENT

Public policy decisions affecting the market system must be made in a complex political environment. Ideas are proposed, rejected, accepted, or amended through the bargaining and compromise of many participants. The President, administrative agencies, congressional leaders, legislative committee chairmen, party leaders, issue experts, state-level political leaders, leaders of organized private groups, and often as a last resort, the courts at both state and federal levels all take part. Legislative decisions often fail to resolve conflicts, and the issues resurface in varying forms. A new law is frequently merely "a verbal formula that a majority of politicians find adequate as a basis for continuing struggle."[2] That is, a law establishes ground rules under which political debate and bargaining may continue as the bureaucracy develops the administrative procedures for implementing policy.

The Constitution empowers the President as the chief executive to see that the laws are properly carried out. In the twentieth century, the President not only enforces laws but also proposes new ones. In addition, Presidential appointees often initiate legislation and have more access to information than those outside the executive branch. For these reasons, they are the direct targets of political pressure groups.

---

1. See Avery Craven, Walter Johnson, and F. Robert Dunn, *A Documentary History of the American People* (Lexington, Mass.: Ginn and Company, 1951), pp. 210, 213, and 226.
2. Raymond A. Bauer, Ithiel de Sola Pool, and Lewis Anthony Dexter, *American Business and Public Policy: The Politics of Foreign Trade* (New York: Atherton Press, 1963), p. 426.

Congress frequently gives the Administration considerable discretion in deciding how a new law will be carried out. Because of the technical nature of much legislation, important policy decisions are therefore made within the bureaucracy. The bureaucracy frequently takes new policy initiatives under existing legislative authority. In fact, a major proportion of all new policies are initiated administratively within existing legislative authority and through the annual budget. Interest groups therefore lobby the agencies to propose policy changes. Such activity does not cease with the passage of a new law; it is never-ending.

Although the President and his Administration are very important in the legislative process, Congress remains the only constitutionally established legislature with the responsibility for enacting and repealing laws. There is no question that its powers remain very great, even relative to those of the President.

The democratic process is based on the recognition that a wide range of interest groups will naturally emerge to represent citizens. This complex system, which permits the participation of so many groups and individuals, can be slow, inefficient, and sometimes inequitable. Interest groups with narrow concerns can harness the political system to promote these concerns. Such groups mobilize public opinion through extensive direct-mail and publicity campaigns. In return for political support, many are able to generate the sizable contributions and favorable publicity that politicians require for election.

Congress often responds to pressure by trying to satisfy a plethora of requests. As a result, conflicting laws have emerged that are detrimental to the health of the nation's economy. Inefficient and inequitable government policies with strong constituencies in Congress and the executive agencies have often been resistant to reform.

To the complexity of the administrative and legislative processes must be added the often unpredictable interventions of the judicial apparatus. The history of court decisions can be as complicated and political as the history of other government decisions. Because laws and administrative decisions are generally the results of compromise among conflicting groups, their implementation can frequently be challenged by the parties who feel adversely and illegally affected. Challenging laws and administrative orders in the courts can delay their enforcement for years. Courts, like administrative and legislative bodies, must be considered an important part of the political process.

PROCESSES THAT DETERMINE POLICY: BUDGET AND APPROPRIATIONS, LEGISLATIVE AND AUTHORIZATION, AND MANAGEMENT ACCOUNTABILITY

Several interrelated processes are involved in the establishment and implementation of policy: the budget and appropriations process, the legislative and authorization process, and the process of making public management accountable. All branches of government participate, and their role in each process determines the extent of government involvement in the market system.[3] Over the years, improvement in these processes has represented slow progress toward more effective decision making.

The most highly developed and systematic process is the Administration's *annual budget.* This process is capable of providing the Administration with a broad perspective on policy priorities and an opportunity to propose changes in government involvement in the market system. Over a number of decades, the evolution of the annual Presidential budget and legislative programs, along with a Presidential agency (the Office of Management and Budget) to do the necessary staff work, has created the ingredients for sound public policy decisions. A basic structure now exists for improving such decisions. Yet, the budget process cannot by itself control government involvement in the economy. Over the past dozen years, there has been a succession of attempts to improve the management of the budget process. However, no formal system can substitute for the assembly of relevant facts, competent analysis of issues, and the exercise of sound judgment by highly qualified personnel. OMB, as presently constituted, is capable of providing the analysis required to develop the

---

3. Within the budget and legislative processes, there has been some attempt to weigh future trends. This concern for forecasting potential problems has been stimulated by the recent failure of policy makers to recognize the importance of demographic change in the areas of health care, retirement, labor force participation, and education. In the executive branch, multiyear planning is used in preparing the annual budget. The Congressional Budget Office now prepares five-year budget projections, and the Joint Economic Committee has initiated a series of studies that forecast economic and social developments into the 1980s.

Foresight is sometimes discussed within the legislative process, and under the House rules, legislative committees are authorized to carry out "futures research" and forecasting. In practice, however, the concept of foresight is still underdeveloped and is not a major consideration in any of the decision-making processes.

complex budget proposals, but it has been much less successful in providing the thoroughgoing evaluations of policies and programs that are necessary to the preparation of the budget. This weakness seriously hampers the executive branch's ability to review the effectiveness of policy.

More recently, Congress has undertaken the development of its own structured budget process, most notably through the Budget Control and Impoundment Act of 1974. In that enactment, Congress adopted a means for establishing overall spending limitations and some priorities among various government activities. In this and other actions, Congress has strengthened its staff capacity for prediction, analysis, and evaluation.

The *appropriations* process provides Congress with considerable potential control over new and existing policies. The Appropriations Committees decide (within the overall budget constraints) the resources that will be allocated to implement policies. The Administration has to defend its requests for funds before Congress approves those funds. Therefore, the appropriations process provides Congress with an opportunity to examine in detail ongoing programs and proposals for program changes and new policies. In practice, the magnitude and complexity of government policies make this opportunity more apparent than real.

The second major systematic process for determining public policy is *legislative*. The authorization of new programs and the reauthorization of existing programs are closely linked to legislative activity. When the executive branch prepares its legislative proposals for submission to Congress, those proposals are reviewed by the agencies and OMB within the Administration's budget review process. Since the 1974 act, legislation proposed by Congress is also supposed to be accompanied by an estimate of its budgetary impact. In practice, however, initial congressional budget limits are not always adhered to.

There are several legitimate reasons why the congressional legislative process is not consistent with the congressional budget and appropriations processes. Determining budget outlays for new policies often results in several estimates, even within the Budget Committees. The economic projections on which the initial budget limits are based may change shortly after these limits are established in the First Budget Resolution. Congress also tends to focus on the first-year costs of new policies instead of on the subsequent costs, which may be much higher. Finally, legislative activity in Congress continues after the date of the Second Budget Resolution (September 15), and if many legislative proposals are passed after this date but before the adjournment of Congress, it is frequently necessary to establish new expenditure limits through a Third Budget Resolution. Consequently, although the 1974 act has resulted in greater coordination of the legislative and budget processes, inconsistencies between the objectives and the financing of policies still emerge, especially within the legislative branch.

The third major decision-making process includes a variety of approaches that attempt to make those responsible for implementing policy *accountable for their performance.*

The implementation of policy through the executive branch requires detailed specifications transforming the broad goals of policy into action. In most cases, the legislative authority provides the federal bureaucracy with only broad guidelines concerning implementation. Detailed administrative decisions are frequently left to the Administration; consequently, appropriate government agencies are left to choose among different methods of implementation.

The administrators of programs are subject to various types of assessments that are supposed to lead to accountability. If management is not achieving the desired policy objectives, either the implementation technique and/or the objectives are supposed to change.

The Administration, Congress, and the courts are involved in this process. Within the executive branch, these assessments involve considerable resources devoted to program monitoring, program evaluation, and some basic research. In Congress, assessments are conducted by the oversight committees. Congress often requests evaluation reports from the executive branch agencies and the appropriate congressional staff units. The courts are only indirectly involved in reviewing performance; they are frequently used in implementing policy, and they may play a role when individuals or groups use the courts in their claim that the government is not carrying out policy according to the law. The results of reviews of program performance can be used to modify, extend, or terminate existing policies.

POLICY REVIEW AND PROGRAM EVALUATION

Within the executive branch, program evaluation and policy reviews are conducted by the government departments and agencies. In some cases, these reviews are conducted by government personnel; in other cases, they are conducted by outside organizations under contract. The results of this work have been useful, but the analysis of performance has been of mixed quality. Experience has shown that objective and useful assessments usually require that internal evaluations to support the budget and legislative processes be complemented by independent research conducted outside the government. Such research is difficult to achieve when government agencies are the single most important source of information concerning program performance. However, reviews to improve the *management* of the programs can be done effectively by the agencies themselves.

Congress, through its oversight responsibilities, is concerned with the implementation and effectiveness of existing public policies. In practice, however, Congress allocates a disproportionately small amount of time to assessing the effectiveness of ongoing programs. The current system of congressional oversight is widely regarded as inadequate because it fails to exercise effective control over the extent and nature of government involvement.[4]

Recent reforms in the budget process have improved fiscal oversight. The contribution of the House and Senate Budget Committees to the requirement of achieving budget limitations by a specific date has increased congressional control over the aggregate level of government expenditures. In addition, the Appropriations Committees review government programs and policies. However, the number and variety of government activities are so numerous that these committees review only a small portion.

In theory at least, oversight is also possible through the authorization process, but the present authorization process has not been effective in this regard. In many cases, authorizing committees have been advocates for special interests, rather than reviewers of legislation. Also, programs with multiyear or permanent appropriations (such as social security) are uncontrollable in the sense that Congress must change current laws in order to modify them.

Most oversight responsibilities are carried out by the standing (authorizing) committees for each house of Congress. These standing committees are in many cases the sources of proposals for the existing

---

4. For a detailed review of current oversight techniques and practices, see *Congressional Oversight,* Report prepared for the Subcommittee on Oversight Procedures, Committee on Governmental Affairs, U.S. Senate (Washington, D.C.: U.S. Government Printing Office, 1976).

programs. Although these committees have the authority to request reports from the appropriate government agencies (or from a nongovernment institution), their judgments are inevitably conditioned by their earlier decision to legislate the program.

The policies of regulatory agencies, including independent regulatory agencies, are also subject to congressional oversight, but not on a regularly scheduled basis. In fact, despite "efforts over the past thirty years to improve the process, Congressional oversight tends to be ad hoc, special-issue oriented, and reactive."[5] Curtailing unjustified expenditure programs and regulations and reshaping those that are justified will therefore require significant improvements in the oversight process.

IMPROVING CONTROL OVER POLICY: CONGRESSIONAL AND EXECUTIVE RECOGNITION OF THE PROBLEM

Congress currently has authority and some responsibility for reviewing both the desirability and the actual effect of major policies. Part of this authority is related to the budget process under the Budget Control and Impoundment Act of 1974, which requires the Budget Committees to exercise their oversight function by "studying the effect of budget outlays on existing and proposed legislation" (*Rules of the House of Representatives*, Rule X). The Appropriations Committees also have general oversight responsibilities within the congressional budget process and may recommend terminating or modifying provisions of laws that provide for spending authority. Since 1975, House rules covering the *general oversight* responsibilities require that each standing committee (except the Budget and Appropriations Committees) determine whether laws and programs under its jurisdiction are being "implemented and carried out in accordance with the intent of Congress and whether such programs should be continued, curtailed or eliminated" [House Rule X, 2(b)(1)]. Similarly, the House Committee on Government Operations is required to "review and study, on a continuing basis, the operation of government at all levels with a view to determining their economy and

---

5. Comptroller General of the United States, *Congressional Oversight Reform Proposals* (Washington, D.C.: U.S. General Accounting Office, 1978), p. 8.

efficiency" [House Rule X, 2(b)(2)] and is responsible for coordinating the oversight activities of the House of Representatives.

Special legislative responsibilities have been given to specific committees of the House. Since 1975, each committee report on each bill or joint resolution must contain an inflationary-impact statement of the effect on "prices and costs in the operation of the national economy" (House Rule XI). Similar authority and responsibility for oversight are contained in the *Rules of the Senate*. In February 1977, the Senate adopted a rule (Senate Rule XXIX) that requires every committee except the Committee on Appropriations, to include an assessment of the regulatory impact in its reports on the assessment of legislation.

Since 1970, Congress has obviously felt the need to strengthen its oversight procedures. If these rules for legislative review and for the oversight of public policies had been implemented effectively, the elimination and modification of a number of unnecessary and ineffective programs might have been accomplished. Unfortunately, the existing congressional oversight rules are too vague. They do not set out specific criteria to be considered by all congressional committees as they review major policies. In addition, there is no explicit recognition of how the committees will acquire high-quality impact evaluations of the policies they are required to review.

The hearings that accompany present oversight procedures tend to be protracted. In addition, they focus insufficient attention on resulting recommended policy changes. Since 1970 (under the authority provided by an amendment of section 116 of the Legislative Reorganization Act), the oversight committees in each house have been required to prepare a biennial report on their oversight activities. However, these reports lack uniform standards and vary in quality; at present, they are of little value to the oversight process.

Several congressional staff organizations provide a limited amount of technical assistance to the oversight committees. The Congressional Budget Office currently uses evaluation results generated elsewhere in its policy analyses for Congress, but most of the resources of the office are devoted to generating data to assist congressional review of the Administration's budget proposal. On the basis of existing studies, the Congressional Research Service provides committees with valuable reviews of policy issues; the Office of Technology Assessment occasionally provides assessments on technically oriented matters.

The General Accounting Office is also in a position to provide Congress with the necessary information for improving oversight. GAO has increasingly evaluated the performance of programs, frequently at the request of Congress. When GAO was established in 1921, its main function was to assist in ensuring that public funds were properly spent by executive agencies. This basic financial auditing function was gradually expanded to reviewing the efficiency of administration (known as *efficiency and economy audits*). Since the mid-1960s and especially with the passage of the Legislative Reorganization Act of 1970, the emphasis of GAO's activities has shifted toward the evaluation of the results of programs (*program results audits and evaluations*). This emphasis on impact evaluation has continued to expand. GAO now provides impact reviews of programs and recommends techniques for conducting evaluations within the executive branch. In recent years, over half of its resources have been devoted to these evaluations.

The government has established procedures that attempt to show the effect of regulatory policies on broad economic goals. For example, the Regulatory Analysis program, established in concept at the end of 1974 (Executive Order 11821), is such an attempt.[6] OMB and the Council on Wage and Price Stability are responsible for reviewing agency submissions under the current Regulatory Analysis program.

Under this program, if an agency proposes to introduce a new regulation that has an effect of $100 million or more on the economy, it must present an analysis of the impact before the regulation is introduced. The analysis must include a description of the problem, an identification of alternate ways to achieve the policy goal, and an analysis of the potential economic impact of the regulation. The purpose of this relatively new program is similar to this Committee's recommendations on criteria for screening proposals for government involvement discussed in Chapter 6. We therefore support this attempt to make agencies justify their regulatory proposals.

Responsibility for control over the most important ten or twenty new regulations each year has been assigned to the Regulatory Analysis Review Group (RARG), established by Presidential directive in February

---

6. At the end of 1976, Executive Order 11949 extended the Regulatory Analysis program and changed the name of the required evaluation from Inflation Impact Statement to Economic Impact Analysis. Finally, in March 1978, Executive Order 12044 changed the name to Regulatory Analysis and tightened up the procedures by requiring that agencies make a draft of the Regulatory Analysis available to the public at the time of proposed rule making.

1978. This cabinet-level body has so far reviewed some six major regulatory standards and has shown some initial promise in bringing important regulatory issues before the public.

The Administration has also tried to strengthen coordination over proposed regulations by setting up the Regulatory Council, which is composed of all executive departments and agencies with major regulatory responsibilities. The council, established by Presidential directive in October 1978, will be chaired the first year by the administrator of the Environmental Protection Agency. Its purpose is to prepare a comprehensive schedule of all proposed major regulations; this calendar of new regulations will be published every six months. The council's effectiveness is still to be tested.

During 1979, many regulatory reform bills, including an Administration bill, have been introduced in Congress. Several bills aimed at controlling the growth of expenditure programs are also currently being proposed. Improvements have been made in the budget process, and both the executive and the legislative branches of government recognize the need for more effective assessment of policies.

Recent changes still fall far short of the nation's need to cope with the cumulative growth of government involvement in the market system. The congressional oversight process is underutilized. Even when it has been used to review ongoing programs, it has rarely proved successful in systematically developing the evidence necessary for evaluating effectiveness. Consequently, any recommendations that emerge from the oversight review generally have only limited impact. Similarly, executive branch reviews of existing programs are relatively ineffective. There are great variations among the departments in the quality of reviews. In many departments, the evaluation is conducted by those responsible for administering the program, and such efforts are not designed to assist in improving program performance or government policy. Further improvements are urgently needed in the framework for policy making.

We regard four steps as necessary to improving the policy-making framework within the political system.

1. Policy makers in the Administration, Congress, and the independent regulatory agencies should use *criteria* to screen proposals for government involvement in the market system, assessing both their likely effect on the market system and their feasibility.

2. Having screened and selected feasible courses of action that will achieve the objective of the specific policy, policy makers should try to choose the one least disruptive to the market system.*

3. With the benefit of hindsight, policy makers should assess the success and failure of the programs and policies within their area of responsibility. This type of evaluation is necessary in order to alter or terminate programs.

4. Policy makers should adopt a *mechanism* to ensure that these steps are taken and that the results of evaluation of major policies are publicized so that policies can be modified.

In Chapter 6, we will examine steps 1 and 2; in Chapter 7, we will examine steps 3 and 4 and discuss the implementation of all four steps.

*See memorandum by E. SHERMAN ADAMS, page 141.

6.

Recommendations for Screening, Adopting, and Designing Government Actions

THE NATION'S POLICY-MAKING PROCESSES do not effectively question the various types of government involvement in the market system. Unless policy makers are required to ask and to answer harder economic questions, the harmful expansion of government into markets will never be brought under control, and effective social policies will not be designed.

This Committee proposes two related sets of recommendations to aid the economic judgments of policy makers. The first set helps screen proposals for government programs by determining first whether government should and can offer a solution to a given problem. The second set helps select and design a specific course of action if policy makers have justified the need for one. Both sets of recommendations require supporters of new and continuing programs to demonstrate that their programs are both necessary to the health of the nation's economy and likely to achieve their specific policy objectives efficiently.

These recommendations are designed to force policy makers to define clearly the precise nature of the problem they are attempting to solve. The criteria for screening and designing government involvement can be applied to proposals for new regulations, expenditure programs, or indirect incentive programs.

This approach has many similarities with the current process within the executive branch, where proposals from government agencies and departments are reviewed by OMB and other groups in the Executive Office of the President. In Congress, our approach can be used by the legislative committees and reviewed in the authorization, budget, and appropriations processes. The independent regulatory agencies should also subject their own proposals to a similar screening; compliance in this case could be verified by either the Congressional Budget Office or the General Accounting Office.

Those proposing new initiatives should comply with the screening process. In addition, our recommendations require that they supply evidence to support their claims. (The procedure for ensuring that the requirements of the criteria are implemented is presented in detail in Chapter 7.)

The appropriate decision-making group in the executive branch, Congress, and the independent regulatory agencies should apply the following criteria to all proposals for government involvement.

RECOMMENDATIONS FOR SCREENING

1. Which type of market limitation (if any) is the government attempting to correct? If one exists:

What is the policy's objective, and how is it related to a market limitation?

Will the policy increase competition by

- eliminating restrictions on entry into the market
- improving the information available to participants in the market
- eliminating restraints on the price mechanism

Is government action required because the market is producing some undesirable side effect such as pollution?

What impact will this government action have on other overall economic objectives?

- Will the policy encourage technological innovation and facilitate the attainment of satisfactory levels of economic growth?
- Will it contribute to reducing inflationary pressure on the aggregate level of prices either in the short run or in the long run, or both?
- Will it encourage growth in the aggregate level of employment?

Proponents of government involvement should document their answers to these questions. Legislators, executive branch policy makers, and independent agency rule makers should be required to list clearly what results they expect from each of their enactments. Only rarely can one find in federal enactments a clear description of the expected results, as opposed to broad, vague, or even inconsistent statements of a problem and its solutions. This deceptive language raises high expectations for programs or activities that have no chance of solving the problem. Such language prevents the public from knowing who to blame later for bad results and allows undisciplined implementation. A clear statement of the objectives, the results to be achieved, and the reasons for selecting among the various possible ways to implement policy is necessary for social or political policies as well as economic policies.

Much existing government involvement has occurred because government has responded, not to a market limitation, but to a special interest or narrow concern. Market limitations are justification for government involvement. Examples include natural monopolies, costs of production or consumption imposed on third parties, and inadequate information.[1]

In the case of a natural monopoly, the market system may be ineffective in the absence of government action. The result may be high prices, reduced output, and excessive profits. In some cases, it may not be feasible to reduce the degree of monopoly. It is sometimes argued that the most appropriate actions may be to regulate against excessive prices and profits and to organize the industry so that the advantage of economies of scale is achieved.

---

1. This discussion is based partly on Comptroller General of the United States, *Government Regulatory Activity: Justifications, Processes, Impacts, and Alternatives* (Washington, D.C.: U.S. Government Printing Office, 1977).

This reasoning has justified government involvement in telephone communications, the network of pipelines, railroads (at some stages in their development), and the radio frequency spectrum. In telecommunications, for example, the Federal Communications Commission was specifically established for the purpose of regulating interstate and foreign commerce in communication by wire and radio so as to make available as far as possible to all the people of the United States a rapid, efficient, nationwide and worldwide wire and radio communications service with adequate facilities at reasonable charges. Changes in technology may, of course, make the original justification for a particular type of government involvement obsolete.

The goal of price stability is sometimes given as a reason for having some form of regulated market in which oligopoly (a small number of large suppliers of the product or service) is protected from the entry of new firms and from price wars. This goal has been used to justify government policy toward railroads, an industry potentially prone to price wars because of its high proportion of fixed to variable costs.

Markets may exhibit a limitation because some of the costs of production or consumption are imposed on unrelated third parties. This imperfection is used to justify government's role in assisting individuals to acquire clean air, to enjoy safety, or to enjoy protection from the actions of others. Protection of the rights of third parties through the market system is difficult if the property rights to the natural resource are difficult to identify. For example, if all whalers pursue their own self-interest, they kill as many whales as possible. Individual whalers will lack an incentive to allow the whales to grow to maturity and reproduce because no *individual* whaler is likely to reap the later benefits. As a result, government may decide to act to ensure that the benefits from certain natural resources are maximized for later generations.

Market limitation may also result from inadequate information. Consumers need to know the quality and prices of a large number of products in the market in order to make their preferences known. Similarly, labor markets must provide adequate information on wage rates, job opportunities, and job hazards if they are to be effective. Government involvement may be justified because of the need to increase the flow of relevant information within the market.

The *possibility* of a market imperfection is not a justification for government involvement. *What evidence is there that the imperfection actually exists and that it generates serious distortions which reduce consumer welfare?*

Government frequently intervenes because of the existence of a limitation in the market, even though its own actions cause equally serious distortions. Consider the government's requirement of safety measures in cars, an action justified by a need to protect third parties and reduce the health and rehabilitation costs arising from auto accidents. Should the government simply provide evidence of the probability that seat belts reduce injuries? The government is going to require the mandatory use of air bags that many consider less effective and that are certainly much more expensive than seat belts. Has adequate evidence been presented to justify this degree of involvement?

Finally, those in government should not consider the objectives of policies in isolation from economic goals. For example, the goal of major improvements in social security benefits should take into account the effect this may have on the availability of funds for business investment. The impact on economic objectives should therefore be taken into account.

2. What social and/or political goal is the government seeking?

What is the policy's objective?

In what manner will the beneficiaries gain?

Which citizens will bear the cost?

What impact will this action have on other overall economic objectives?

Government is responsible for several functions that are not directly related to improving the economy. Providing national security, protecting the basic rights of citizens, influencing the distribution of the output of the economic system to provide for the welfare of those in need are all legitimate concerns of government. However, before the government embarks on policies to fulfill these concerns, it should be quite clear about who is going to benefit from these policies and who is going to pay for them. It should also specify how these policies are going to affect the economic system.

3. Is the policy's goal feasible?

Recent economic history makes it clear that the distinction between desirable goals and feasible goals is not always obvious to policy makers or their constituencies. Until legislators and the public appreciate this distinction, new policies and programs risk being wasteful and misleading. There is, of course, no foolproof guarantee that proposed government action will succeed. *If government is to avoid costly mistakes and intervene constructively in the economy*, it must systematically evaluate a proposal's probable success.

> Could the stated goal of the proposed government involvement be achieved more efficiently by eliminating an existing government involvement?

This issue must be considered in order to avoid endless new legislation designed to correct the shortcomings of prior legislation. We believe much mischief can be avoided if this question is posed at the outset.

> Can the stated goal be achieved by government action?

The importance of this question has been demonstrated by the nation's experience with prohibition and, more recently, when in some instances the government apparently attempted to achieve an almost riskless work environment. At the very least, the posing of this question may serve to force legislators and Presidents to define the goals by which the effectiveness of their programs may be evaluated.

> *4. What will the stated goal cost? How does the cost compare with the probable benefits?*

No one would propose government action without advertising its benefits, but too many propose government action without appraising its costs. Yet, the costs will be real; whereas the benefits may not be. Every government involvement imposes a cost, either overt or hidden. That cost should be calculated and publicized by those who propose government action, so that legislators and the public can weigh it against the purported benefits.

> What are the proposal's probable side effects, and what will they cost?

A suitable government action may be shown to be excessively damaging to the economy as a whole when its side effects are appraised. The benefit of a particular government action will help some groups, but it may harm others. There are only limited resources in the economy. If, for example, government assigns considerable medical resources to cure a particular disease, it will have fewer medical resources left for solving other problems. Similarly, raising the U.S. price above the world price of sugar may benefit U.S. sugar beet growers, but it also results in a misallocation of resources toward sugar beet production and away from investment in the production of other goods. The result is higher prices to the U.S. consumer.

New proposals for government action must clearly examine the side effects, the groups that will be harmed, and the action's overall effect on the economic system.

RECOMMENDATIONS FOR SELECTING AND DESIGNING A SPECIFIC KIND OF GOVERNMENT INVOLVEMENT IN THE MARKET SYSTEM

Proponents of government action should present convincing evidence of the need for action. *We believe the key to improving government involvement is to ask less of government and more of the market whenever there is a problem in the economy.*

This Committee recommends the following five criteria to the legislative and executive branches of government and the independent regulatory agencies when they are designing programs that will intervene directly or indirectly in the market system. These criteria are especially relevant to designing new regulations.

1. The market mechanism should be used to achieve policy objectives wherever possible.

This principle is fundamental. It applies to all government policies, including those designed to assure the production of public goods, to protect citizens against the adverse effects of production, to provide equal opportunity, and to stimulate technology and productivity. The burden of proof should always be on the proponents (government agency, legislator, or regulator) to show that government involvement will be more effective than the market mechanism.

For example, partial deregulation is feasible in most areas in which government has used the command-and-control type of rules and standards to achieve social goals. Preliminary evidence suggests this is one of the lessons to be learned from the recent partial deregulation initiated by the Civil Aeronautics Board. Similarly, continued subsidization of some sectors of an industry may simply result in misallocation of resources within the industry and within the economy as a whole without stimulating the desired innovations.

2. Before intervening directly, government should first try to solve the problem of informing the public about the issue and/or the institutions in question.

Even when there is a perceived problem with particular products or services, it is frequently unnecessary for the government to try to mandate changes in these products or services. If consumers are provided adequate information, their behavior in the market will automatically resolve questions about the quantity and reliability of products.

3. When policy makers want to achieve performance goals, they should try to devise incentives and penalties, rather than dictate one path industry must follow in order to comply.

It is possible to reach some of the goals of environmental policy and of occupational safety and health policy through incentives and penalties. Less government regulation could still reward firms that meet the goal of public policy and punish those who do not. Although some policy goals cannot be met through this mechanism and some mandatory standards may be required to supplement it, the mechanism of incentives is nevertheless powerful.[2]

Incentives may take the form of subsidies or credit guarantees. However, two decades of housing policy have shown the risks in this approach. Subsidies, credit guarantees, and differential tax treatment may produce some benefits, but they can also involve substantial costs. Because this form of government involvement provides a direct benefit to a specific segment of the population, it is politically difficult to eliminate or even modify. Nevertheless, such incentives are preferable to detailed rules and regulations.

---

2. Charles L. Schultze, *The Public Use of Private Interests* (Washington, D.C.: Brookings Institution, 1977).

4. Whenever it is absolutely necessary for government to establish detailed goals for institutions and individuals to achieve within the economic system, government should avoid prescribing how these goals should be met.

In some cases, mandatory *minimum* standards may be necessary. Institutions should be free to pursue these standards in the way they believe most efficient, provided they meet the minimum standards. However, whenever there is a legitimate case for mandatory standards, government should be certain that institutions are given a *reasonable* time to achieve them. Goals that have to be achieved too rapidly result in increased costs of production and other undesirable side effects, such as reduced employment opportunities.

Once government has set minimum performance goals, it should, wherever feasible, consider identifying broad groups of goals with which employers would be required to certify compliance. This approach would have to be accompanied by a system of penalties for inaccurate certification.

5. Public production should be used only when no other technique will be more effective.

Government's legitimate responsibility for providing goods and services can frequently be met through contracting arrangements with the private sector. This approach can capture many of the efficiencies of the market mechanism. Public production should be the path of last resort.

METHODS OF INVOLVEMENT THAT SHOULD BE REASSESSED: FOUR CASE STUDIES

The following brief case studies suggest weaknesses in the implementation of several government programs and demonstrate the need to expose them to the type of screening and review process described in our recommendations. These case studies illustrate principles underlying our criteria for selecting and designing better methods of government involvement in the market system. The descriptions of the potential weaknesses are not meant to prejudge the outcome of the recommended review.

Utilizing the Price Mechanism: Environmental Policy*

The case for public policy to enhance environmental quality is a clear and compelling one. As is true of anything that is free for the taking, water and air are abused by both producers and consumers (and

---

IMPLICATIONS OF THE ZERO-RISK PRINCIPLE

The concept of zero risk is currently influential in determining public policies regarding occupational safety and health, the environment, and consumer products. The source of this concept is the 1958 Delaney Amendment to the Food, Drug and Cosmetic Act, which prohibits the use of any chemical substance (*in any amount*) as a food additive if that substance has been found, by "appropriate tests," to induce cancer in human beings or laboratory animals.

The goal of reducing hazardous substances in workplaces, the environment, and consumer products is laudable, but the goal of eliminating *all* risks is foolish. A risk-free environment is impossible to achieve. Even when a substance is known to be potentially dangerous, it may be so only in substantial quantities. Although minimum threshold levels of dangerous substances are highly desirable, policies that ban any measured trace of the substance can impose a high cost on industries, their employees, and the public generally.

A case in point is the FDA's outright ban on acrylonitrile (AN) in beverage bottles (effective January 1978). The FDA considered AN a "food additive" and forbade more than 300 parts per billion. Monsanto (the company with the largest investment in the AN bottle) states their tests detected no migration of AN from the bottle to the beverage after six months at room temperature, using a test method having a sensitivity of 10 parts per billion. Monsanto stated the lowest level of feeding showing harm to test animals requires, in human terms, that a child drink 3,000 bottles of soda every day for life in order to duplicate the test conditions.

---

*See memorandum by J. W. McSWINEY, page 141.

public agencies as well). To protect the environment, the government can choose between two basic approaches: direct controls that place specific restrictions on producers and consumers and indirect controls that create monetary incentives to protect the environment. Government administrators have chosen to rely on direct controls; however, sub-

---

Even though the original standard (300 parts per billion) was established in 1976, FDA proposed dropping this to 50 parts per billion in 1977. FDA now states that tests show there is no safe level of ingestion. Over a three-year period, FDA has changed its standards and now appears to be claiming that in order to achieve zero risk, there must be virtually no migration of AN. The zero-risk approach and continual changes in standards may lead to investment losses to the firms producing the product and imposes costs on the economy.

The pursuit of zero risk is also an ineffective strategy for improving the aggregate quality of the work environment, the physical environment, and consumer products generally. The *extra* costs (research, engineering design, compliance, and reduced productivity) of achieving *zero risk,* rather than an *acceptable threshold of risk,* are often enormous. The pursuit of zero risk forces the government and the private sector to allocate a disproportionate share of their limited resources to eliminating risk in a very small segment of total economic activity. The pursuit of *reduced* risk generally, according to the benefits achieved per unit of investment, would reap much greater reward. This approach would be less damaging to the economy and would yield greater benefits to employers, workers, and citizens generally.

"If we look back at the world of a century ago, we find that expectation of life was 50 years; now it is 70 years. Therefore the sum of all the risks to which we are now exposed must be less than it was."*

---

* Richard Wilson, "Analyzing the Risks of Daily Life," *Technology Review* (February 1979): 41.

stantial evidence suggests that reliance on pricing incentives can frequently be more efficient and just as effective in achieving environmental objectives.[3]

Current environmental policy in the United States involves the issuance of permits to individual polluters and the *determination by public authorities of the best available technology for pollution control* in individual industries. Confrontations, legal battles, and painful delays in the realization of environmental goals have resulted, in addition to excessive abatement costs running into billions of dollars. It might be far more efficient to charge polluters for their waste emissions into our environment and to require industry itself to determine and develop the least expensive way to reduce pollution. Do such programs work? They do. The widespread response to the adoption of refillable beverage containers is one example. The return rate on these containers is running well in excess of 90 percent, and the added cost associated with this program is modest. Potential applications for the similar use of pricing incentives are many. Some have already been implemented abroad: effluent fees on waste discharges into the air or waters, landing fees based on noise levels and waste emissions of aircraft, and higher peak-load prices that shift usage of congested facilities away from periods of peak use. In each instance, the idea is the same: Make pollution unprofitable.

Pricing incentives are not the whole answer. There are surely important roles for direct controls (and even moral suasion) in a comprehensive program for protection of the environment. The question is: What is the most effective combination of policies? Pricing incentives should be the first weapon during normal times because they also stimulate the development of improved and less expensive techniques for lessening pollution. However, the system of fees could be supplemented with a set of direct controls to

regulate polluting activities where metering is not feasible

prohibit emissions of wastes that pose grave threats to humanity

---

3. For documentation and more extended examination of these issues, see William J. Baumol, Wallace E. Oates, and Sue Anne Batey Blackman, *Economics, Enviromental Policy, and the Quality of Life* (Englewood Cliffs, N.J.: Prentice-Hall, 1979). CED has previously urged greater reliance on market incentives for environmental protection in *More Effective Programs for a Cleaner Environment* (1974).

provide additional restrictions on waste discharges during emergency periods of adverse environmental conditions

Existing attempts by government to forge an environmental policy without enlisting the direct support of market forces have greatly reduced the effectiveness of policy and, at the same time, generated substantial waste of resources.*

Avoiding Undesirable Side Effects of a Subsidy: Housing

Since the depression, the federal government has been increasingly involved in providing housing through subsidies and public housing efforts. For many reasons, these efforts to provide housing for the poor have rarely succeeded. In the early stages of the nation's public housing policy, middle-income families paid for the operating costs of public housing projects, and the poor were excluded. As the government began to aid the poor, it found housing projects alone were insufficient and fashioned extensive federal subsidies.

The Housing Act of 1968, which focused on the nation's poor, mandated broad subsidies for home ownership and rental assistance. Although initially successful in helping thousands of families gain comfortable housing, the programs were eventually suspended. Among the concerns raised by the subsidies were their high cost ($200 billion estimated over the life of the mortgage guarantees), their tendency to contribute to inflation, their failure to aid in the rehabilitation of existing housing, their vulnerability to administrative fraud, and the conversion of the federal government into the nation's largest slumlord (through abandonment and default caused in part by not taking into account future operating costs). Moreover, the subsidy programs seemed inequitable because they served only some of the poor and because they asked middle-income taxpayers to support housing that was often better than their own.

An underlying fault in the design of housing programs was their scope; they often tried to do more than help the poor; they also tried to increase housing construction and employment. Housing experts have concluded that these two goals should be dealt with separately. Although construction of new housing for the poor has often led to a boom in the housing industry and positive overall impacts for the economy, the poor have also suffered from the perverse side effects of the programs that were formulated primarily to help them.

*See memorandum by J. W. McSWINEY, page 142.

It is extremely difficult to design a multipurpose subsidy in a field such as housing, in which there are competing vested interests. The subsidy program for housing clearly did not meet its expectations. A voucher program or offer of housing assistance to the poor in a reformed welfare program would provide more direct help. Either of these approaches might avoid the undesirable side effects that resulted in a major misallocation of the nation's resources. However, recent studies have shown that voucher programs have not been particularly successful. Government involvement in the housing industry to assist low-income families has so far been one of the most ineffective examples of public policy.

Internalizing the Costs of Accidents and Illness: OSHA[4]

In the 1960s, the federal government moved to reduce the number of industrial and work-related hazards and accidents. Once the decision was made to use direct controls, an enormous number of detailed rules and regulations concerning work equipment and materials and the work environment were inevitable.

Although no one agrees about the precise cost of all these direct controls, all agree that costs are sometimes substantial, even enormous, compared with the benefits achieved. For example, it has been estimated that the standard eighty-five decibels proposed by the government to control noise in workplaces will require the expenditure of $18.5 billion in capital costs over a five-year period.

Both the cost and the chosen method of achieving the standards set by the government raise questions. The government not only sets the goal but also prescribes almost exactly how to achieve it. The government requires an almost noise-free environment and forces expensive conversion of the capital plant and equipment without leaving employers the option of offering employees and requiring them to wear (less expensive) protective gear as a way of reducing the risk of hearing impairment. The government's approach to reducing risk from occupational disease is similarly weak.

---

4. *Making Prevention Pay* (Washington, D.C.: U.S. Government Printing Office, 1978). The Interagency Task Force on Work Place Safety and Health report was released in December 1978. It supports most of the changes suggested in this case study.

A policy that uses direct controls provides employers and employees with neither incentives for improving health and safety nor penalties for failure to do so. Direct controls dealing with a complex problem inevitably lead to an enormous number of detailed standards and a complicated procedure in which employer groups and others are involved in lengthy challenges to the application of the controls. The government then must mount a massive compliance effort that has an inevitably slight probability of success.

There are alternatives to this adversary approach to improving the health and safety of workers. For example, policy makers should consider the following approaches: The government may develop a strategy that requires employees or their representatives to participate in employer policies for improving worker health and safety. It may be possible to internalize the cost of *some* types of workplace accidents. An expanded disability insurance system and/or an improved workers' compensation scheme in which premium rates are more closely linked to an individual business or industry safety record would be examples. This approach also implies that the current social security benefits for injured workers should be incorporated into worker compensation programs.

If policy moves in this direction, it will pay employers to reduce work-related injuries. Workers will also have the same incentive because production cost increases resulting from high injury rates will reduce potential real wage increases as well as employment opportunities.

Economic incentives will not be effective in *all* areas of health and safety. For example, it is difficult for government and business to predetermine standards for the work environment because of the problems of determining the precise causes of certain occupational diseases and the long latency periods for many of them. Nevertheless, for workers' health the government should, whenever possible, avoid prescribing precisely how production should be carried out. It should adopt an approach that identifies hazards through a clearinghouse for scientific research and product information and that prescribes a goal but permits employers to achieve that goal in a variety of ways. In addition to a system of penalties and incentives, the government should consider requiring businesses to certify their own compliance with its prescribed goals.

These alternative techniques would reduce the number of detailed rules and regulations, would reduce direct enforcement costs, and would permit employers to decide the type of capital costs required to improve health and safety. In essence, the government should consider setting performance standards and permit employers to decide how to meet them.

Coordinating Involvement Techniques: Transportation

For many decades, government has used every type of regulation to influence transportation in the United States. Price controls and special tax arrangements have been justified in the interest of safety in air and sea navigation. Capital construction and maintenance costs have been completely or partially borne by the government for highway, airport, and coastal and inland waterway improvements. These costs have been met in some cases directly out of government revenues and in others gradually through taxes on users. Subsidies have been made available to all forms of transportation, including ship construction, urban mass transit, and railroads. Credit guarantees have been provided to cover the unsubsidized portions of ship construction.

A very complex network of regulations affects the entry and exit of firms in various segments of the transportation industry and in their submarkets. Regulations have drawn the government deeply into the day-to-day operation of airlines, railroads, trucking, and shipping. These detailed regulations affect the fares and rate charges of public carriers and the allocation of routes among carriers, as well as the specifications of the capital equipment and the related manning requirements of that equipment.

Many justifications are cited for such a detailed and prescriptive form of government involvement. National security, the need to serve all communities, the need to unify the country, the need to avoid wasteful competition, and the need to avoid excessive profits from the monopoly position of firms have all been used as justifications for vast government involvement. The government has an important stake in fostering a national transportation system that links all areas of the country and encourages the economic development of the nation. Nevertheless, many current policies are questionable and should be reviewed. For example, railroads are sometimes unable to abandon uneconomic lines despite the existence of alternate means of transportation; an integrated system is not possible because there are restrictions limiting companies' ability to operate in more than one form of transportation.

There is now general agreement that the effect of government policy on competition within the transportation industry needs to be reexamined. Expensive subsidies, lack of competition, and potential overregulation of prices may all have contributed to an uncoordinated and inefficient system. Subsidies for urban mass transit and government proposals for reorganizing railroads have also resulted in expensive protection provisions for workers without necessarily improving the effectiveness of the transportation system. Government should consider reducing its role in transportation and should permit the market to be the main allocator of resources among and within the major modes of transportation.

CONCLUSIONS

If policy makers systematically apply the criteria described in this chapter, they will gradually stem the unproductive expansion of government into the market system. The questions that should be answered before an attempt is made to correct a market limitation are especially relevant for reviewing regulatory policy proposals. If the proponents of new regulations are made to respond to these questions in a serious way *before* new rules are published and the answers are reviewed at public hearings, many potentially harmful regulations will be avoided.

The market limitation questions are also important when indirect policies such as subsidies, loans, and loan guarantees are being considered by policy makers. Before the government intervenes through an indirect incentive, it should be clear that the market limitation actually exists.

The questions associated with the social and political goals are important to all forms of government involvement, especially when a new direct expenditure program is proposed. Experience has shown that expenditure programs introduced without a definition of who the program is supposed to benefit and who is going to bear the cost frequently end up failing to help those intended to benefit from the program. The feasibility questions we recommend apply to all forms of government involvement.

Once expenditure programs and regulatory policies are in existence, a variety of vested interests will resist their elimination even when their weaknesses are obvious. It is therefore essential to avoid potentially harmful government intervention before it occurs. To do this, it is necessary for the political system to develop procedures that will force policy makers to ask harder questions when screening and designing new government policies. This will require the political system to initiate procedural changes in the policy-making process. Chapter 7 discusses the procedural changes that we believe will improve the role of public policy in the market system.

SUMMARY OF CRITERIA
FOR SCREENING, ADOPTING, AND DESIGNING
GOVERNMENT ACTIONS

Recommendations for Screening Proposals for Government Involvement

Which type of market limitation (if any) is the government attempting to correct? If one exists:

- What is the policy's objective, and how is it related to a market limitation?

- Will the policy increase competition by eliminating restrictions on entry, improving information, or eliminating restraints on the price mechanism?

- Is government action required because the market is producing some undesirable side effect such as pollution?

- What impact will this have on other overall economic objectives such as improved technological innovation, satisfactory economic growth, reducing the rate of inflation, and high employment?

What social and/or political goal is the government seeking?

- What is the policy's objective?

- In what manner will the beneficiaries gain?

- Which citizens will bear the cost?

- What impact will this have on other overall economic objectives? Is government's goal feasible?

- Could the stated goal of the proposed government involvement be achieved more efficiently by eliminating an existing government involvement?
- Can the stated goal be achieved by *any* conceivable government action?

What will the stated goal cost?

- What are the proposal's side effects, and what will they cost?
- How do the costs and hoped-for benefits compare?

Recommendations for Selecting and Designing a Specific Kind of Government Involvement (criteria especially relevant for selecting cost-effective regulatory techniques)

The market mechanism should be used to achieve policy goals wherever possible.

Before intervening directly, the government should educate the public about the issues and/or the institutions in question.

When policy makers want to achieve specific goals, they should devise incentives and penalties, rather than dictate one path that industry must follow in order to comply.

Whenever it is absolutely necessary for government to establish detailed goals for institutions and individuals to achieve within the economic system, government should avoid prescribing how these goals should be met.

Public production should be used only when no other technique will be more effective.

A Comprehensive Approach for Disciplining Policy Decisions

POLITICIANS IN THE ADMINISTRATION and Congress and administrators in the independent regulatory agencies are now responding to public concern about the growth of government. Over the years, the role of government in the market system has emerged from within the political system because it was politically attractive to support new direct expenditure programs and regulations, some of which often unintentionally (and sometimes intentionally) reduced the effectiveness of markets. Because the effect of much of this government expansion into markets is now recognized as detrimental to the long-term performance of the economy, it has become politically attractive to seek ways to reduce the growth of government and to eliminate or modify ineffective public policies. The Administration and Congress are now actively seeking new legislative approaches to achieve this purpose.

If this Committee's criteria for screening and reviewing public policy are to be implemented by policy makers in the executive branch, Congress, and the independent regulatory agencies, it is necessary to reform the policy-making process. Procedural changes in the policy-making process are no guarantee that unnecessary and ineffective government actions will be curtailed, but these changes do provide elected officials with a framework for improving policies.* *Our recommendations support the efforts of political leaders in the Administration and Congress who are seriously concerned about strengthening the market system and eliminating inefficient government activities.*

Our recommendations for redefining government's role in the market system emphasize a process that includes the following phases: screening the objective and the particular method the government should adopt to implement a new policy and estimating the impact of the proposed policy; evaluating results to eliminate, expand, or modify existing policy; ensuring that systematic program evaluation leads to policy changes; and finally, periodically reviewing the decision-making process.

The reformed process for policy making includes procedures for analyzing all economically significant legislative and administrative proposals prior to their adoption and systematically evaluating them after implementation so that ineffective policies can be eliminated or modified. This Committee's recommended approach is comprehensive: Proposals from every branch of government (the executive, Congress, and the independent regulatory agencies) would be subjected to the four-phase process. The proponents of each major policy proposal would be required to respond satisfactorily to similar questions before proposals would be considered for adoption. (The recommended screening questions that apply to all proposals for government involvement are discussed in Chapter 6.) The responses to these questions would be submitted to specific administrative units within each branch of government. Consequently, although similar screening questions are asked about proposals from all branches of government, the responses justifying compliance and the final decision to approve or disapprove the policy proposal involve different procedures for each branch of government.

We strongly recommend that all types of government involvement discussed in this statement be subjected to this process. This Committee believes that other types of public policies may also benefit from a similar systematic review. Initially, only new policies, whether enacted in legislation or resulting from existing administrative authority, are included in the review process. New policy proposals are usually closely related to one or more existing government programs. Consequently, the review process will also be applied to existing programs selectively on the basis

*See memorandum by ROY L. ASH, page 139.

of their relevance to new policy issues. Existing programs or regulations of major economic significance should also be gradually subjected to systematic review.

The only reason for excluding a policy from the review process is practical: It is important to concentrate on those proposed policies and groups of existing programs that are of major economic significance. Experience with congressional oversight and the preparation of inflationary- and economic-impact statements have shown that any attempt to subject *all* policy proposals to systematic review will simply result in superficial pro forma assessments.[1]

The definition of *major* policies should be determined by the Administration on the basis of the Council on Wage and Price Stability's most recent attempts to assess the impact of regulations. For the executive branch, the President could define the specifications of a major policy in an executive order or incorporate them into legislation. Congress should also be guided by recent experience in attempting to assess the impact of regulations.[2] Specifications for Congress to follow in defining major policies could be contained in a Presidential message or in legislation. We recommend that the definition applied by Congress be followed by the independent regulatory agencies in defining their major policy proposals and that this definition be contained in appropriate legislation.

Our entire set of recommendations aims at impelling better consideration of the long-range as well as the short-range costs and benefits of any proposed major action *before* it is taken and careful periodic efforts to learn from the past successes and mistakes of major programs *after* they are introduced. The recommendations are specifically adapted to the current organization of the federal government. That means they respect the constitutional division of powers between the executive and legislative branches and the current allocation of functional responsibilities within each. Furthermore, the recommendations themselves contain various checks and balances on their own workings to guard against omissions, failures to perform, or consistently erroneous patterns of action. To ac-

---

1. See Congressional Research Service, *Economic and Inflation Impact Statements: The Use by the Executive and Legislative Branches* (Washington, D.C.: U.S. Library of Congress, 1978).

2. The standard for defining *major* under the current assessment of the inflationary impact of regulations is $100 million in direct and indirect costs imposed on the economy.

complish all this takes a sizable number of specific recommended measures that are interrelated in a comprehensive approach.

PHASE 1: SCREENING THE OBJECTIVE, METHOD, AND IMPACT OF PROPOSED POLICIES

Major policy changes proposed by an agency within the executive branch, a congressional legislative committee, or an independent regulatory agency should provide answers to the type of questions proposed in Chapter 6 (see page 108). These criteria for screening proposals require proponents of new policies to justify the need for government action. As has been pointed out, these criteria have to be adapted to the type of government action being proposed—regulations, indirect incentives, or direct expenditures. Unless these criteria are satisfied, the policy should not be initiated or continued. Once the case for involvement is made, proponents should justify their choice of method of involvement according to our suggested priorities.

In addition, every major new government policy or regulation should state its objectives in a form that will permit future evaluation and should estimate its primary and secondary results. The purpose of framing these objectives is to establish standards for the future evaluation of the program's success or failure. At present, much government legislation and administrative regulation are launched with excessively broad and sometimes internally inconsistent objectives. This vagueness frequently leads to unrealistic expectations about what the proposal is likely to achieve. Unless the objectives are stated in specific terms, there will be no standards by which to assess success or failure. The estimate of potential side effects should include the impact on overall economic objectives. We suggest that these objectives might include reducing inflation, encouraging high employment, and technological and productivity improvements as well as general economic growth. To be effective, the Administration and Congress would have to define these objectives in law and should require that they be taken into account in the design of new policies.

The estimate of the proposal's likely effect on economic goals should go beyond the cost estimates currently required by the budget process. The direct cost of new policies, whether regulations or new programs, is important, but the total impact on the economy may in the long run be greater or less than the budgetary outlay. The net cost of a new regulation is almost always more inflationary than its official budget. For example, new health programs may involve only small expenditures by the federal government but large costs to individuals and employers. The process of screening proposals must allow time for the evidence to be questioned and analyzed by others.

Specific recommendations for how phase 1 might be implemented are presented in this section. As indicated, it should be required by law that major policy proposals be subjected to specific screening procedures. Consequently, policy decisions must give due weight to the effect of the proposal on economic objectives as well as to the primary objective of the policy. In order to avoid pro forma compliance with this legal requirement, there should also be guidelines specifying acceptable standards of evidence to be included in impact statements.

The procedure for certifying compliance is different for each branch of government. For proposals from executive agencies (and executive regulatory agencies), evidence answering the screening questions would be reported to an administrative unit within OMB or some other part of the Executive Office of the President. This administrative unit would certify that the evidence accompanying the proposal is in compliance with the standards identified in the guidelines. If these standards are not met, the proponents of the proposal would have to resubmit the proposal. In order to implement this procedure, it might in some cases be necessary to amend the enabling legislation for some regulatory agencies.

The decision whether or not to proceed toward implementing the proposal would be made within the existing decision-making process in the executive branch of government. But in the case of rule making within existing legislative authority, we recommend that the executive branch and regulatory agencies provide greater opportunity for public comment on those proposals that the Administration intends to implement. For major changes in rule making, it is not sufficient simply to publish the proposal in the *Federal Register*. The public must be involved in the discussion *before* the Administration decides to implement a new regulation.

Proposals for new policies from the legislative branch must include evidence in response to the screening questions for the legislative proposals from congressional committees. We recommend that the congressional Rules Committees verify that the evidence presented meets the standards necessary for compliance. We also suggest that the Congressional Budget Office or the General Accounting Office review new policy proposals and assist the Rules Committees in making their compliance decisions. Provided the evidence is in compliance, the decision concerning implementation would follow the normal legislative process.

We believe that the Rules Committees should perform this function when legislation is reported out of the committee *and* when amendments of major significance are introduced on the floor of either the Senate or the House.

New rules (or groups of rules) proposed by the independent regulatory agencies would also be reviewed for compliance. The review should be designed so that it does not conflict with the independent regulatory agencies' legislative responsibilities for rule making. We therefore recommend that either the Congressional Budget Office or the General Accounting Office review proposals for new regulations for compliance with the screening requirements for proposed major new regulations. CBO or GAO should be required to make their compliance report available at the public hearing held prior to new rule changes. In the past, the Council on Wage and Price Stability has in a few cases used a similar approach when the Administration was concerned about the potential inflationary impact of new regulations.

The advantage of this compliance review is that the public and interested parties are provided with additional information prior to the implementation of new regulations. The regulatory agency is still free to initiate the proposed rule change, but the review will highlight any potential adverse effects of the proposal. Even if implemented, the new regulation can be monitored, and the evaluation phase of our recommendations provides an opportunity to determine whether these adverse effects actually materialize.

PHASE 2: EVALUATING THE EFFECTIVENESS OF POLICIES

Evaluating the effectiveness of policies (or groups of policies) and related programs is a crucial phase in any attempt to improve decision making. In this phase, determining the effectiveness of policies requires a systematic review of the program or groups of programs that have been used to implement the policy. In the case of regulatory policy, the specific regulations should be evaluated.

The need for a comprehensive system for improving policy decisions is not unique to public policies; businesses also require a systematic approach to decision making. Business screens new policies through an elaborate process of financial analysis, product testing, and market analysis, including projections of the future demand for goods and services.

IMPLEMENTING PHASE 1: RECOMMENDATIONS FOR SCREENING THE OBJECTIVE, METHOD, AND IMPACT OF PROPOSED POLICIES

For any proposed major policy change (legislative or administrative) that has significant economic consequences, the Administration, Congress, and the independent regulatory agencies should implement the following (or similar) procedures:

1. Establish guidelines for defining major legislative and administrative proposals for policy and program changes.
2. Require that all proposals be screened according to this Committee's (or similar) criteria (summarized on page 108). Provide evidence to justify compliance with particular criteria.
3. Require that all proposals meet this Committee's (or similar) criteria for selecting and designing a specific kind of government involvement. Justify the method of involvement chosen, and explain why no higher-ranked method was adequate for the task.
4. Direct that each proposal briefly and clearly express its objectives (in a format that permits future evaluation) and anticipated results, direct and indirect, as well as summarizes its justifications.
5. Review statements of anticipated results submitted with each new proposal, recommending any modification deemed necessary to describe more fairly the likely results, including the impact on overall economic objectives such as reducing inflation, high employment, technological and productivity improvements, and general economic growth. This might best be accomplished by defining these objectives by law, with the legislative history providing guidelines for the type of evidence required for new proposals. Similarly, effective implementation also suggests that there be a legal requirement to take these objectives into account in the implementation of new policies.
6. Develop arrangements for selectively subjecting major ongoing programs to the same criteria specified in steps 1 to 5 for new major policy proposals.

7. Provide funds for future program evaluation. If legislation is required, funding arrangements for evaluation should be included in the bill reported out of committee.

Implementation Procedures

Executive. Through the appropriate legal instrument, it should be made mandatory for all major policy proposals to be subjected to this (or a similar) screening process. In the executive branch, the President should be free, within the mandatory requirements, to establish the appropriate institutional arrangements for reviewing new proposals by government agencies. OMB could be required to review agencies' compliance with the screening process, including preparation of the schedule for *selectively* reviewing ongoing programs.

Congress. Congress should have the legal basis for requiring that each legislative proposal reported out of committee conform to the screening process. The Government Operations and Governmental Affairs Committees could prepare a schedule for *selectively* reviewing existing programs and assigning oversight responsibility. The Rules Committee, assisted by CBO or GAO, should ensure that evidence required in the screening process, including the main focus of future evaluations, is included in each committee report accompanying legislation. Major amendments modifying proposals from the legislative committee should also be accompanied by answers to the screening questions.

Independent Regulatory Agencies. Congress should consider enacting legislation requiring these agencies to follow the screening process. However, such legislation should be flexible enough to permit an agency to adapt the screening process to any unique features in its responsibilities. Compliance with the screening process would be certified through a review by either CBO or GAO that could be reported at the public hearing *prior* to the implementation of any new major regulation.

There are, however, important distinctions. In the market system, determining a policy's success is a matter of accurate cost accounting to determine economic viability because the market automatically determines success or failure, and the authority system within business makes it relatively easy to change policy once failure is identified. In the public sector, there is no such automatic measurement of success or failure. Programs that implement policy have to be evaluated to determine whether they are successful in achieving their goals. In addition, public officials are likely to experience considerable resistance to the elimination of established programs from public employees and the beneficiaries of the programs. Even when evaluation identifies policy weaknesses, the decision to eliminate or modify programs has to emerge from a political environment in which compromise among political interests may prevent any action being taken. *It is for this reason that evaluation results must become part of the public debate.*

Evaluating the effectiveness of policies involves several interrelated types of measurements. Evaluation is essential to the effective administration of programs. Executive branch agencies devote considerable resources to assessing how well programs are being implemented. This type of *process* evaluation determines whether the funds were spent according to the legislative authority and whether the administration of the program was efficient. Process evaluation is therefore an essential management technique that should be used to modify the administration of programs. **This Committee believes that all agencies, including the independent regulatory agencies, should initiate or continue to conduct process evaluations and should use the results of these reviews in the internal management of their programs.**

In recent years, there has been a rapid growth in *impact* evaluation within the executive branch agencies. This type of evaluation tries to determine whether the program has made a difference. Did the program in fact achieve its objectives? Some of this type of evaluation has been carried out by the agencies responsible for administering the programs. The participation of those responsible for the day-to-day operation of programs contributes to successful impact evaluations by providing the basic information on program performance. However, this is not a reliable source of objective evaluations. **This Committee recommends that impact evaluation by the operational agencies be supplemented within the entire department.** Objective in-house evaluation of a program (or, preferably, groups of programs) also *requires that evaluations be conducted or at least systematically reviewed by those outside the agency responsible for* *administering the program.* The executive departments and the independent regulatory agencies should, therefore, have a centralized evaluation unit that conducts its own evaluations and reviews agency evaluations. This central evaluation unit should report to the top management of the department or independent regulatory agency. *In addition, agencies should be encouraged to contract with nongovernment independent researchers for objective evaluations of program success or failure.* Comparing program objectives with program results will also require considerable strengthening of the evaluation functions currently performed by the Office of Management and Budget and other units within the Executive Office of the President.

Congress is now beginning to recognize that its own efforts to evaluate policy through congressional oversight are inadequate. Unlike the executive branch, Congress has rarely requested the funds to finance independent evaluations. It relies primarily on the government agencies responsible for administering the program being reviewed for information on program effectiveness. One effective way to remedy this unsatisfactory arrangement is to require that all legislation affecting major policy changes reported out of committee contain provision for future evaluation with the necessary funding to evaluate program effectiveness.

If Congress is to perform its oversight functions effectively, it also requires staff support from professional evaluators. Existing congressional committee staffs can synthesize the results of evaluation reports, but they are rarely in a position to conduct evaluation studies. *However, the key staff support in Congress can be strengthened without creating a new bureaucratic structure.*

Successful evaluation depends more on the quality of personnel than on their number. The necessary staff for strengthening congressional oversight is potentially available from several sources. The agencies of government have information that can be used for impact evaluations, although it would be inappropriate to rely wholly on agency evaluations without inviting independent evaluators to review carefully their assumptions, specifications, and methodology. GAO currently provides policy and program analyses to congressional committees. *Strengthening GAO to support its increasing emphasis on evaluation of programs is a logical way to increase staff support to the oversight committees.* Congress should also consider using nongovernment sources for expertise on particular topics. *Other groups in Congress are capable of contributing to the evaluation process, including the Congressional Budget Office, the Congressional Research Service, the Office of Technology Assessment, the*

IMPLEMENTING PHASE 2: RECOMMENDATIONS FOR EVALUATING THE EFFECTIVENESS OF POLICIES

For major policies and related programs that have significant economic consequences:

The *Administration* should

1. Require the appropriate agency to report to the President on the second and thereafter on every fifth anniversary of any major policy and related programs, appraising the difference between actual and anticipated results. Each of these evaluations is reviewed by OMB and includes recommendations for improvement, modification, or termination of programs that the Administration can put into effect at its discretion (including proposals for termination if appropriate) or by proposing legislation to Congress.

Congress should

1. Assign primary oversight responsibility for each major policy and related government programs (and regulatory policies) to a specific committee of each house of Congress, and direct each committee to hold comprehensive oversight hearings to evaluate the performance of such major programs and regulations at least once every five or six years, or more frequently if the committee deems necessary. Insofar as possible, the hearings should be held in the first year of the appropriate Congress and, except for those with permanent authorization, prior to the reauthorization date.

2. For each policy (or policies), ensure that the chairman of the oversight committee requests an evaluation report from the relevant agency and/or GAO. This report would determine how the policy measured up to its objectives. CBO, CRS, and the House and Senate Budget and

Appropriations Committees would be invited to comment on the implications of the evaluation report. The evaluation report would be discussed at the oversight hearings, with the committee stating its agreement or disagreement.

3. Require that the oversight committee's recommendations for improving, modifying, or terminating programs be forwarded to the appropriate legislative committee, the Appropriations Committees, the Budget Committees, the Ways and Means Committee, the Senate Finance Committee, and the Administration for consideration in their future actions.

4. Coordinate the expiration dates of all related programs so that evaluations of groups of programs can be conducted prior to expiration. Permanently authorized programs should also be included in the group evaluations.

The *independent regulatory agencies* should be required (conceivably through appropriate legislation) to

1. Establish an internal evaluation unit, independent of those drafting and implementing regulations, to monitor the impact of regulations in view of their stated objectives. The evaluation unit should recommend changes on the basis of the evaluation.

2. Report to their respective congressional oversight committees on the second and fifth anniversaries of the effective date of any major new policy or program, conveying its appraisal of the impact of policies compared with their objectives. Recommendations for legislative improvement, modification, or termination of programs judged to be deficient should also be reported.

House and Senate Budget Committees, and the House and Senate Appropriations Committees.

One way of implementing the evaluation phase is outlined on page 120. Because the recommendations in this policy statement apply to major new policy proposals, evaluation policies would not be initiated for several years after this (or a similar) comprehensive approach was adopted. However, we have also recommended that the comprehensive approach should be *selectively* applied to existing major policies. Consequently, the evaluation phase should be gradually implemented by reviews of the most significant major policies. Selection of these policies could be made by the Government Operations Committee and the Governmental Affairs Committee in Congress and by OMB for the Administration.

We recommend strengthening congressional review by requiring the chairman of each oversight committee to request an evaluation report from the appropriate agency within the Administration, an outside group, or from the General Accounting Office. The evaluation report should review a major policy by examining the program or group of programs used to implement it. The report should determine whether or not the programs are achieving the policy objectives and make recommendations for continuing, terminating, or modifying the programs. The oversight committee should also indicate whether or not it agrees with the evaluation report and why. On the basis of the report, the oversight committee can make its own recommendations on the future of programs and assess what changes are necessary in the overall policy. However, before the committee makes its judgment, the Congressional Budget Office, the House and Senate Budget Committees, the House and Senate Appropriations Committees, the Congressional Research Service, and the agency responsible for the program should be invited to comment on the evaluation. The advantage of inviting these groups to comment is that each will contribute a different perspective to the review of policy.

Finally, this Committee believes the oversight committee's recommendations for modifying policy must be incorporated into the debates within congressional committees that are in a position to change policy. Policy recommendations should therefore be made to the appropriate legislative committee, the Budget and Appropriations Committees, the House Ways and Means Committee, and the Senate Finance Committee. The oversight committees should also request policy changes of the Administration. This request should be made to OMB and the head of the appropriate department; in the case of the independent regulatory agencies, the request would be made to the head of the agency. The Administration would be asked to respond to recommendations of the oversight committee and explain if and how it intends to implement changes in programs and overall policy.

ADDITIONAL PROCEDURES FOR SCREENING AND EVALUATING PUBLIC POLICIES

Several additional changes in the policy-making process can be made to complement this Committee's recommendations for screening and evaluating policies. The specific changes vary according to the type of government involvement.

Direct Expenditure Programs

We recommend that the existing budget and appropriations reviews of direct expenditure programs be strengthened. This is necessary because only major programs will be evaluated every five or six years; the remaining programs will not be evaluated on a regular basis.

Several steps can be taken to strengthen the budget and appropriations processes:

Improving Coordination between the Budget and Appropriations Processes

We believe that the budget process should be made more complementary to the appropriations process. In preparing the budget resolution on the overall budget level, the Budget Committees now examine the proposed funding level of groups of related programs within the nineteen traditional budget categories.[3] Strengthening fiscal oversight would be achieved if the Budget Committees recommended budget ceilings for groups of programs related to a specific policy. This would

---

3. The following are the nineteen categories: national defense; international affairs; general science, space, and technology; energy; natural resources and environment; agriculture; commerce and housing credit; transportation; community and regional development; education, training, employment, and social services; health; income security; veterans benefits and services; administration of justice; general government; general-purpose fiscal assistance; interest; allowances; undistributed offsetting receipts.

provide the Appropriations Committees with guidance as they review programs within policy areas and make program spending decisions.

Within the appropriations process, there is a greater need to evaluate the contribution of groups of programs to particular policies before spending decisions are made. Congress recognizes that the current line items in the budget are not appropriate for determining the scope of policy reviews prior to appropriation of funds. We therefore support the trend toward appropriations decisions that take into account related groups of programs that may be included within one or more budget line items.

Implementing the Intent of the Budget Impoundment and Control Act of 1974

This Committee believes that the growth in expenditure programs can be slowed down significantly by implementing authority existing under the Budget Impoundment and Control Act. The key to improving the budget process is to strengthen the First Budget Resolution. The process of developing the first resolution involves considerable debate over the budget authority for new policy initiatives and changes in the budget requirement for existing policies and programs. Subsequent budget resolutions are largely determined by changes in economic projections and changes in spending and revenue rates. If the growth in expenditures is to be contained, it is therefore necessary to improve the quality of analysis used in preparing the First Budget Resolution and to ensure that the longer-term implications of budget-level decisions are taken into account.

The First Budget Resolution can be strengthened in several ways. Deviations from the original budget ceilings should be permitted only when economic projections change between February and the date of the Second Budget Resolution in September or in the event that the government has to respond to an emergency.

Each year, a number of individual waivers are granted to specific programs; the result is overall expenditures above the budget ceilings established in the Second Budget Resolution. The budget process would also be strengthened if the Budget Committees, as a regular practice, encouraged compensating reductions in other programs to offset the waiver or granted a waiver only in case of an emergency.

The budget process would also be more effective if Section 308(a), "Reports on Legislation Providing New Budget Authority," was fully implemented. This section was intended to give the Budget Committees and Congress detailed information on the immediate *and* future effects of each bill on the overall budget. This is necessary when the Budget Committees are making budget-level and allocation decisions for the current budget resolution. This section of the act was meant to deal with the problem of new legislation that may involve significant variations between first-year and subsequent expenditures.

Section 308(a)(2) requires that reports accompanying any bill or resolution providing new budget authority include in detail "a projection of the outlays which will result from the bill or resolution in each of the five ensuing years, beginning with the year in which the outlays first occur." For the 1980 Presidential budget, estimates are being made for a three-year period. The Senate Budget Committee reports include five-year projections, but the House Budget Committee reports do not include projections for future years. Despite the intent of the act, future-year estimates are not regarded as part of the current-year budget resolution.

This Committee recommends that for all new bills or resolutions, the information required under the act be submitted to the Budget Committees. This means that the Budget Committees should incorporate the five-year projected outlays into the nineteen functional budget categories so that the budget resolution includes the five-year projected outlays for all expenditure programs. In addition to including out-year projections, we recommend that these estimates be voted on. This recommendation should apply to the First Budget Resolution, as well as to subsequent resolutions.

We recommend that under Section 302 of the act, the Budget Committees include in the annual budget resolution the current budget authority and outlays *along with the five-year estimates allocated among the nineteen functional categories of the total budget.* Under the same section of the act, the Appropriations Committee of each house is required to subdivide the Budget Committee's allocations among its subcommittees and proceed to make spending decisions. Because the Budget Committees will have voted on the estimates for future years, those estimates could be used as a standard for the preparation of budget resolutions in subsequent years. Deviations from the estimates would have to be justified by the Budget Committees. Therefore, the five-year estimates by functional area would become provisional budget ceilings.

If Section 308(a) of the 1974 act is implemented, it would clearly identify the future-cost implications of new expenditure programs. Policy makers would then be forced to recognize the full implications of their decisions at the time those decisions are being made. The future-expenditure implications of existing programs can easily be incorporated into the five-year estimates because the Congressional Budget Office currently makes five-year estimates for *total* budget authority and outlays, as well as estimates for functional categories.

If the Budget Committees utilize their existing authority and submit the current and five-year budget estimates to the Appropriations Committees, it will also strengthen the Appropriations Committees' ability to control spending levels and review the effectiveness of expenditure programs. **This Committee strongly recommends that the philosophy underlying Section 308(a)(2) be implemented because it is an extremely effective way of improving expenditure decisions and controlling the growth of federal expenditures.**

Alternate Approaches to Controlling the Aggregate Growth of Federal Expenditures

Several approaches to controlling the growth of federal expenditures have been proposed in recent years. One suggests restricting the growth of revenue available to government for administration and funding of expenditure programs. The adjustment of tax rates in a program of gradual tax reduction has been proposed in Congress. However, a federal tax cut does not by itself guarantee a reduction in the growth of federal expenditures. Government may simply continue to finance expenditures through borrowing. In addition, the benefits of a tax cut may be illusory, particularly when the tax cut contributes to inflation. Rising prices reduce real income and are likely to offset increases in real income resulting from lower taxes.

Another approach advocates control of government expenditures rather than revenue. It is possible to place specific limits on the aggregate growth of expenditures by varying increases according to the growth of GNP and the rate of inflation.

A combination of the revenue and expenditures approaches may be used by linking tax cuts to a reduction in expenditure growth. This combination is more likely to be effective than controlling either revenue or expenditures alone. Proposals for constitutional amendments that mandate a balanced budget by a specific date are currently popular. These proposals attempt to force policy makers to choose among alternative expenditure proposals and reduce federal government involvement in the economy. Although we share this goal, we believe there are several serious questions about the workability of such proposals that need to be carefully studied before any final conclusions are reached. For example, the relationship between federal revenues and expenditures is an important component of fiscal policy. Rigid expenditure and revenue constraints or strict requirements to balance the budget thus sacrifice flexibility in macroeconomic policy, a sacrifice that could be damaging to the economy. On the other hand, there is the question of the degree to which budgetary ceilings could be circumvented by resorting to off-budget authority for funding particular government activities directly or indirectly through federal guarantees and the like. Thus, even if the expenditure ceiling controls the growth of expenditures in the current budget year, it may not avoid the problem of the automatic growth of funding for particular programs in future years. There is, in addition, the issue of how effective budget restraints might be in preventing the growth of government pressure through regulatory policies.

None of the proposals for revenue or expenditure ceilings provide assurance that policy makers will eliminate or restrict the growth of the least efficient expenditure programs. Powerful political interests within the Administration (including the federal bureaucracy), Congress, and interest groups may combine to preserve the ineffective programs.

This Committee recognizes that although it may be possible to define an effective expenditure ceiling policy, these difficulties must first be overcome. The recommendations in this policy statement for strengthening the budget process will contribute substantially to reducing the growth of government expenditures. Whatever may be done to control total government revenues and expenditures, we believe there is an urgent need to screen and to conduct independent evaluations of expenditure programs and regulatory policies. This approach to policy making should also include procedures ensuring that these evaluations result in the elimination or modification of ineffective programs and regulations.

Improving Public Policy through Sunset Proposals

The concept underlying many sunset proposals is the requirement that after a number of years, specified government programs, including regulations, would be terminated unless specifically reauthorized by the legislature.

Although new in its scope and mechanics, sunset legislation at the federal level is not a new idea. Many federal programs and activities are now authorized for limited periods, usually from one to five years. Only selected programs, such as social security, and certain activities, such as the independent regulatory commissions, are authorized in permanent law, and many of these programs are subject to annual legislative appropriations.

There are many practical problems associated with the sunset approach. Total and immediate termination is such a drastic action that it may rarely be exercised. It is also possible that if every program and policy is subject to possible termination, it will be impossible to review all programs or groups of programs prior to the specified termination date. Thus, although it is desirable to review the effectiveness of policies periodically, the threat of termination may be very disruptive to program implementation. Because some current decisions are made on the basis of future expectations, many policies obviously should not be subject to termination, even though they may be periodically reviewed and modified.

Despite these weaknesses, this Committee believes that sunset proposals represent a serious attempt to improve the efficiency and effectiveness of government policies and therefore deserve serious consideration by Congress. However, we believe that the process outlined in this policy statement, which incorporates some of the desirable features of several sunset proposals, is a much more practical way of improving public policy.

Indirect Incentive Policies

The major issue concerning indirect incentive policies such as loans and loan guarantees is how to improve control over these policy instruments. We believe that many programs which are currently off budget should be included in the process we have suggested for improving public policies. This Committee also supports in principle changes in the budget process that would enhance the controllability of all off-budget items.

In the 1980 Presidential budget, the Administration reviews this problem and suggests a way for achieving more effective control over the growth of federal credit programs. The Administration suggests imposing limitations on each individual credit program and on their aggregate total. It also suggests that aggregate ceilings be set in congressional budget resolutions and that legally binding limitations for each individual budget account be included in regular annual appropriations acts.

This approach would help moderate the *growth* of federal credit programs and would link policy decisions on broad categories of credit programs more closely with the budget. **However, in order to improve** control over these policy instruments, we recommend that all major existing credit programs be systematically reviewed to determine their effectiveness.

Because it is impossible to have dependable evaluations of *all* government programs and policies, this Committee supports proposals to strengthen the authorization procedure. At present, the authorization procedure is relatively ineffective for reviewing policies because many policies have multiyear authorizations. Congress should consider introducing a two-year authorization period for all programs. This would provide the authorizing committees with more time to review programs prior to reauthorization. More important, it would provide these committees with more time to perform their oversight function under the new comprehensive review process that we have outlined in our recommendations. We would also support changes in the congressional committee structure aimed at greater coordination among the committees and subcommittees and at reduction of inefficient jurisdictional overlap of their responsibilities.

Regulations

This Committee has not made any specific recommendations that would coordinate the cost of regulations with the budget process. However, we do believe that attempts should be made to develop the concept of a regulatory budget. This concept has been actively discussed within government for several years. The regulatory budget is an estimate of the administrative costs and the private costs imposed on the economy by all forms of federal regulation. If such a budget were available, its year-to-year growth could be monitored. A regulatory budget would help check the growth of this form of government activity. However, major measurement difficulties must be overcome before reliable budget estimates can be prepared. Any useful regulatory budget must incorporate indirect costs imposed on the private sector.

It is difficult to measure these indirect costs and even more difficult to aggregate them within the budget system. Yet, failure to estimate them is similar to permitting the government to levy a tax without knowing its magnitude. We support developmental work on a regulatory budget and urge that an estimate of the benefits of regulation accompany estimates of the costs of regulation.

Several current regulatory reform proposals propose to periodically evaluate the job performance of appointed members of regulatory agencies. Under specified circumstances, unsatisfactory performance can, under some current legislative proposals, lead to dismissal of the member of the agency. Our committee did not specifically address the problem of the qualifications and job performance of members of regulatory agencies. We do, however, support the intent of these proposals. **We believe that failure of regulatory agencies to effectively implement our screening and evaluation procedures should be considered evidence of inadequate job performance within any job evaluation process applied to members of independent regulatory agencies.**

PHASE 3: ENSURING THAT PROGRAM EVALUATION LEADS TO POLICY CHANGES

Evaluations of the results of major federal programs are neither systematic nor rigorous enough. Even more serious is the lack of a strong mechanism to ensure that policy makers learn from mistakes. We encourage broadly based representative organizations to speak out on specific issues where their vital interests are *not* at stake. For example, such organizations should take positions on policy proposals that have significant impact on the economy and recognize that all groups in society will benefit from a healthy market system. In addition, this Committee perceives the *need for greater media attention* to the oversight hearings and evaluation of major government policies and to the *actions taken within Congress and the executive branch to implement recommended policy changes.*

There is a strong tendency to continue existing policies and programs without challenging their basic purpose or administration. It is essential that the Administration examine the effectiveness of its own programs and be required to justify its assessments. **One way of achieving this self-examination and focusing public attention on the results is to require executive branch agencies and the independent regulatory agencies to rank their programs according to effectiveness.**[4] These ordinal rankings,

---

4. The concept of ranking program effectiveness was originated by Lawrence A. Silberman and was incorporated into a sunset bill (Sunset Act of 1978) as an amendment by Senator Charles Percy and the late Congressman William Steiger. A similar approach is included in HR 2, a bill recently introduced in the House of Representatives.

along with their justifications, could be reported to the appropriate congressional oversight committee. On the basis of the agency rankings, OMB should identify which programs should be eliminated or improved. The rankings can be used to guide Congress in determining which programs require oversight reviews and modification.

Such a strategy will expose the worst examples of government activities to criticism within the political system. This exposure will result in pressure for policy changes from the media and the public generally. At the very least, it will force major changes in the implementation of ineffective policies.

A systematic public accounting of what happens as a result of the oversight findings will focus public attention on both appropriate and inappropriate government activities. **We recommend that each house prepare an annual oversight report.** These reports should contain

> a summary of the major recommendations of the evaluation report and the recommendations of the oversight committee
>
> estimates of the budget and private costs of these recommendations, compared with the costs of current programs
>
> a review of the action taken by the appropriate legislative committees and of the response of the Administration

The contents of the reports on the oversight of major policies would be brief scorecards of recommended actions and their financial implications and of the responses from the appropriate legislative committees, Congress as a whole, and the Administration.

The Government Operations Committee in the House and the Governmental Affairs Committee in the Senate would be responsible for preparing the reports. These committees should call upon GAO, CBO, and CRS to assist in designing a format for the reports and in preparing them.

There are several important reasons for including this information in public documents. *Publicizing the response to an evaluation of program effectiveness prevents it from becoming just another report to be disregarded by policy makers.* Because the positions of all the major participants in the review of policy are clearly identified, each participant can be held responsible for his or her actions. At present, even if oversight hearings result in recommendations for policy changes, it is often difficult to identify whether failure to implement change is due to inaction within Congress or within the bureaucracy, which may resist modifying or terminating long-established policies. Finally, annual oversight reports will permit the public and all parts of government to know *who* is responsible for continuing, modifying, or terminating a given program and whether he or she has fulfilled that responsibility.

PHASE 4: RECOMMENDATIONS FOR REVIEWING THE POLICY-MAKING PROCESS

This comprehensive approach to appraising policy decisions requires systematically related efforts at all levels of the executive branch, Congress, and the independent regulatory agencies. Such widespread change is unlikely to be perfect. Future experience will suggest further improvements. The entire process of analysis and evaluation should itself be subject to periodic review. Its practitioners should conduct periodic self-reviews, but in addition, more disinterested authorities should periodically scrutinize the process. **We recommend that every four years, Congress conduct a review of its own oversight process. In addition, in order to ensure some general perspective and balance with regard to government's role in the economy, a Presidential commission should appraise government's involvement in the market system.**

CONCLUSIONS

Changes in the government's decision-making process probably could not produce immediate and across-the-board improvement. Beneficial changes are more likely to evolve and be sustained over the years, as has been true with the development of the congressional budget process.

Although improvements resulting from the type of reforms in policy making we are recommending in this statement are likely to be gradual, we believe that over a period of years they will be substantial and involve a relatively low cost.

Implementation of our recommendations requires no new agency. However, our proposals for screening, designing, and adopting public policies and for periodically evaluating them will require some strengthening of congressional-support staff.

In the executive branch of government, our proposals can be implemented by a reallocation of existing resources. Most agencies already

IMPLEMENTING PHASE 3: RECOMMENDATIONS FOR ENSURING THAT PROGRAM EVALUATION LEADS TO POLICY CHANGES

Congress should:

1. Through legislation, require executive branch agencies and the independent regulatory agencies periodically (within two to four years) to submit to Congress a ranking of the effectiveness of their major programs. These ordinal rankings should be based on the reviews conducted by evaluation units within the agencies. Programs should be ranked on a continuum ranging from excellent to unsatisfactory, with explanations of the ranks. The criteria for determining the rankings should include clarity of statutory design and objective, design of the implementation procedures, quality of the management of the program, and the perceived impact of the program. The ranking should be reported to the Government Operations Committee and the Governmental Affairs Committee. These committees would request the appropriate oversight committee to recommend the steps that should be taken to remedy programs the Administration ranks in the unsatisfactory range of the continuum.

2. Require the Government Operations Committee and the Governmental Affairs Committee to prepare annual congressional oversight reports for the House and Senate, respectively. The reports should constitute brief scorecards of the actions recommended by the oversight reports of each major policy, a summary of the financial implications, and scorecards of the actions taken by the legislative committees, Congress as a whole, and the Administration in response to the oversight recommendations. The expertise of GAO, CBO, and CRS should be used in designing and preparing the reports.

have substantial budgets for research and evaluation. We believe these funds can be reallocated effectively to provide the evidence required to screen, design, and adopt new proposals and to evaluate existing programs. Modest additional staff with analytic skills will be required to strengthen some of the congressional-support organizations such as CBO and GAO. In addition, Congress will be required to allocate more time to oversight activities and to respond to recommended changes in the oversight process. *Essentially, oversight must become one of the most important components of the policy-making process.*

Our proposals contain several concepts which will ensure that policy makers justify their actions and implement the results of the improved policy process. For each branch of government, there is provision for certifying that proponents of new policies are in compliance with the requirements for the screening, designing, and adopting of proposals. In the executive branch, certification is provided by the Office of Management and Budget or some other unit within the Executive Office of the President. In Congress, the Rules Committees would perform this task based on the advice of one of the congressional-support organizations (either CBO or GAO).

Compliance with the screening process by the independent regulatory agencies is encouraged through requiring CBO or GAO to review proposed major regulations for compliance with the recommended procedures. The congressional-support organization (CBO or GAO) could present the public with its assessment of whether the agency has considered the proposed rule's potential impact on overall economic objectives and on the stated purpose of the regulation. This requirement does not restrict the statutory authority of the independent regulatory agencies to issue new rules; it does, however, provide the public with information on the potential effect of proposed rules before they are implemented.

This Committee's recommendations also contain evaluation procedures that will clearly identify the successes and failures of major existing programs and regulatory policies. The results of these evaluations will become part of the public debate. Of course, ineffective programs and regulations may survive this debate, but any failure of policy makers to correct failures will become obvious.

If an approach similar to the one we are recommending is adopted, we are confident that there will be substantial improvements in public policies. The reason for our optimism is that there is now considerable bipartisan support for many legislative proposals that are similar in intent to many of our recommendations. These proposals, now emerging

> ## IMPLEMENTING PHASE 4: RECOMMENDATIONS FOR REVIEWING THE POLICY-MAKING PROCESS
>
> *Congress* should:
> 1. Authorize the Speaker of the House, the House minority leader, and the presiding officer of the Senate to appoint, every four years, a bipartisan commission of outstanding congressional experts to appraise the effectiveness of the congressional oversight process and to make any recommendations for desired improvement. Dissenting views of any members of the commission are to be published in the commission's report.
>
> The *President* should:
> 1. Appoint, once every eight years, a Presidential commission of public and private leaders who represent views across the political spectrum to consider the current relationship between public policy and the market system, to review government's methods of involving itself in the economy, and to make recommendations to the President and Congress for such improvements as it thinks wise.

both from the Administration and from within Congress, demonstrate that public officials desire to improve the policy-making process.

The proposals presented in this statement offer practical steps to increase government's sensitivity to the need for a healthy, competitive market system. Administrators, politicians, and voters should consider the effect of public policy decisions on the long-term performance of the economy. There are encouraging signs of a growing understanding that social progress depends on economic progress. Public decisions must strike a balance between respecting and fostering the market system and improving social programs. Unless they do, the nation will achieve neither its social nor its economic goals.

Memoranda of Comment, Reservation, or Dissent

Page 15, by E. SHERMAN ADAMS

While I definitely agree with the general thrust of this CED policy statement, it seems unfortunate that it does not deal more specifically with international trade policies, which certainly have an enormous direct impact on the operation of a number of our important markets. Not only the *concept* of periodic evaluation but also most of the criteria and procedures recommended in this statement for evaluating other types of governmental policies that directly affect the operation of markets should be applied to our trade policies.

Page 18, by ROBERT R. NATHAN

The expression that government has a responsibility to restore competition when it is absent is an important, constructive statement, but this report does not truly deal adequately with this responsibility. Rather, it focuses nearly exclusively on government regulation and spending, which are important but do not tell the whole story.

If competition is absent because of a breakdown of a competitive environment, then certainly the government should restore competition. It also is desirable to prevent the erosion of competition through government policies and actions relating to mergers and a variety of anticompetitive practices. Prevention of monopoly may be more fruitful and more feasible than restoration of competition once it has been destroyed.

It is in the area of preventing anticompetitive conditions where the government and the private sector lock horns in bitter and frustrating confrontations. Unfortunately, less attention has been given in this report to the preventative or restorative activities of government in preserving or strengthening competition than has been given to many other government economic functions that bear adversely on the marketplace. It is in the interest of the free enterprise system that the marketplace function effectively and efficiently, and that does not mean a license to destroy competition under the banner of free enterprise.

Consideration should be given to encouraging or facilitating private triple-damage antitrust suits. This would provide a sort of marketplace determination, within the judiciary system, whereby businesses harmed by anticompetitive practices would be well compensated for harm done to them and defendants found guilty would be heavily penalized financially for anticompetitive and monopolistic behavior.

Page 20, by PHILIP M. KLUTZNICK, *with which* E. SHERMAN ADAMS, CHARLES P. BOWEN, JR., *and* FLETCHER L. BYROM *have asked to be associated*

I believe that this policy statement has overcome tremendous handicaps and produced a very helpful and constructive document, which I favor. I have one reservation: It does not really address itself to the substance but rather to the tone of the first chapter, "Introduction and Summary." There are appropriate references in several places to the adverse effect of the work of "organized interest groups," "the political system," "excessive, ill-planned regulation and excessive, poorly designed government expenditures," and to the role of the government generally. Certainly, the government carries a weighty responsibility in having created a mass of regulations, an accumulation of subsidies and loan programs that to a greater or lesser degree impede the operations of the market system. I believe it is incomplete, however, not to call attention to the fact that in all too many cases, some of these actions have been induced by business interests who felt that the benefit to a particular business or activity was special and should be favorably acted upon by the government. There are records of cases where the industry involved has either resisted the elimination of regulation or induced its passage. In short, the private sector cannot be completely absolved of the role that it has played over the years in helping to create this morass.

Page 20, by FRAZAR B. WILDE

Our statement, *Redefining Government's Role in the Market System*, has much value in it. I approve it with this reservation: that it is far too long and lacks much in the way of specific solutions. I would hope that enough people would read it so that it would have some public value.

Page 23, by ROBERT R. NATHAN, *with which* E. SHERMAN ADAMS *has asked to be associated*

Certainly government involvement should only be considered if the market system is incapable of dealing with important problems. But this raises the basic question of the degree of effective functioning of the marketplace. Few questions of government involvement in market system performance come anywhere near providing a black-or-white choice. It is obviously fruitless to contend that each and every government intervention is adverse or destructive, as some spokesmen for the business community claim. It is likewise absurd to argue that the performance of the marketplace is nearly always perfect and effective. Advocates of government intervention whenever or wherever there is any indication of marketplace inadequacies are equally irresponsible.

The name of the game is competition because that is the key to good market performance and the basis for less government intervention. It is certainly in the interest of the general public as well as business to foster and strengthen and preserve competition. Unfortunately, government policies and actions designed to achieve this objective are not usually welcomed by business and are often attacked for their imperfections, which may not be as bad as the imperfections of business practices that undermine and weaken competition.

It might be noted that the effective functioning of the marketplace may be eroded not only by anticompetitive practices and greater concentration of economic power among producers and distributors but also by less price and quality consciousness among consumers. If our affluence is making consumers function less and less like the "economic man" described in theoretical treatises, the marketplace will not do the job expected of it.

Pages 24 and 111, by ROY L. ASH, *with which* CHARLES P. BOWEN, JR., FLETCHER L. BYROM, TERRANCE HANOLD, CHARLES KELLER, JR., *and* D. C. SEARLE *have asked to be associated*

The statement deals with one of the most important issues in this country today. It provides some very useful information and makes a number of good points and recommendations, especially for improving government program evaluation and oversight.

Unfortunately, its main recommendations (summarized in Chapter 1 and detailed in Chapters 6 and 7) are politically unrealistic, especially as applied to the Congress.

The imposition of the proposed additional procedures within the government for "screening, adopting, and designing government actions" is not the solution. Realistically, we cannot expect to "discipline policy decisions"; that is, no procedure can require politicians to be systematic, logical, analytical, and objective, especially if that would cost the loss of votes.

The answer has to be found within the existing political process, untidy as it is. Those who are a part of that process can benefit from the information and thinking reflected in this statement, but only when our elected officials sense that more votes can be gained by reining in undue regulation and expenditures than continuing the present course will progress be made. And it will be made without new "disciplining" procedures of the kinds suggested. In that direction is our challenge.

Page 34, by FLETCHER L. BYROM

I question this statement. Competition can be implied rather than existent, threatened rather than real. The implied abuse of consumers due to lack of competition would result in excessive returns and would invite new entry by others or substitution of materials in today's technological environment. The only lack of protection would be in terms of limited periods, not in terms of long-term action in the market.

Page 34, by FLETCHER L. BYROM

This should be recognized as the means by which the inefficient or the noncontributors are denied the availability of resources which if allocated to them would be a wasteful use of society's resources.

Page 34, by ROBERT R. NATHAN, *with which* E. SHERMAN ADAMS *has asked to be associated*

It is regrettably true that few advocates of the market system openly or actively support antitrust policy. Those who believe in the free enterprise system and the benefits of the competitive market might be expected to recognize that a most serious threat to the system derives from monopolistic and anticompetitive practices in the business world. Therefore, the business community ought to support the practices as well as principles of antitrust policy.

There may be some exceptions, but no evidence comes to mind of any single expression in support of any specific antitrust actions by any business group, whether it be the Chamber of Commerce or the National Association of Manufacturers or the Business Roundtable or, perhaps, even the Committee for Economic Development. It would be wholesome and helpful if from time to time some group in the business community openly commended the government for some antitrust action, even if these commendations were confined only to actions against the most blatant and significant violations of antitrust policy. Instead of such support, there is a common tendency for business organizations and individual businessmen to characterize every antitrust prosecution as a persecution.

Since this report deals with the government's role in the market system, it should give more emphasis to that role in strengthening competition and the marketplace. Implicit in all of the analyses and policy implications in this report is faith in the functioning of the market system. That faith may or may not be warranted just because of the presence of some businessmen who preach free enterprise and practice monopoly.

The few paragraphs on "The Market System's Limitations" are important and reflect a commendable degree of realism. However, the report would carry more credibility if there were fuller recognitions of how these limitations arise and how they might be coped with by minimal but appropriate government policies and actions.

Page 48, by E. SHERMAN ADAMS

Broadly defined, subsidies obviously also include tariffs, import quotas, and other governmental restrictions on the competition of foreign goods in our markets, thereby subsidizing particular industries and their workers at the expense of American consumers, who are forced to pay artificially high prices for both imported and domestically produced goods.

Page 63, by E. SHERMAN ADAMS, *with which* ROY L. ASH, WILLIAM F. MAY, *and* D. C. SEARLE *have asked to be associated*

In considering increases in production costs resulting from government regulations, three points deserve special emphasis. One, practically all of these increased production costs necessarily result in higher prices that will have to be paid by American consumers. Two, most of them are not simply one-time payments but become imbedded in the price structure indefinitely. Three, not only will some of these costs be continuing, they will tend to be compounded over time as they become injected into the self-perpetuating wage-price spiral.

Page 63, by DAVID L. FRANCIS

The coal industry has been plagued since the early Roosevelt Administration, when all mines were unionized under NRA. Shortly thereafter, the federal Guffey Act was enacted, establishing federal price controls. This was a dismal failure and fortunately was declared unconstitutional.

In the past ten years, duplicate federal and state environmental and safety laws have cut the daily production per man-day in half and raised prices eight to tenfold and greatly increased start-up lead time, capital requirements, and closing off millions of tons of reserves on government-owned lands.

If the above government laws and regulations had been of a reasonable nature, the coal industry would be geared to carry a larger part in alleviating the present energy crisis.

Page 90, by E. SHERMAN ADAMS, *with which* D. C. SEARLE *has asked to be associated*

In choosing among alternative courses of action, policy makers should also give careful consideration to their probable inflationary effects.

Page 100, by J. W. McSWINEY, *with which* FLETCHER L. BYROM *has asked to be associated*

While I share the general concern expressed throughout the report that the expansion of the government's role into the operation of the market system has in many cases impaired the performance of the U.S. economy, I find myself in disagreement with the thrust of some of its conclusions and recommendations in the areas of health, safety, and the environment.

I find no evidence in the report or elsewhere that leads me to believe that government has demonstrated any greater expertise for manipulating market forces to implement public policy than through its use of direct controls. The role of government involvement in the economy should, therefore, be kept to an absolute minimum consistent with the execution of its legitimate task of achieving those objectives of public policy that do not flow naturally from the free market system.

Page 103, by J. W. McSWINEY

For the most part, standards of protection should be set forth in terms of the end results that are desired, not by defining the process of achieving them. However, if, as is almost always the case, there is a wide variation of costs for achieving different levels of protection among different dischargers, the use of effluent fees as the regulatory mechanism will either result in a shortfall of protection in some cases or a gross overexpenditure in others. Public health and environmental protection should be determined by direct regulation, rather than economic optimization. The examples of effluent charges used abroad, to the best of my knowledge, have been in reality user charges or taxes to pay for the use or construction of treatment facilities provided or supplied by the government. They have not been a basis for determining the economic level of pollution. Our own system of user charges for industrial use of publicly owned treatment works is a similar use and allows a company to choose between private or public treatment of its effluent. It is not, and should not be, the basis for deciding the level of treatment to be achieved by industrial dischargers by a process of economic optimization, as the recommendation suggests.

This position does not mean that I believe that government has always established controls or regulations in the most effective or prudent manner. Indeed, there is much evidence to the contrary. In the environmental area, examples abound where social ideology and prescription have replaced objectivity and performance in standard setting. The answer is to replace ideology and prescription with objectivity and performance standards rather than replace regulation with market manipulation.

The malady today is that we have too much government and in areas where its involvement is not needed or is being counterproductive to the public interest. The report correctly identifies environment, housing, safety, and transportation as four examples where excessive governmental regulation has attempted to prescribe methods of achievement, rather than objective standards, and it rightly recommends a change. It is in the nature of that change where I part company with some of the recommendations. The idea is not "to make pollution unprofitable," but it is to protect the public with the minimum of government intervention in the operation of the marketplace.

Objectives of the Committee for Economic Development

For thirty-five years, the Committee for Economic Development has been a respected influence on the formation of business and public policy. CED is devoted to these two objectives:

To develop, through objective research and informed discussion, findings and recommendations for private and public policy which will contribute to preserving and strengthening our free society, achieving steady economic growth at high employment and reasonably stable prices, increasing productivity and living standards, providing greater and more equal opportunity for every citizen, and improving the quality of life for all.

To bring about increasing understanding by present and future leaders in business, government, and education and among concerned citizens of the importance of these objectives and the ways in which they can be achieved.

CED's work is supported strictly by private voluntary contributions from business and industry, foundations, and individuals. It is independent, nonprofit, nonpartisan, and nonpolitical.

The two hundred trustees, who generally are presidents or board chairmen of corporations and presidents of universities, are chosen for their individual capacities rather than as representatives of any particular interests. By working with scholars, they unite business judgment and experience with scholarship in analyzing the issues and developing recommendations to resolve the economic problems that constantly arise in a dynamic and democratic society.

Through this business-academic partnership, CED endeavors to develop policy statements and other research materials that commend themselves as guides to public and business policy; for use as texts in college economics and political science courses and in management training courses; for consideration and discussion by newspaper and magazine editors, columnists, and commentators; and for distribution abroad to promote better understanding of the American economic system.

CED believes that by enabling businessmen to demonstrate constructively their concern for the general welfare, it is helping business to earn and maintain the national and community respect essential to the successful functioning of the free enterprise capitalist system.

CED Board of Trustees

Chairman
FLETCHER L. BYROM, Chairman
Koppers Company, Inc.

Vice Chairmen
WILLIAM S. CASHEL, JR., Vice Chairman
American Telephone & Telegraph Company
E. B. FITZGERALD, Chairman
Cutler-Hammer, Inc.
PHILIP M. KLUTZNICK
Klutznick Investments
RALPH LAZARUS, Chairman
Federated Department Stores, Inc.
WILLIAM F. MAY, Chairman
American Can Company
ROCCO C. SICILIANO, Chairman
Ticor

Treasurer
CHARLES J. SCANLON, Vice President
General Motors Corporation

A. ROBERT ABBOUD, Chairman
The First National Bank of Chicago
RAY C. ADAM, Chairman and President
NL Industries, Inc.
WILLIAM M. AGEE, Chairman and President
The Bendix Corporation
ROBERT O. ANDERSON, Chairman
Atlantic Richfield Company
WILLIAM S. ANDERSON, Chairman
NCR Corporation
ROY L. ASH, Chairman
AM International, Inc.
THOMAS G. AYERS, Chairman
Commonwealth Edison Company
ROBERT H. B. BALDWIN, President
Morgan Stanley & Co. Incorporated
JOSEPH W. BARR
Washington, D.C.
ROSS BARZELAY, President
General Foods Corporation
HARRY HOOD BASSETT, Chairman
Southeast Banking Corporation
WILLIAM O. BEERS, Chairman
Kraft, Inc.
GEORGE F. BENNETT, President
State Street Investment Corporation
JACK F. BENNETT, Senior Vice President
Exxon Corporation
JAMES F. BERE, Chairman
Borg-Warner Corporation
DAVID BERETTA, Chairman
Uniroyal, Inc.
JOHN C. BIERWIRTH, Chairman
Grumman Corporation
HOWARD W. BLAUVELT
Consultant and Director
Continental Oil Company

WILLIAM W. BOESCHENSTEIN, President
Owens-Corning Fiberglas Corporation
DEREK C. BOK, President
Harvard University
JOHN F. BONNER, President
Pacific Gas and Electric Company
CHARLES P. BOWEN, JR., Honorary Chairman
Booz, Allen & Hamilton Inc.
ANDREW F. BRIMMER, President
Brimmer & Company, Inc.
ALFRED BRITTAIN III, Chairman
Bankers Trust Company
THEODORE F. BROPHY, Chairman
General Telephone & Electronics Corporation
R. MANNING BROWN, JR., Chairman
New York Life Insurance Co., Inc.
JOHN L. BURNS, President
John L. Burns and Company
FLETCHER L. BYROM, Chairman
Koppers Company, Inc.
ALEXANDER CALDER, JR., Chairman
Union Camp Corporation
ROBERT D. CAMPBELL, Chairman
Newsweek, Inc.
ROBERT J. CARLSON, Senior Vice President
Deere & Company
RAFAEL CARRION, JR., Chairman and President
Banco Popular de Puerto Rico
THOMAS S. CARROLL, President
Lever Brothers Company
FRANK T. CARY, Chairman
IBM Corporation
SAMUEL B. CASEY, JR., President
Pullman Incorporated
WILLIAM S. CASHEL, JR., Vice Chairman
American Telephone & Telegraph Company
FINN M. W. CASPERSEN, Chairman
Beneficial Corporation
JOHN B. CAVE, Senior Vice President
Finance and Administration
Schering-Plough Corporation
HUNG WO CHING, Chairman
Aloha Airlines, Inc.
*EMILIO G. COLLADO, President
Adela Investment Co., S.A.
ROBERT C. COSGROVE, Chairman
Green Giant Company
JOSEPH F. CULLMAN, 3rd
Chairman, Executive Committee
Philip Morris Incorporated
RICHARD M. CYERT, President
Carnegie-Mellon University
W. D. DANCE, Vice Chairman
General Electric Company
JOHN H. DANIELS, Chairman
National City Bancorporation
RONALD R. DAVENPORT, Chairman
Sheridan Broadcasting Corporation
RALPH P. DAVIDSON, Vice President
Time Inc.
ARCHIE K. DAVIS, Chairman of the Board (Retired)
Wachovia Bank and Trust Company, N.A.

*Life Trustee

R. HAL DEAN, Chairman and President
Ralston Purina Company

WILLIAM N. DERAMUS, III, Chairman
Kansas City Southern Industries, Inc.

JOHN DIEBOLD, Chairman
The Diebold Group, Inc.

ROBERT R. DOCKSON, Chairman
California Federal Savings and Loan Association

EDWIN D. DODD, Chairman
Owens-Illinois, Inc.

VIRGINIA A. DWYER, Assistant Treasurer
American Telephone & Telegraph Company

ALFRED W. EAMES, JR., Chairman
Del Monte Corporation

W. D. EBERLE, Special Partner
Robert A. Weaver, Jr. and Associates

WILLIAM S. EDGERLY, Chairman and President
State Street Bank and Trust Company

ROBERT F. ERBURU, President
The Times Mirror Company

THOMAS J. EYERMAN, Partner
Skidmore, Owings & Merrill

WALTER A. FALLON, Chairman
Eastman Kodak Company

FRANCIS E. FERGUSON, President
Northwestern Mutual Life Insurance Company

JOHN T. FEY, Chairman
The Equitable Life Assurance Society
of the United States

JOHN H. FILER, Chairman
Aetna Life and Casualty Company

WILLIAM S. FISHMAN, Chairman
ARA Services, Inc.

E. B. FITZGERALD, Chairman
Cutler-Hammer, Inc.

CHARLES F. FOGARTY, Chairman
Texasgulf Inc.

CHARLES W. L. FOREMAN, Senior Vice President
United Parcel Service

JOHN M. FOX, Retired Chairman
H. P. Hood Inc.

DAVID L. FRANCIS, Chairman
Princess Coals, Inc.

*WILLIAM H. FRANKLIN
Chairman of the Board (Retired)
Caterpillar Tractor Co.

DON C. FRISBEE, Chairman
Pacific Power & Light Company

DONALD E. GARRETSON
Vice President, Finance
3M Company

CLIFTON C. GARVIN, JR., Chairman
Exxon Corporation

RICHARD L. GELB, Chairman
Bristol-Myers Company

LINCOLN GORDON, Senior Research Fellow
Resources for the Future, Inc.

THOMAS C. GRAHAM, President
Jones & Laughlin Steel Corporation

HARRY J. GRAY, Chairman and President
United Technologies Corporation

JOHN D. GRAY, Chairman
Hart Schaffner & Marx

JOHN D. GRAY, Chairman
Omark Industries, Inc.

WILLIAM C. GREENOUGH, Chairman
TIAA-CREF

DAVID L. GROVE
Armonk, New York

JOHN D. HARPER, Retired Chairman
Aluminum Company of America

SHEARON HARRIS, Chairman
Carolina Power & Light Company

FRED L. HARTLEY, Chairman and President
Union Oil Company of California

ROBERT S. HATFIELD, Chairman
Continental Group, Inc.

GABRIEL HAUGE
Director and Retired Chairman
Manufacturers Hanover Trust Company

PHILIP M. HAWLEY, President
Carter Hawley Hale Stores, Inc.

H. J. HAYNES, Chairman
Standard Oil Company of California

H. J. HEINZ II, Chairman
H. J. Heinz Company

LAWRENCE HICKEY, Chairman
Stein Roe & Farnham

RODERICK M. HILLS
Latham, Watkins and Hills

WAYNE M. HOFFMAN, Chairman
Tiger International, Inc.

ROBERT C. HOLLAND, President
Committee for Economic Development

FREDERICK G. JAICKS, Chairman
Inland Steel Company

EDWARD R. KANE, President
E. I. du Pont de Nemours & Company

HARRY J. KANE, Executive Vice President
Georgia-Pacific Corporation

CHARLES KELLER, JR.
New Orleans, Louisiana

DONALD P. KELLY, President
Esmark, Inc.

J. C. KENEFICK, President
Union Pacific Railroad Company

TOM KILLEFER, Chairman and President
United States Trust Company of New York

PHILIP M. KLUTZNICK
Klutznick Investments

HARRY W. KNIGHT, Chairman
Hillsboro Associates, Inc.

RALPH LAZARUS, Chairman
Federated Department Stores, Inc.

FLOYD W. LEWIS, President
Middle South Utilities, Inc.

FRANKLIN A. LINDSAY, Chairman
Itek Corporation

J. EDWARD LUNDY, Executive Vice President
Ford Motor Company

J. PAUL LYET, Chairman
Sperry Rand Corporation

*Life Trustee

RICHARD W. LYMAN, President
Stanford University

RAY W. MACDONALD, Honorary Chairman
Burroughs Corporation

IAN MacGREGOR, Honorary Chairman and
Chairman, Finance Committee
AMAX Inc.

BRUCE K. MacLAURY, President
The Brookings Institution

MALCOLM MacNAUGHTON, Chairman
Castle & Cooke, Inc.

JOHN D. MACOMBER, President
Celanese Corporation

G. BARRON MALLORY
Jacobs Persinger & Parker

ROBERT H. MALOTT, Chairman
FMC Corporation

AUGUSTINE R. MARUSI, Chairman
Borden Inc.

WILLIAM F. MAY, Chairman
American Can Company

JEAN MAYER, President
Tufts University

*THOMAS B. McCABE
Chairman, Finance Committee
Scott Paper Company

C. PETER McCOLOUGH, Chairman
Xerox Corporation

GEORGE C. McGHEE, Corporate Director and
former U.S. Ambassador
Washington, D.C.

JAMES W. McKEE, JR., Chairman
CPC International Inc.

CHARLES A. McLENDON
Executive Vice President
Burlington Industries, Inc.

CHAMPNEY A. McNAIR, Vice Chairman
Trust Company of Georgia

E. L. McNEELY, Chairman
The Wickes Corporation

RENE C. McPHERSON, Chairman
Dana Corporation

J. W. McSWINEY, Chairman
The Mead Corporation

BILL O. MEAD, Chairman
Campbell Taggart Inc.

CHAUNCEY J. MEDBERRY, III, Chairman
Bank of America N.T. & S.A.

RUBEN F. METTLER, Chairman
TRW, Inc.

CHARLES A. MEYER
Senior Vice President, Public Affairs
Sears, Roebuck and Co.

LEE L. MORGAN, Chairman
Caterpillar Tractor Co.

ROBERT R. NATHAN, Chairman
Robert R. Nathan Associates, Inc.

EDWARD N. NEY, Chairman
Young & Rubicam Inc.

WILLIAM S. OGDEN, Executive Vice President
The Chase Manhattan Bank

THOMAS O. PAINE, President
Northrop Corporation

EDWARD L. PALMER, Chairman, Executive Committee
Citibank, N.A.

RUSSELL E. PALMER, Managing Partner
Touche Ross & Co.

VICTOR H. PALMIERI, Chairman
Victor Palmieri and Company Incorporated

DANIEL PARKER
Washington, D.C.

JOHN H. PERKINS, President
Continental Illinois National Bank
and Trust Company of Chicago

HOWARD C. PETERSEN,
Philadelphia, Pennsylvania

C. WREDE PETERSMEYER,
Bronxville, New York

MARTHA E. PETERSON, President
Beloit College

PETER G. PETERSON, Chairman
Lehman Brothers Kuhn Loeb, Inc.

JOHN G. PHILLIPS, Chairman
The Louisiana Land and Exploration Company

CHARLES J. PILLIOD, JR., Chairman
The Goodyear Tire & Rubber Company

JOHN B. M. PLACE, President
Crocker National Bank

DONALD C. PLATTEN, Chairman
Chemical Bank

EDMUND T. PRATT, JR., Chairman
Pfizer Inc.

JOHN R. PURCELL, Senior Vice President
CBS, Inc.

R. STEWART RAUCH, JR., Chairman
The Philadelphia Saving Fund Society

DONALD T. REGAN, Chairman
Merrill Lynch & Co., Inc.

DAVID P. REYNOLDS, Chairman
Reynolds Metals Company

JAMES Q. RIORDAN, Executive Vice President
Mobil Oil Corporation

FELIX G. ROHATYN, General Partner
Lazard Freres & Company

AXEL G. ROSIN, Retired Chairman
Book-of-the-Month Club, Inc.

WILLIAM M. ROTH
San Francisco, California

JOHN SAGAN, Vice President-Treasurer
Ford Motor Company

TERRY SANFORD, President
Duke University

JOHN C. SAWHILL, President
New York University

CHARLES J. SCANLON, Vice President
General Motors Corporation

HENRY B. SCHACHT, Chairman
Cummins Engine Company, Inc.

ROBERT M. SCHAEBERLE, Chairman
Nabisco Inc.

J. L. SCOTT, Chairman
Great Atlantic & Pacific Tea Company

*Life Trustee

D. C. SEARLE, Chairman, Executive Committee
G. D. Searle & Co.

RICHARD B. SELLARS
Chairman, Finance Committee
Johnson & Johnson

ROBERT V. SELLERS, Chairman
Cities Service Company

ROBERT B. SEMPLE, Chairman
BASF Wyandotte Corporation

MARK SHEPHERD, JR., Chairman
Texas Instruments Incorporated

RICHARD R. SHINN, President
Metropolitan Life Insurance Company

GEORGE P. SHULTZ, President
Bechtel Corporation

ROCCO C. SICILIANO, Chairman
Ticor

ANDREW C. SIGLER, Chairman and President
Champion International Corporation

WILLIAM P. SIMMONS, President
First National Bank & Trust Company

L. EDWIN SMART, Chairman
Trans World Airlines

DONALD B. SMILEY, Chairman
R. H. Macy & Co., Inc.

RICHARD M. SMITH, Vice Chairman
Bethlehem Steel Corporation

ROGER B. SMITH, Executive Vice President
General Motors Corporation

ELVIS J. STAHR, President
National Audubon Society

CHARLES B. STAUFFACHER, President
Field Enterprises, Inc.

EDGAR B. STERN, JR., President
Royal Street Corporation

J. PAUL STICHT, Chairman
R. J. Reynolds Industries, Inc.

GEORGE A. STINSON, Chairman
National Steel Corporation

*WILLIAM C. STOLK
Weston, Connecticut

WILLIS A. STRAUSS, Chairman
Northern Natural Gas Company

DAVID S. TAPPAN, JR., Vice Chairman
Fluor Corporation

WALTER N. THAYER, President
Whitney Communications Corporation

WAYNE E. THOMPSON, Senior Vice President
Dayton Hudson Corporation

CHARLES C. TILLINGHAST, JR.
Managing Director, Capital Markets Group
Merrill Lynch, Pierce, Fenner & Smith, Inc.

HOWARD S. TURNER
Chairman, Executive Committee
Turner Construction Company

L. S. TURNER, JR., Executive Vice President
Texas Utilities Company

THOMAS A. VANDERSLICE, Senior Vice President
and Sector Executive, Power Systems Sector
General Electric Company

ALVIN W. VOGTLE, JR., President
The Southern Company, Inc.

JOHN WILLIAM WARD, President
Amherst College

SIDNEY J. WEINBERG, JR., Partner
Goldman, Sachs & Co.

WILLIAM H. WENDEL, President
Kennecott Copper Corporation

GEORGE L. WILCOX, Director-Officer
Westinghouse Electric Corporation

*FRAZAR B. WILDE, Chairman Emeritus
Connecticut General Life Insurance Company

J. KELLEY WILLIAMS, President
First Mississippi Corporation

JOHN H. WILLIAMS, Chairman
The Williams Companies

*W. WALTER WILLIAMS
Seattle, Washington

MARGARET S. WILSON, Chairman
Scarbroughs

RICHARD D. WOOD, Chairman and President
Eli Lilly and Company

*Life Trustee

Honorary Trustees

E. SHERMAN ADAMS
New Preston, Connecticut

CARL E. ALLEN
North Muskegon, Michigan

JAMES L. ALLEN, Hon. Chairman
Booz, Allen & Hamilton, Inc.

FRANK ALTSCHUL
New York, New York

O. KELLEY ANDERSON
Boston, Massachusetts

SANFORD S. ATWOOD, President Emeritus
Emory University

JERVIS J. BABB
Wilmette, Illinois

S. CLARK BEISE, President (Retired)
Bank of America N.T. & S.A.

HAROLD H. BENNETT
Salt Lake City, Utah

WALTER R. BIMSON, Chairman Emeritus
Valley National Bank

JOSEPH L. BLOCK, Former Chairman
Inland Steel Company

ROGER M. BLOUGH
Hawley, Pennsylvania

FRED J. BORCH
New Canaan, Connecticut

MARVIN BOWER, Director
McKinsey & Company, Inc.

THOMAS D. CABOT, Hon. Chairman of the Board
Cabot Corporation

EDWARD W. CARTER, Chairman
Carter Hawley Hale Stores, Inc.

EVERETT N. CASE
Van Hornesville, New York

WALKER L. CISLER
Detroit, Michigan

JOHN L. COLLYER
Vero Beach, Florida

STEWART S. CORT, Director
Bethlehem Steel Corporation

GARDNER COWLES, Hon. Chairman of the Board
Cowles Communications, Inc.

GEORGE S. CRAFT
Atlanta, Georgia

JOHN P. CUNNINGHAM
Hon. Chairman of the Board
Cunningham & Walsh, Inc.

DONALD C. DAYTON, Director
Dayton Hudson Corporation

DOUGLAS DILLON, Chairman, Executive Committee
Dillon, Read and Co. Inc.

ROBERT W. ELSASSER
New Orleans, Louisiana

EDMUND FITZGERALD
Milwaukee, Wisconsin

WILLIAM C. FOSTER
Washington, D.C.

CLARENCE FRANCIS
New York, New York

GAYLORD FREEMAN
Chicago, Illinois

PAUL S. GEROT, Hon. Chairman of the Board
The Pillsbury Company

CARL J. GILBERT
Dover, Massachusetts

KATHARINE GRAHAM, Chairman
The Washington Post Company

WALTER A. HAAS, JR., Chairman
Levi Strauss and Co.

MICHAEL L. HAIDER
New York, New York

TERRANCE HANOLD
Minneapolis, Minnesota

J. V. HERD, Director
The Continental Insurance Companies

WILLIAM A. HEWITT, Chairman
Deere & Company

OVETA CULP HOBBY, Chairman
The Houston Post

GEORGE F. JAMES
Cos Cob, Connecticut

HENRY R. JOHNSTON
Ponte Vedra Beach, Florida

GILBERT E. JONES, Retired Vice Chairman
IBM Corporation

THOMAS ROY JONES
Consultant, Schlumberger Limited

FREDERICK R. KAPPEL
Sarasota, Florida

DAVID M. KENNEDY
Salt Lake City, Utah

JAMES R. KENNEDY
Essex Fells, New Jersey

CHARLES N. KIMBALL, Chairman
Midwest Research Institute

SIGURD S. LARMON
New York, New York

ROY E. LARSEN, Retired Vice Chairman of the Board
Time Inc.

DAVID E. LILIENTHAL, Chairman
Development and Resources Corporation

ELMER L. LINDSETH
Shaker Heights, Ohio

JAMES A. LINEN, Consultant
Time Inc.

GEORGE H. LOVE
Pittsburgh, Pennsylvania

ROBERT A. LOVETT, Partner
Brown Brothers Harriman & Co.

ROY G. LUCKS
Del Monte Corporation

FRANKLIN J. LUNDING
Wilmette, Illinois

FRANK L. MAGEE
Stahlstown, Pennsylvania

STANLEY MARCUS, Consultant
Carter Hawley Hale Stores, Inc.

JOSEPH A. MARTINO, Hon. Chairman
N L Industries, Inc.

OSCAR G. MAYER, Retired Chairman
Oscar Mayer & Co.

L. F. McCOLLUM
Houston, Texas

JOHN A. McCONE
Los Angeles, California

JOHN F. MERRIAM
San Francisco, California

LORIMER D. MILTON
Citizens Trust Company

DON G. MITCHELL
Summit, New Jersey

ALFRED C. NEAL
Harrison, New York

J. WILSON NEWMAN,
Chairman, Finance Committee
Dun & Bradstreet Companies, Inc.

AKSEL NIELSEN,
Chairman, Finance Committee
Ladd Petroleum Corporation

JAMES F. OATES, JR.
Chicago, Illinois

W. A. PATTERSON,
Honorary Chairman
United Air Lines

EDWIN W. PAULEY, Chairman
Pauley Petroleum, Inc.

MORRIS B. PENDLETON
Vernon, California

JOHN A. PERKINS
Bay View, Michigan

RUDOLPH A. PETERSON,
President (Retired)
Bank of America N.T. & S.A.

PHILIP D. REED
New York, New York

MELVIN J. ROBERTS
Colorado National Bankshares, Inc.

GEORGE RUSSELL
Bloomfield Hills, Michigan

E. C. SAMMONS
Chairman of the Board (Emeritus)
The United States National Bank of Oregon

JOHN A. SCHNEIDER
New York, New York

ELLERY SEDGWICK, JR.
Chairman, Executive Committee
Medusa Corporation

LEON SHIMKIN, Chairman
Simon and Schuster, Inc.

NEIL D. SKINNER
Indianapolis, Indiana

ELLIS D. SLATER
Landrum, South Carolina

S. ABBOT SMITH
Boston, Massachusetts

DAVIDSON SOMMERS,
Vice Chairman
Overseas Development Council

ROBERT C. SPRAGUE,
Hon. Chairman of the Board
Sprague Electric Company

FRANK STANTON
New York, New York

SYDNEY STEIN, JR., Partner
Stein Roe & Farnham

ALEXANDER L. STOTT
Fairfield, Connecticut

FRANK L. SULZBERGER
Chicago, Illinois

CHARLES P. TAFT
Cincinnati, Ohio

C. A. TATUM, JR., Chairman
Texas Utilities Company

ALAN H. TEMPLE
New York, New York

LESLIE H. WARNER
Darien, Connecticut

ROBERT C. WEAVER
Department of Urban Affairs
Hunter College

JAMES E. WEBB
Washington, D.C.

J. HUBER WETENHALL
New York, New York

A. L. WILLIAMS
Ocean Ridge, Florida

*WALTER W. WILSON
Rye, New York

ARTHUR M. WOOD, Director
Sears, Roebuck and Co.

THEODORE O. YNTEMA
Department of Economics
Oakland University

*CED Treasurer Emeritus

Trustees on Leave for Government Service

W. GRAHAM CLAYTOR, JR.
Secretary of the Navy

A. L. McDONALD, JR.
Deputy Special Representative for Trade Negotiations

Research Advisory Board

Chairman
THOMAS C. SCHELLING
John Fitzgerald Kennedy School of Government
Harvard University

GARDNER ACKLEY
Henry Carter Adams University
Professor of Political Economy
Department of Economics
The University of Michigan

MARTIN FELDSTEIN, President
National Bureau of Economic Research, Inc.

CARL KAYSEN
Vice Chairman and Director of Research
The Sloan Commission on Government
and Higher Education

ANNE O. KRUEGER
Professor of Economics
The University of Minnesota

ROGER G. NOLL, Chairman and Professor of Economics
Division of the Humanities and Social Sciences
California Institute of Technology
ANTHONY G. OETTINGER, Director
Program on Information Resources Policy
Harvard University

GEORGE L. PERRY, Senior Fellow
The Brookings Institution
WILLIAM POOLE, Professor of Economics
Brown University
ARNOLD R. WEBER, Provost
Carnegie-Mellon University

CED Professional and Administrative Staff

ROBERT C. HOLLAND
President

FRANK W. SCHIFF
*Vice President
and Chief Economist*

KENNETH McLENNAN
Director of Industrial Studies

SOL HURWITZ
*Vice President,
Information/Administration*

KENNETH M. DUBERSTEIN
*Director of Business-Government
Relations and Secretary,
Research and Policy Committee*

ELIZABETH J. LUCIER
Comptroller

S. CHARLES BLEICH
*Vice President, Finance
and Secretary, Board of Trustees*

R. SCOTT FOSLER
Director of Government Studies

Research

SEONG H. PARK
Economist

JACK B. LIPTON
Policy Analyst

Business-Government Relations

MARGARET J. HERRE
Staff Associate

Conferences

RUTH MUNSON
Manager

Information and Publications

CLAUDIA P. FEUREY
Associate Director

ROBERT F. CORYELL
Associate Director

MARY C. MUGIVAN
Publications Coordinator

HECTOR GUENTHER
Staff Associate

SANDRA KESSLER
Staff Associate

Finance

PATRICIA M. O'CONNELL
Deputy Director

HUGH D. STIER, JR.
Associate Director

Administrative Assistants to the President

THEODORA BOSKOVIC
SHIRLEY R. SHERMAN

Statements on National Policy
Issued by the Research and Policy Committee
(publications in print)

Redefining Government's Role in the Market System *(July 1979)*

Improving Management of the Public Work Force:
 The Challenge to State and Local Government *(November 1978)*

Jobs for the Hard-to-Employ:
 New Directions for a Public-Private Partnership *(January 1978)*

An Approach to Federal Urban Policy *(December 1977)*

Key Elements of a National Energy Strategy *(June 1977)*

The Economy in 1977-78: Strategy for an Enduring Expansion *(December 1976)*

Nuclear Energy and National Security *(September 1976)*

Fighting Inflation and Promoting Growth *(August 1976)*

Improving Productivity in State and Local Government *(March 1976)*

*International Economic Consequences of High-Priced Energy *(September 1975)*

Broadcasting and Cable Television: Policies for Diversity and Change *(April 1975)*

Achieving Energy Independence *(December 1974)*

A New U.S. Farm Policy for Changing World Food Needs *(October 1974)*

Congressional Decision Making for National Security *(September 1974)*

*Toward a New International Economic System:
 A Joint Japanese-American View *(June 1974)*

More Effective Programs for a Cleaner Environment *(April 1974)*

The Management and Financing of Colleges *(October 1973)*

Strengthening the World Monetary System *(July 1973)*

Financing the Nation's Housing Needs *(April 1973)*

Building a National Health-Care System *(April 1973)*

*A New Trade Policy Toward Communist Countries *(September 1972)*

High Employment Without Inflation:
 A Positive Program for Economic Stabilization *(July 1972)*

Reducing Crime and Assuring Justice *(June 1972)*

Military Manpower and National Security *(February 1972)*

The United States and the European Community *(November 1971)*

Improving Federal Program Performance *(September 1971)*

Social Responsibilities of Business Corporations *(June 1971)*

Education for the Urban Disadvantaged:
From Preschool to Employment *(March 1971)*

Further Weapons Against Inflation *(November 1970)*

Making Congress More Effective *(September 1970)*

Training and Jobs for the Urban Poor *(July 1970)*

Improving the Public Welfare System *(April 1970)*

Reshaping Government in Metropolitan Areas *(February 1970)*

Economic Growth in the United States *(October 1969)*

Assisting Development in Low-Income Countries *(September 1969)*

*Nontariff Distortions of Trade *(September 1969)*

Fiscal and Monetary Policies for Steady Economic Growth *(January 1969)*

Financing a Better Election System *(December 1968)*

Innovation in Education: New Directions for the American School *(July 1968)*

Modernizing State Government *(July 1967)*

*Trade Policy Toward Low-Income Countries *(June 1967)*

How Low Income Countries Can Advance Their Own Growth *(September 1966)*

Modernizing Local Government *(July 1966)*

Budgeting for National Objectives *(January 1966)*

Educating Tomorrow's Managers *(October 1964)*

Improving Executive Management in the Federal Government *(July 1964)*

**Statements issued in association with CED counterpart organizations in foreign countries.*

CED Counterpart Organizations in Foreign Countries

Close relations exist between the Committee for Economic Development and independent, nonpolitical research organizations in other countries. Such counterpart groups are composed of business executives and scholars and have objectives similar to those of CED, which they pursue by similarly objective methods. CED cooperates with these organizations on research and study projects of common interest to the various countries concerned. This program has resulted in a number of joint policy statements involving such international matters as energy, East-West trade, assistance to the developing countries, and the reduction of nontariff barriers to trade.

CE — Círculo de Empresarios
Serrano Jover 5-2°, Madrid 8, Spain

CEDA — Committee for Economic Development of Australia
139 Macquarie Street, Sydney 2001, New South Wales, Australia

CEPES — Europäische Vereinigung für Wirtschaftliche und Soziale Entwicklung
Reuterweg 14, 6000 Frankfurt/Main, West Germany

IDEP — Institut de l'Entreprise
6, rue Clément-Marot, 75008 Paris, France

経済同友会 — Keizai Doyukai
(Japan Committee for Economic Development)
*Japan Industrial Club Bldg.
1 Marunouchi, Chiyoda-ku, Tokyo, Japan*

PSI — Policy Studies Institute
1–2 Castle Lane, London SW1E 6DR, England

SNS — Studieförbundet Näringsliv och Samhälle
Sköldungagatan, 2, 11427 Stockholm, Sweden